The

Microsoft® Excel®

Step-By-Step Training Guide

Book Bundle

C.J. Benton

ISBN-10: 1518628753
ISBN-13: 978-1518628757

DEDICATION

To users searching for a comprehensive
Microsoft® Excel® Formulas & Features book!

CONTENTS

	Preface	i
1	How To Use This Book	1
2	Formula Basics (Sum, Subtraction, Multiplication, & Division)	6
3	Formula = AVERAGE	12
4	Formulas = MIN & MAX	15
5	Formulas = TODAY & NETWORKDAYS	24
6	Formula = SUMIF	30
7	Introduction to Pivot Tables	37
8	Introduction To Dashboards	69
9	Updating Existing Pivot Tables With New Or Modified Data	90
10	Pivot Tables (Advanced)	96
11	Pivot Tables Error Messages and How To Resolve Them	117

CONTENTS CONTINUED:

12	Feature = Data Sorting	**120**
13	Feature = Formula Trace	**124**
14	Feature = Text To Columns	**132**
15	Feature = Conditional Formatting	**137**
16	Formula = LEN	**145**
17	Formula = TRIM	**151**
18	Formula = PROPER, UPPER, & LOWER	**156**
19	Formula = MID & CONCATENATION	**159**
20	Formula = IF & NESTED IF	**168**
21	Introduction To The VLOOKUP Formula	**178**
22	Enhanced VLOOKUP Formulas	**193**
23	Applying the VLOOKUP Across Multiple Sheets & Workbooks	**208**
24	VLOOKUP Troubleshooting	**220**

CONTENTS CONTINUED:

25 Excel Shortcuts & Tips **230**

Currency formatting **231**

A Message From The Author **235**

PREFACE

For nearly twenty years, I worked as a Data & Systems Analyst for three different Fortune 500 companies, primarily in the areas of Finance, Infrastructure Services, and Logistics. During that time I used Microsoft® Excel® extensively developing hundreds of different types of reports, analysis tools, and several forms of Dashboards.

I've utilized many Microsoft® Excel® features, including Pivot Tables, VLOOKUP, IF formulas, and much more. The following are the functions and features I used and taught the most to fellow colleagues.

CHAPTER 1
HOW TO USE THIS BOOK

This book can be used as a tutorial or quick reference guide. It is intended for users who are just getting started with the fundamentals of Microsoft® Excel®, as well as for users who understand the basics and now want to build upon this skill by learning the more common intermediate level Excel® formulas and features.

While this book is intended for beginners, it does assume you already know how to create, open, save, and modify an Excel® workbook, and have a general familiarity with the Excel® toolbar.

All of the examples in this book use Microsoft® Excel® 2013, however, most of the functionality and formulas can be applied with Microsoft® Excel® version 2007 or later.

Please always **back-up your work** and **save often**. A good best practice when attempting any new functionality is to **create a copy of the original spreadsheet** and implement your changes on the copied spreadsheet. Should anything go wrong, you then have the original spreadsheet to fall back on. Please see the diagram below.

Diagram 1:

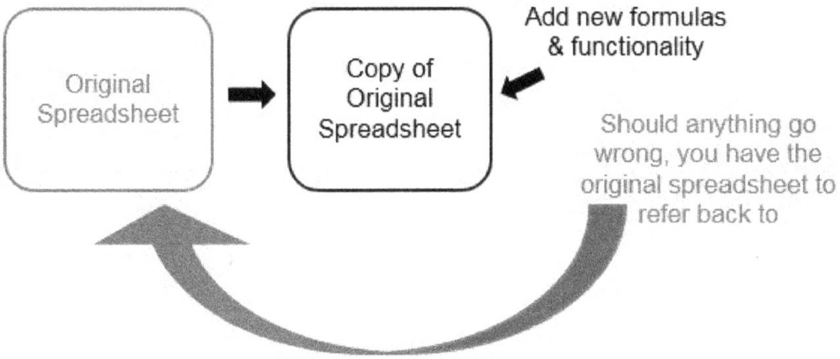

Original Spreadsheet

Copy of Original Spreadsheet

Add new formulas & functionality

Should anything go wrong, you have the original spreadsheet to refer back to

This book was written in the United States, therefore many of the examples use the US dollar currency symbol **$**. For instructions on how to change the currency symbol, for example to the **British Pound £** or **Euro €**, please see chapter 25 'Excel Shortcuts & Tips', page 231.

This book is structured into six parts. Part one focuses on basic formulas. This is where users who are just beginning to learn Excel® would typically start. The next three parts are intended for intermediate level users, they examine the features of Pivot Tables, data sorting, conditional formatting, and supporting formulas that can be used when troubleshooting Pivot Table report results and other spreadsheets. Concluding with parts five and six, which introduces some advanced Excel® functionality of the VLOOKUP, IF, and Nested IF formulas.

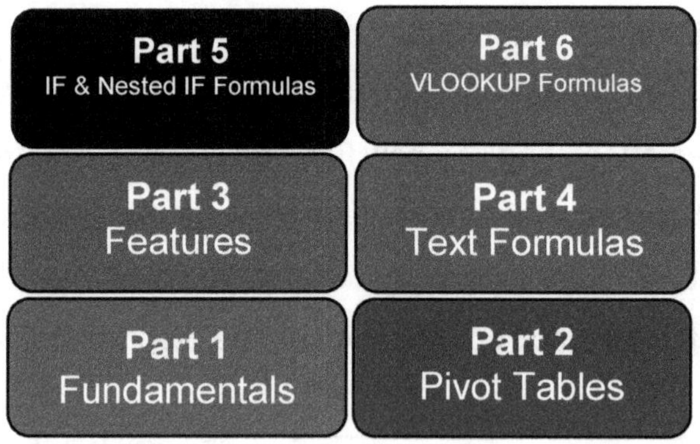

The below tables provide a summary of the functionality and features detailed in each section:

PART 1 - Fundamentals	
Chapters 2 - 6	• Sum, Subtraction, Multiplication, & Division • Average, Minimum, & Maximum • Today(), & Networkdays • SumIF
PART 2 - Pivot Tables & Introduction To Dashboards	
Chapter 7 Pivot Table Basics	• Organizing & summarizing data • Formatting results • Inserting Pivot Charts • Displaying averages & percentages • Ranking data
Chapters 8 & 9 Dashboards	• How to create a basic Dashboard • Optional instructions for protecting Dashboard data and hiding tabs • Updating Pivot Table or Dashboard data, while keeping the existing formatting and presentation intact
Chapter 10 Pivot Tables Advanced	• Grouping data • Inserting calculated fields
Chapter 11 Pivot Table Error Messages	• Common Pivot Table error messages and how to resolve them
PART 3 – Excel® Features	
Chapters 12 - 15	• Data Sorting • Formula Trace • Text-To-Columns • Conditional Formatting

PART 4 – Text Functions	
Chapters 16 - 19	• LEN & TRIM • CONCATENATE & MID • PROPER, UPPER, & LOWER
PART 5 – Logic Formulas	
Chapter 20	• IF (formula) • Nested IF (formula)
PART 6 – VLOOKUP	
Chapter 21 VLOOKUP Basics	• What the VLOOKUP formula does • The parts of a VLOOKUP formula • Two detailed examples with screenshots using a basic VLOOKUP formula
Chapter 22 Taking the VLOOKUP to the next level	• Incorporating the IFERROR functionality into your VLOOKUP formula • What to do when you attempt to lookup a value in the table_array, but none exists • What to do when you don't have a unique lookup_value • What to do when the unique lookup_value is listed more than once in the table_array
Chapter 23 Applying the VLOOKUP across tabs & workbooks	• Detailed example with screenshots applying the VLOOKUP formula across multiple workbooks and tabs
Chapter 24 VLOOKUP Troubleshooting	• A review of five common VLOOKUP error messages / issues and how to resolve them

To enhance readability and for those who want to skip to specific areas, each chapter consists of <u>*one or more*</u> of the following sections:

Diagram 2:

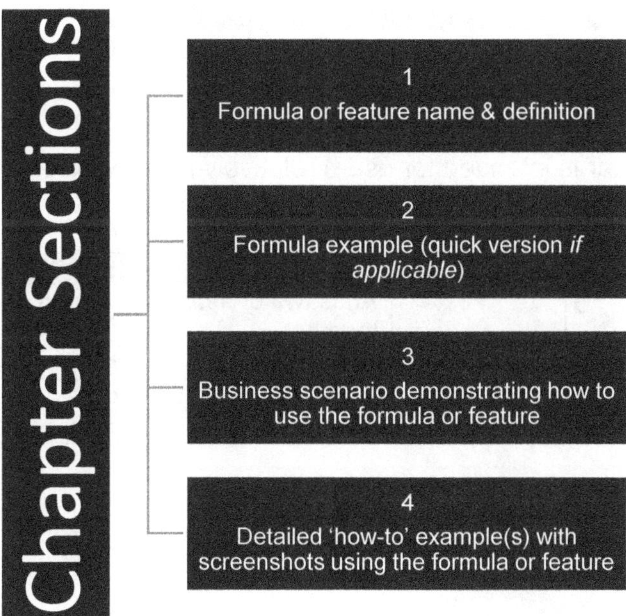

<u>SECTION 1:</u>

Provides the formula or feature name and definition for that chapter.

<u>SECTION 2:</u>

Gives a quick example of how to use the formula and the results. This is intended for intermediate level users who do not require a detailed step-by-step example. Also, this section can be used as a quick reference of the syntax.

<u>SECTION 3:</u>

Offers one or more business scenarios demonstrating how the formula or feature may be used.

<u>SECTION 4:</u>

Presents detailed instructions with screenshots explaining how to answer each chapter's scenario.

(PART 1) - CHAPTER 2

SUM, SUBTRACTION, MULTIPLICATION, & DIVISION

This chapter is intended for users relatively new to Excel®. These are the fundamental formulas that everyone starts with.

FORMULA	OPERATOR	DEFINITION
Sum	+	Adds two or more cells or numbers together
Subtraction	-	Subtracts two or more cells or numbers
Multiplication	*	Multiplies two or more cells or numbers
Division	/	Divides two or more cells or numbers

Detailed examples of how to use each basic formula:

SUM

1. Begin by creating a new blank Excel® spreadsheet
2. Enter the following numbers into **column 'A'**
    a. Cell '**A1'** enter the number **2**
    b. Cell '**A2'** enter the number **3**
    c. Cell '**A3'** enter the number **1**
    d. Cell '**A4'** enter the number **2**

The spreadsheet should look similar to the following:

	A
1	2
2	3
3	1
4	2
5	

3. Click cell **'A5'**
4. From the toolbar select **Formulas**
5. Click ∑ **AutoSum**

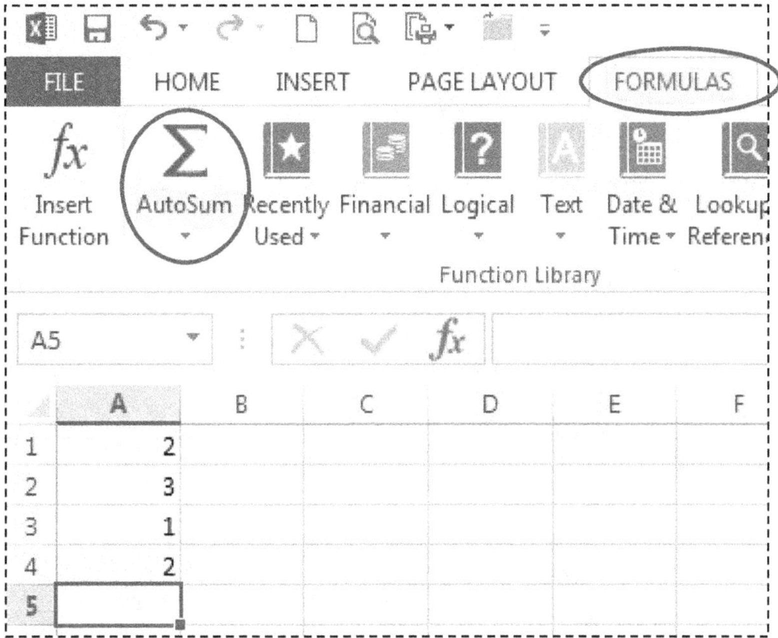

The result should be **8**:

A5 | =SUM(A1:A4)

	A	B	C	D	E
1	2				
2	3				
3	1				
4	2				
5	8				

Alternatively, you may also enter the following into cell **'A5'**:

1. Enter the **equal (=)** symbol from your keyboard
2. Type **sum(**
3. Highlight rows **'A1-A4'**
4. Press the **'Enter'** button on your keyboard

SUBTRACTION

Using the same the sample data as the 'Sum' section:

1. Start by clicking cell **'B3'**
2. Enter the **equal (=)** symbol from your keyboard
3. Click cell '**A2'**
4. Enter the **minus (-)** symbol from your keyboard
5. Click cell '**A3'**
6. Press the **'Enter'** button on your keyboard

	A	B
1	2	
2	3	
3	1	=A2-A3
4	2	
5	8	

The result should be **2**:

B3 | fx =A2-A3

	A	B	C	D
1	2			
2	3			
3	1	2		
4	2			
5	8			

MULTIPLICATION

Using the same the sample data as the 'Sum' section:

1. Start by clicking cell **'B4'**
2. Enter the **equal (=)** symbol from your keyboard
3. Click cell '**A4'**
4. Enter the **asterisk (*)** symbol from your keyboard
5. Click cell '**A1'**
6. Press the **'Enter'** button on your keyboard

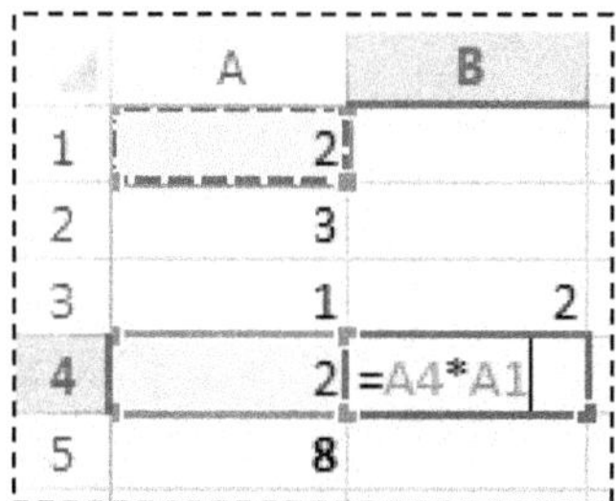

	A	B
1	2	
2	3	
3	1	2
4	2	=A4*A1
5	8	

The result should be **4**:

B4 | fx =A4*A1

	A	B	C	D
1	2			
2	3			
3	1	2		
4	2	4		
5	8			

DIVISION

Using the same the sample data as the 'Sum' section:

1. Start by clicking cell **'C4'**
2. Enter the **equal (=)** [+ =] symbol from your keyboard
3. Click cell '**B4'**
4. Enter the **backslash (/)** [? /] symbol from your keyboard
5. Click cell '**B3'**
6. Press the **'Enter'** [Enter ↵] button on your keyboard

	A	B	C
1	2		
2	3		
3	1	2	
4	2	4	=B4/B3
5	8		

The result should be **2**:

C4 =B4/B3

	A	B	C	D
1	2			
2	3			
3	1	2		
4	2	4	2	
5	8			

☑ Additional Information:

To access the Microsoft® Excel® **Help** function, press (**F1**) on your keyboard or click the **'?'** icon above the menu ribbon:

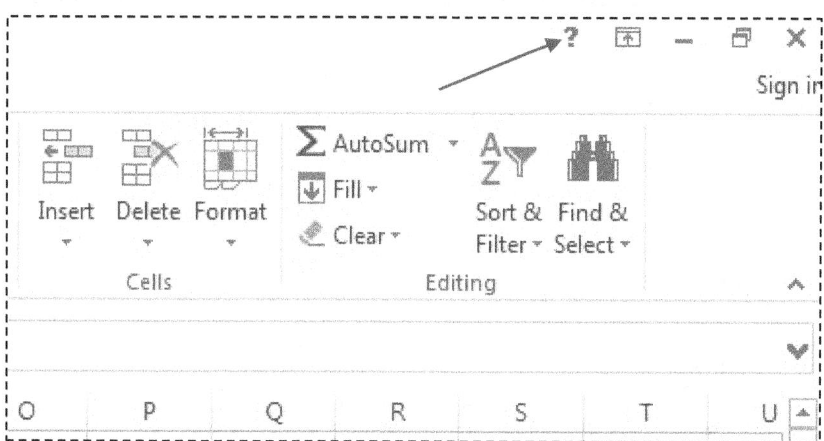

(PART 1) - CHAPTER 3

FORMULA = AVERAGE

Formula:

- AVERAGE

Definition:

- Returns the average number in a range of values, does not include text in the evaluation.

Quick Example:

```
Formula Syntax:
AVERAGE(number1, [number2], ...)
Number1 is required, subsequent numbers are optional
```

A4 | =AVERAGE(A2:A3)

	A	B	C	D	E
1	SALES				
2	$100				
3	$200				
4	$150				

Scenario:
You have a list of sales numbers and would like to determine the average of all the sales.

Detailed Example How To Use The Formula:

1. Begin by creating a new blank Excel® spreadsheet

2. Enter the following numbers into **column 'A'**
    a. Cell '**A1'** enter the label **'SALES'**
    b. Cell '**A2'** enter the number **$100**
    c. Cell '**A3'** enter the number **$200**
    d. Cell '**A4'** enter the number **$300**
    e. Cell '**A5'** enter the number **$400**

The spreadsheet should look similar to the following:

	A
1	SALES
2	$100
3	$200
4	$300
5	$400

3. Click cell **'A6'**
4. From the toolbar select **Formulas**
5. Click **AutoSum** drop-down box and select **'Average'**

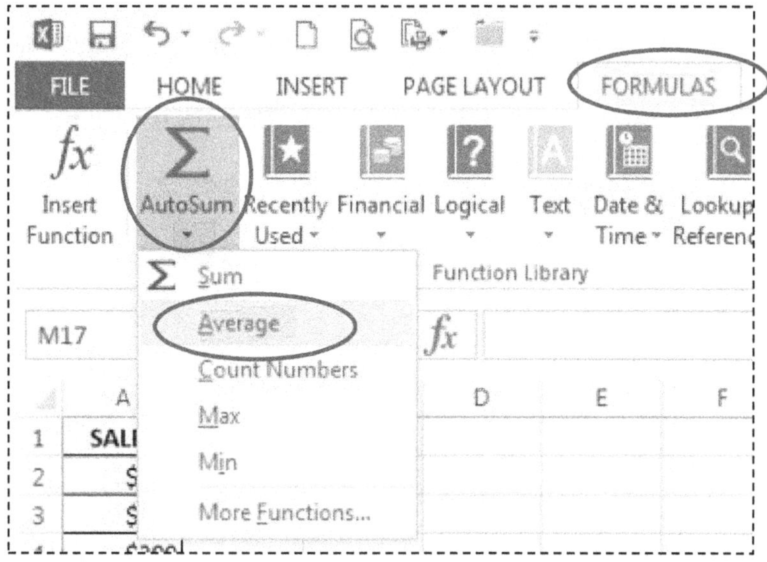

The result should be **250**:

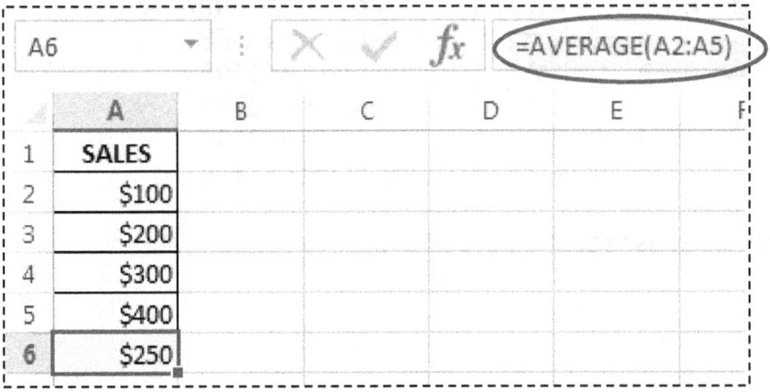
A6
fx
=AVERAGE(A2:A5)
A
B
C
D
E
F
1 SALES
2 $100
3 $200
4 $300
5 $400
6 $250

Alternatively, you may also enter the following into cell **'A6'**:

1. Enter the **equal (=)** 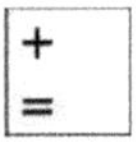
+
=
symbol from your keyboard
2. Type **average(**
3. Highlight rows **'A2 - A5'**
4. Press the **'Enter'** 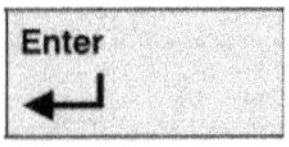
Enter
button on your keyboard

You've now determined the average sales from the list above.

(PART 1) - CHAPTER 4

FORMULAS = MIN & MAX

Formulas:

- MIN & MAX

Definition:

- **MIN:** Returns the ***lowest number*** in a range of values, does not include text in the evaluation.
- **MAX:** Returns the ***largest number*** in a range of values, does not include text in the evaluation.

Quick Example: MIN

```
Formula Syntax:
MIN(number1, [number2], ...)
Number1 is required, subsequent numbers are optional
```

B2 | fx | =MIN(A2:A6)

	A	B	C	D	E
1	LIST	MIN	MAX		
2	1	1			
3	2				
4	3				
5	4				
6	5				

Quick Example: MAX

```
MAX(number1, [number2], ...)
Number1 is required, subsequent numbers are optional
```

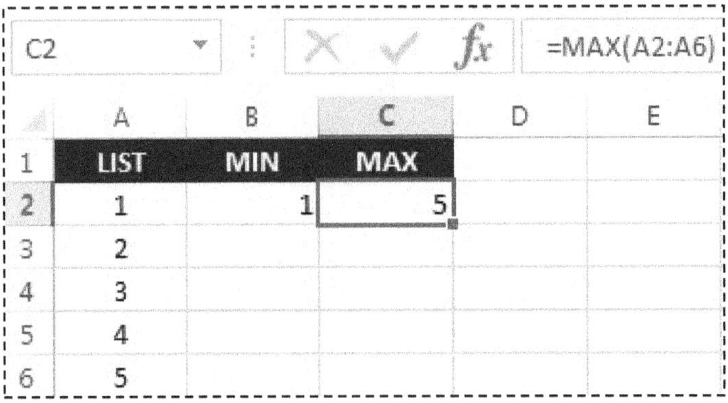

C2 =MAX(A2:A6)

	A	B	C	D	E
1	LIST	MIN	MAX		
2	1	1	5		
3	2				
4	3				
5	4				
6	5				

Scenario:
You've been given a spreadsheet that contains the total fruit sales by quarter and sales person. You've been asked to provide the top and worst performing sales person by quarter.

Detailed Example How To Use The Formula:

Sample data:

	A	B	C	D
1	SALES PERSON FIRST NAME	SALES PERSON LAST NAME	QTR	TOTAL
2	Jack	Smith	1	343
3	Jack	Smith	2	1,849
4	Jack	Smith	3	2,653
5	Jack	Smith	4	5,494
6	Joe	Tanner	1	377
7	Joe	Tanner	2	2,404
8	Joe	Tanner	3	3,980
9	Joe	Tanner	4	39,631
10	Helen	Simpson	1	457
11	Helen	Simpson	2	4,062
12	Helen	Simpson	4	8,954
13	Helen	Simpson	4	20,459
14	Billy	Winchester	1	552
15	Billy	Winchester	2	6,865
16	Billy	Winchester	3	16,558
17	Billy	Winchester	4	8,516

1. Insert three labels:
    a. Cell '**F1**' label '**BEST**'
    b. Cell '**G1**' label '**QTR.**'
    c. Cell '**H1**' label '**SALES**'
    d. Leave two blank rows (rows 2 & 3)

2. Insert three more labels:
    a. Cell '**F4**' label '**WORST**'
    b. Cell '**G4**' label '**QTR.**'
    c. Cell '**H4**' label '**SALES**'
    d. Leave one blank row (row 5)

Please see screenshot below for an example:

	A	B	C	D	E	F	G	H
1	SALES PERSON FIRST NAME	SALES PERSON LAST NAME	QTR	TOTAL		BEST	QTR.	SALES
2	Jack	Smith	1	343				
3	Jack	Smith	2	1,849				
4	Jack	Smith	3	2,653		WORST	QTR.	SALES
5	Jack	Smith	4	5,494				
6	Joe	Tanner	1	377				
7	Joe	Tanner	2	2,404				
8	Joe	Tanner	3	3,980				
9	Joe	Tanner	4	39,631				
10	Helen	Simpson	1	457				
11	Helen	Simpson	2	4,062				
12	Helen	Simpson	4	8,954				
13	Helen	Simpson	4	20,459				
14	Billy	Winchester	1	552				
15	Billy	Winchester	2	6,865				
16	Billy	Winchester	3	16,558				
17	Billy	Winchester	4	8,516				

3. Next, apply the '**MAX**' function for cell '**H2**'

4. From the toolbar select **Formulas : Insert Function**

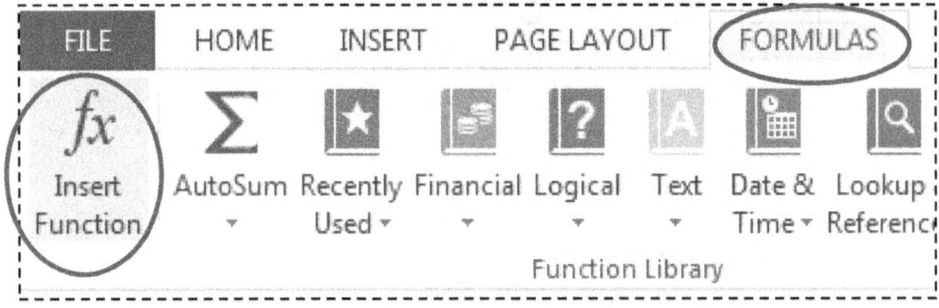

5. Type '**MAX'** in the 'Search for a function:' dialogue box

6. Click the '**Go**' button

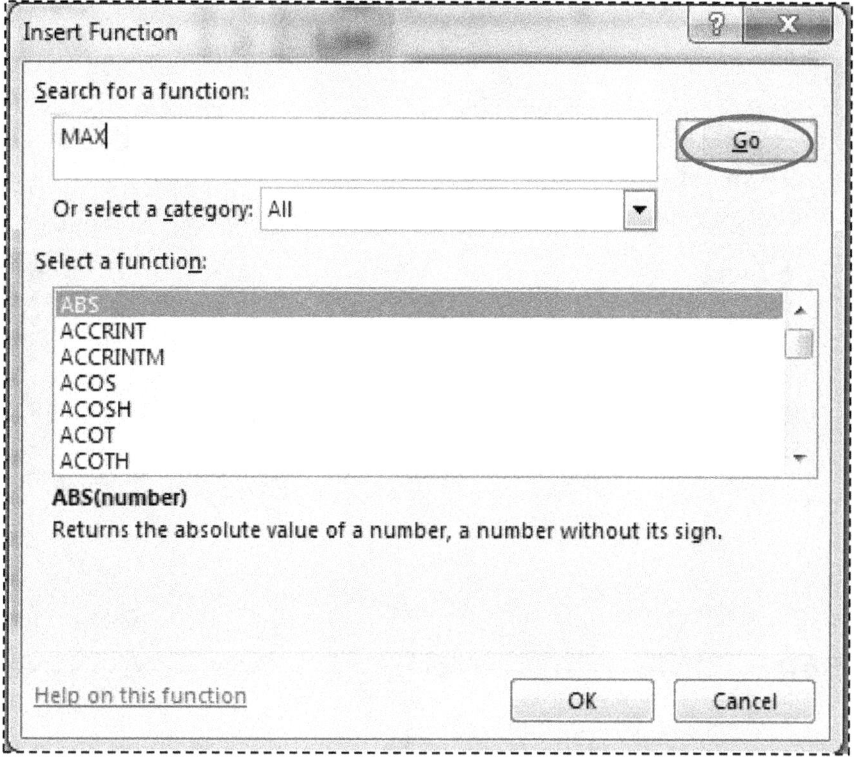

The following dialogue box should now appear:

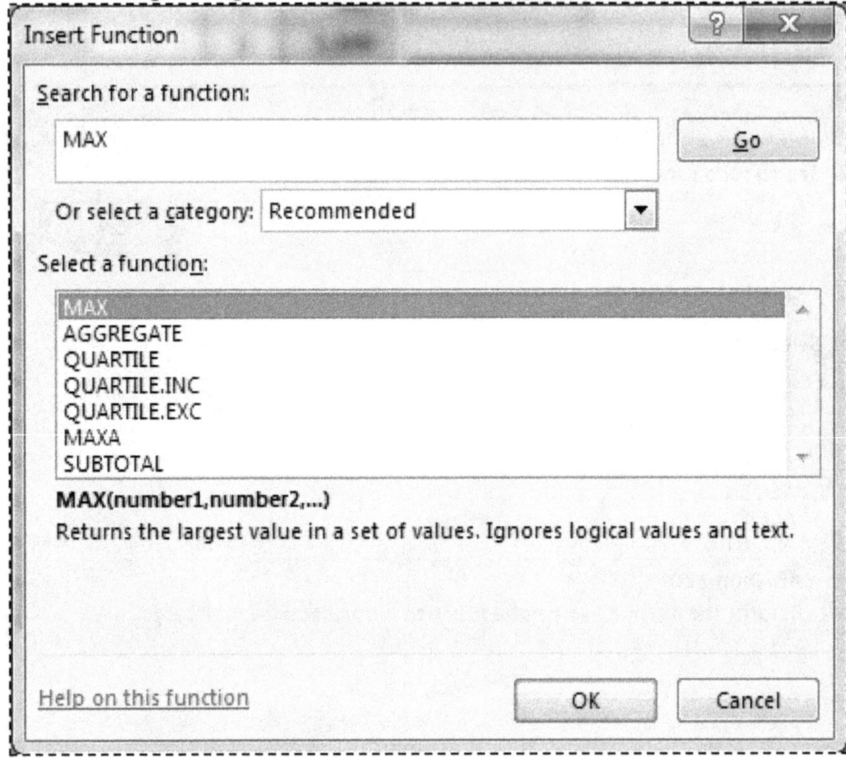

7. Click the '**OK**' button

8. For the **Number1** click the **column 'D'** *(this column lists the sales)*
9. Click the '**OK**' button:

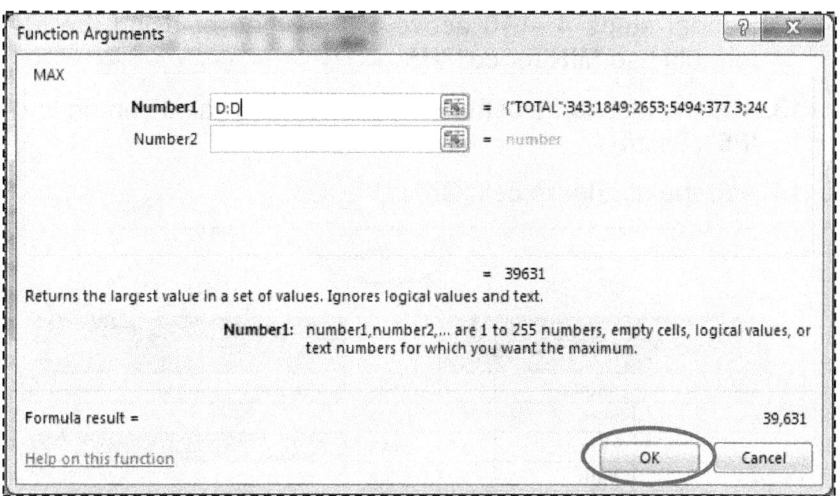

The result is **39,631**:

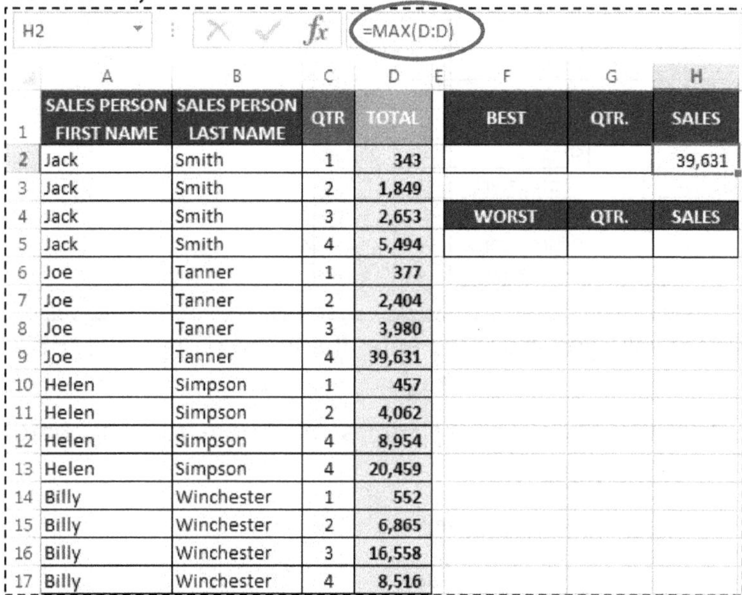

	A	B	C	D	E	F	G	H
1	SALES PERSON FIRST NAME	SALES PERSON LAST NAME	QTR	TOTAL		BEST	QTR.	SALES
2	Jack	Smith	1	343				39,631
3	Jack	Smith	2	1,849				
4	Jack	Smith	3	2,653		WORST	QTR.	SALES
5	Jack	Smith	4	5,494				
6	Joe	Tanner	1	377				
7	Joe	Tanner	2	2,404				
8	Joe	Tanner	3	3,980				
9	Joe	Tanner	4	39,631				
10	Helen	Simpson	1	457				
11	Helen	Simpson	2	4,062				
12	Helen	Simpson	4	8,954				
13	Helen	Simpson	4	20,459				
14	Billy	Winchester	1	552				
15	Billy	Winchester	2	6,865				
16	Billy	Winchester	3	16,558				
17	Billy	Winchester	4	8,516				

10. Add the last name of the best performing sales person to cell **'F2'** *(Tanner)*
11. Add the quarter to cell **'G2'** *(4)*
12. Repeat steps 4 – 10 above, but instead of using the MAX formula use **MIN** for cell **'H5'**
13. Add the last name of the worst performing sales person to cell **'F5'** *(Smith)*
14. Add the quarter to cell **'G5'** *(1)*

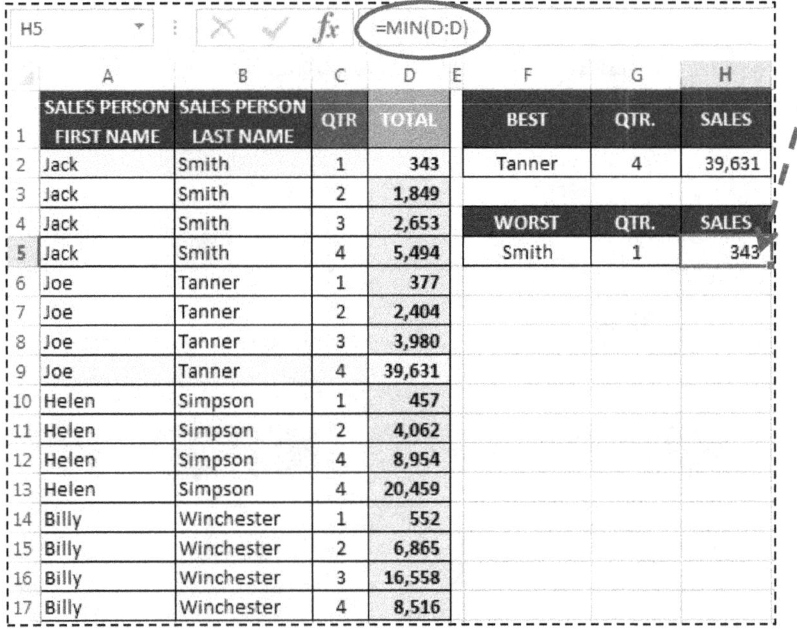

H5 =MIN(D:D)

	A	B	C	D	E	F	G	H
1	SALES PERSON FIRST NAME	SALES PERSON LAST NAME	QTR	TOTAL		BEST	QTR.	SALES
2	Jack	Smith	1	343		Tanner	4	39,631
3	Jack	Smith	2	1,849				
4	Jack	Smith	3	2,653		WORST	QTR.	SALES
5	Jack	Smith	4	5,494		Smith	1	343
6	Joe	Tanner	1	377				
7	Joe	Tanner	2	2,404				
8	Joe	Tanner	3	3,980				
9	Joe	Tanner	4	39,631				
10	Helen	Simpson	1	457				
11	Helen	Simpson	2	4,062				
12	Helen	Simpson	4	8,954				
13	Helen	Simpson	4	20,459				
14	Billy	Winchester	1	552				
15	Billy	Winchester	2	6,865				
16	Billy	Winchester	3	16,558				
17	Billy	Winchester	4	8,516				

Alternatively, you may also enter the following into cell **'H5'**:

1. Enter the **equal (=)** [+ =] symbol from your keyboard
2. Type **min(**
3. Highlight column **'D'**
4. Press the **'Enter'** [Enter ↵] button on your keyboard

or for **MAX**:

You may enter the following into cell **'H2'**:

1. Enter the **equal (=)** [+ =] symbol from your keyboard
2. Type **max(**
3. Highlight column **'D'**
4. Press the **'Enter'** [Enter ↵] button on your keyboard

You've now determined the top and worst performing sales person by quarter.

☑ Additional Information:

All of the formulas reviewed in chapters 2 – 4 can also be accomplished using Pivot Tables, which are introduced in chapter 7. However, sometimes it is quicker to use one of the above formulas when your sample size is small or you're simply providing these results in an email, IM (instant message), or text.

Similarly, these are very useful formulas when you want to quickly double check your Pivot Table results. It's always a good practice to validate your results to ensure you're not missing any values. By taking just a few extra minutes to verify your calculations, you'll likely catch any mistakes, improve your creditability with customers, and have the confidence to defend your work should it ever be questioned.

(PART 1) - CHAPTER 5

FORMULAS = TODAY & NETWORKDAYS

Formulas:

- TODAY
- NETWORKDAYS

Definition:

- **TODAY**: provides today's date. *NOTE: this formula will update each day, it is always the current date.*
- **NETWORKDAYS**: calculates the number of ***workdays*** (Monday – Friday) between two dates.

Quick Example: TODAY

There is no syntax for the **'Today()'** formula. Alternatively, you may also use the **'Now()'** function, the results would be as follows:

	A	B
1	FORMULA	RESULT
2	=TODAY()	7/13/2015
3	=NOW()	7/13/2015 10:28 AM

Quick Example: NETWORKDAYS

Formula Syntax:

```
NETWORKDAYS(start_date, end_date, [holidays])

start_date and end_date are required, holidays is
optional
```

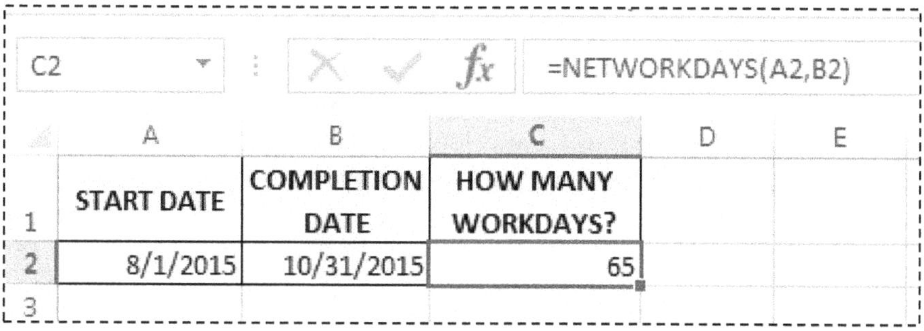

C2 =NETWORKDAYS(A2,B2)

	A	B	C	D	E
1	START DATE	COMPLETION DATE	HOW MANY WORKDAYS?		
2	8/1/2015	10/31/2015	65		
3					

Scenario:

You've been asked to determine how many resources are needed to complete a project by specific date.

1. The start of the project is 08/01/2015 and needs to be completed by 10/31/2015
2. The project is estimated to take 1,040 hours
3. Assume each resource would work one 8 hour shift per day, Monday – Friday

It would take 1 resource 130 days to complete the project including weekends:

```
(1040 hours / 8 hour shift = 130 days)
```

Therefore we know we need more resources, but how many?

Detailed Example How To Use The Formula:

First, we need to determine how many *workdays* there are between 08/01/2015 and 10/31/2015. Once we know this amount, we can then multiply this value with the number of hours per shift to determine the appropriate total of resources needed to complete the project by 10/31/2015.

1. Begin by creating a new Excel® spreadsheet

2. Enter the following:
   a. Cell '**A1'** enter the label **'START DATE'**
   b. Cell '**A2'** enter the date '**8/1/2015'**
   c. Cell '**B1'** enter the label **'COMPLETION DATE'**
   d. Cell '**B2'** enter the date '**10/31/2015'**
   e. Cell '**C1'** enter the label **'HOW MANY WORKDAYS?'**

3. Place your cursor in cell **'C2'**:

	A	B	C
1	START DATE	COMPLETION DATE	HOW MANY WORKDAYS?
2	8/1/2015	10/31/2015	
3			
4			

4. From the toolbar select **Formulas : Insert Function**

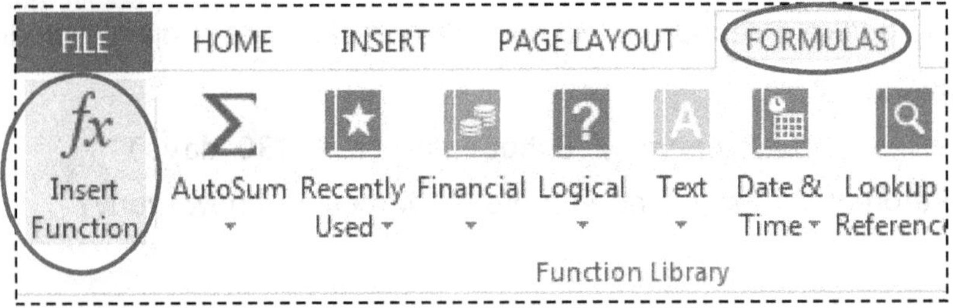

5. Type "**NETWORKDAYS**" in the **'Search for a function:'** dialogue box
6. Click the '**Go**' button

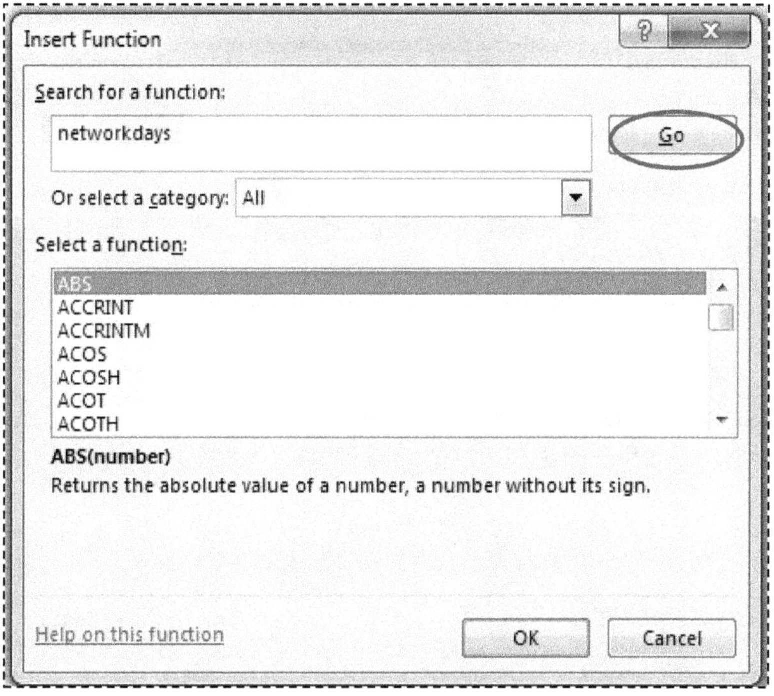

The following dialogue box should now appear:

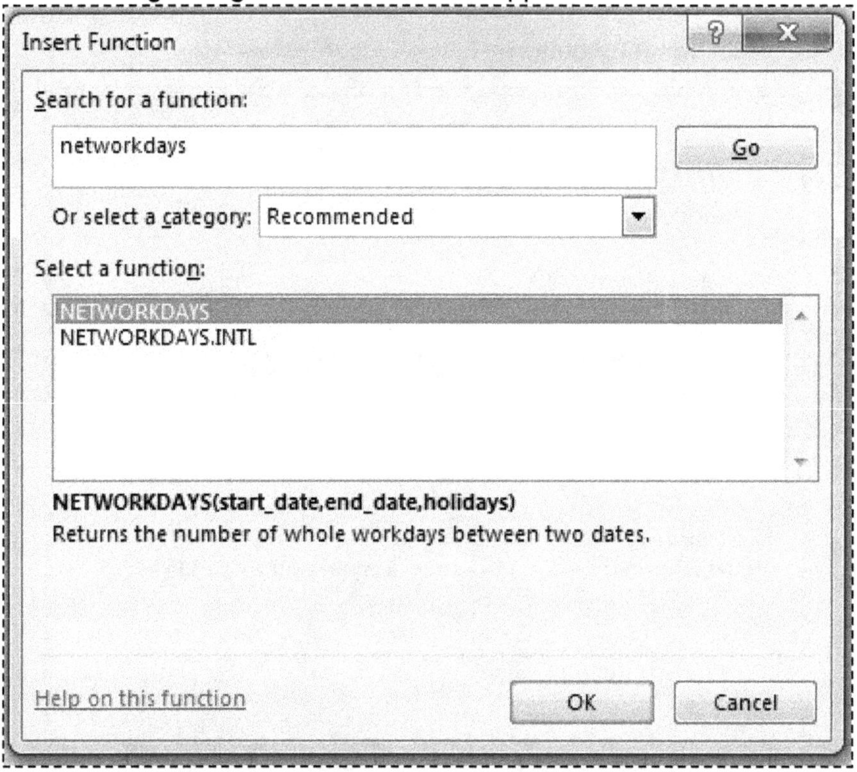

7. Click the '**OK**' button:

8. For the **Start_date** click cell '**A2**' or enter **A2**
9. For the **End_date** click cell '**B2**' or enter **B2**
10. Click the '**OK**' button

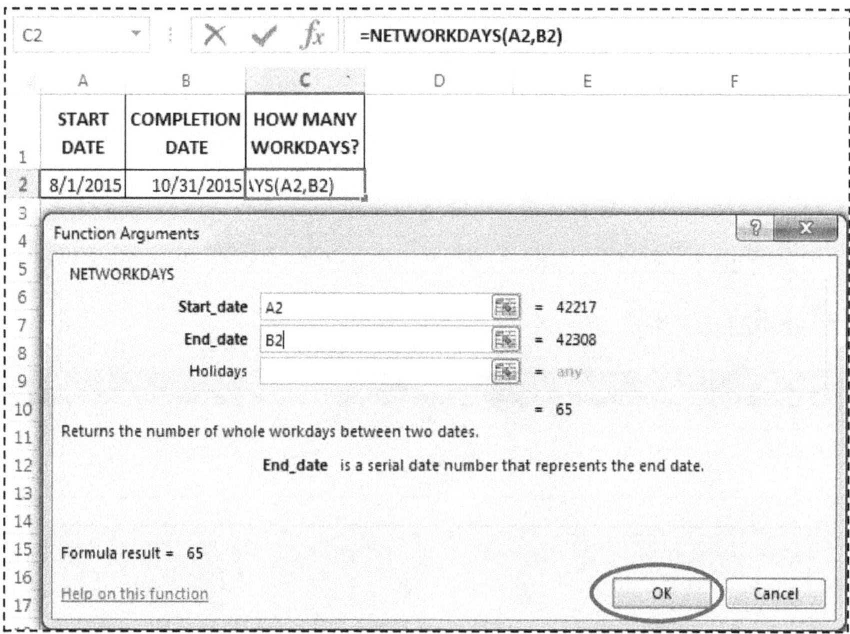

The result is **65 days:**

11. Next, we apply the basic calculations to determine the appropriate amount of resources needed to complete the project (please see screenshot below):

	A	B	C	D	E	F
1	START DATE	COMPLETION DATE	HOW MANY WORKDAYS?	NUMBER OF HOURS WORKED FOR 1 RESOURCE FOR 65 DAYS	ESTIMATED PROJECT HOURS	RESOURCES NEEDED TO COMPLETE BY 10/31/2015
2	8/1/2015	10/31/2015	65	520	1,040	2
3	*Formulas used in the above cel*			*C2*8 = 520*		*E2/D2 = 2*
4						
5						

The result is **2 resources** are needed to complete a project by 10/31/2015.

(PART 1) - CHAPTER 6

FORMULAS = SUMIF

Formula:

- SUMIF

Definition:

- Sums the values in a range based on the criteria you identify.

Quick Example:

```
Formula Syntax:
SUMIF(range, criteria, [sum_range])
range and criteria are required, sum_range is optional
```

F2 =SUMIF(B2:B13,1,C2:C13)

	A	B	C	D	E	F	G
1	REGION	QUARTER	APPLES SALES		QUARTER	APPLE SALES	
2	Central	1	111		Q1	751	
3	Central	2	161				
4	Central	3	183				
5	Central	4	243				
6	East	1	263				
7	East	2	313				
8	East	3	335				
9	East	4	395				
10	West	1	377				
11	West	2	427				
12	West	3	449				
13	West	4	509				

Scenario:

You've been given a spreadsheet that contains the Apple sales by quarter for three regions. You've been asked to summarize the data and provide the total apples by quarter.

Detailed Example How To Use The Formula:

Sample data:

	A	B	C
1	REGION	QUARTER	APPLES SALES
2	Central	1	111
3	Central	2	161
4	Central	3	183
5	Central	4	243
6	East	1	263
7	East	2	313
8	East	3	335
9	East	4	395
10	West	1	377
11	West	2	427
12	West	3	449
13	West	4	509

1. Add two columns:
   a. Cell '**E1**' label '**QUARTER**'
   b. Cell '**F1**' label '**APPLE SALES'**
   c. Add rows for **Quarters Q1 – Q4**

Please see below screenshot for an example:

	A	B	C	D	E	F
1	REGION	QUARTER	APPLES SALES		QUARTER	APPLE SALES
2	Central	1	111		Q1	
3	Central	2	161		Q2	
4	Central	3	183		Q3	
5	Central	4	243		Q4	
6	East	1	263			
7	East	2	313			
8	East	3	335			
9	East	4	395			
10	West	1	377			
11	West	2	427			
12	West	3	449			
13	West	4	509			

2. Next, apply the '**SUMIF**' function for 'Apple Sales' in row '**F2**'

3. From the toolbar select **Formulas : Insert Function**

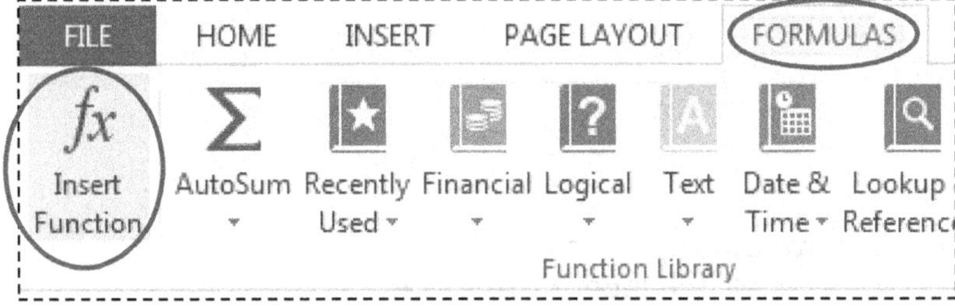

4. Type '**SUMIF'** in the **'Search for a function:'** dialogue box
5. Click the '**Go**' button

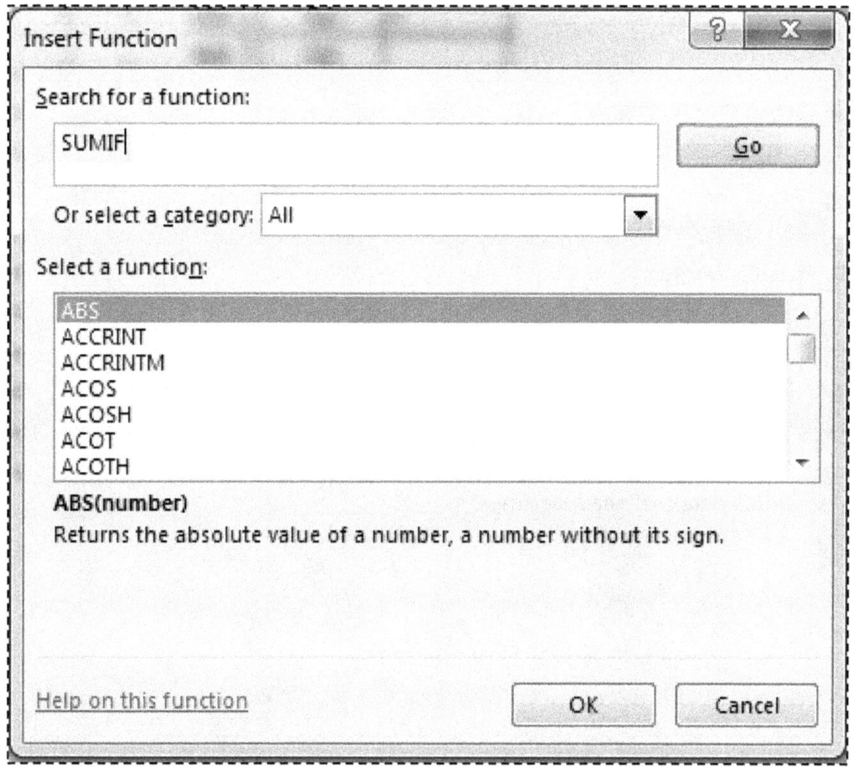

The following dialogue box should now appear:

6. Click the '**OK**' button:

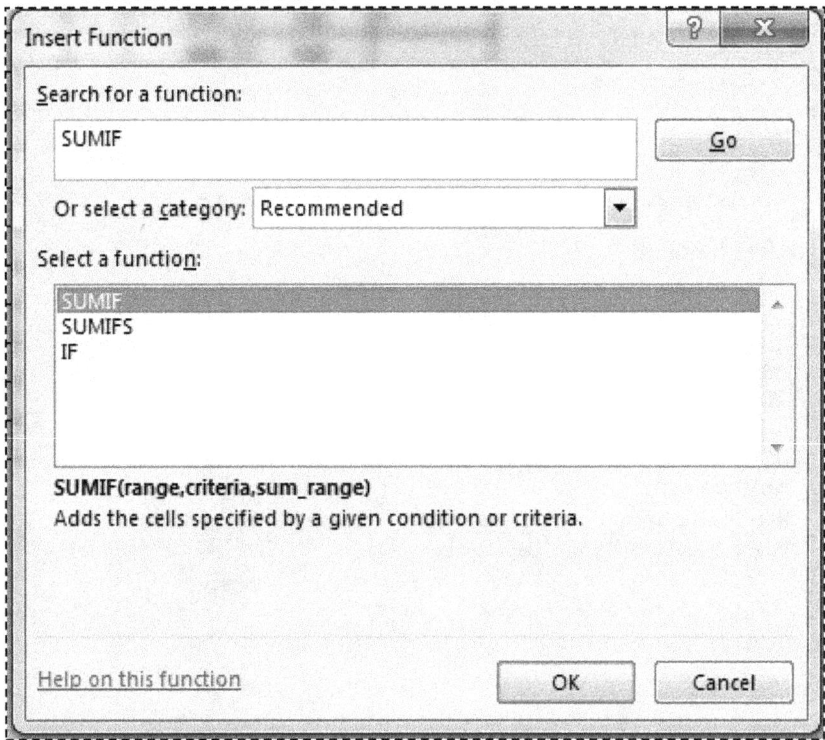

7. For the **Range** click the **column 'B'** *(this column lists the quarter)*
8. For the **Criteria** enter **'1'** for Quarter 1 *(note: if this were a text field, you would encapsulate the text with double quotes " ")*
9. For the **Sum_Range** click the **column 'C'** *(this column list the apple sales)*
10. Click the '**OK**' button:

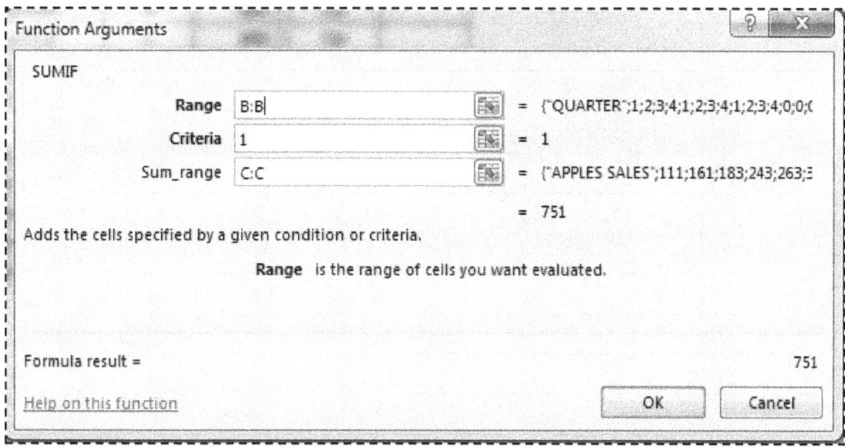

The result for **Q1** is **751** sales:

F2 | =SUMIF(B:B,1,C:C)

	A	B	C	D	E	F
1	REGION	QUARTER	APPLES SALES		QUARTER	APPLE SALES
2	Central	1	111		Q1	751
3	Central	2	161		Q2	
4	Central	3	183		Q3	
5	Central	4	243		Q4	
6	East	1	263			
7	East	2	313			
8	East	3	335			
9	East	4	395			
10	West	1	377			
11	West	2	427			
12	West	3	449			
13	West	4	509			

11. From here, we can copy the formula down through cells **'F3' – 'F5'** and change the **'Criteria'** value for the appropriate quarter *(i.e. **2,3, & 4 for quarters 2-4**)*.

SUMIF | =SUMIF(B:B,4,C:C)

SUMIF(range, crite

	A	B	C	D	E	F
1	REGION	QUARTER	APPLES SALES		QUARTER	APPLE SALES
2	Central	1	111		Q1	751
3	Central	2	161		Q2	901
4	Central	3	183		Q3	967
5	Central	4	243		Q4	IIF(B:B,4,C
6	East	1	263			
7	East	2	313			
8	East	3	335			
9	East	4	395			
10	West	1	377			
11	West	2	427			
12	West	3	449			
13	West	4	509			

☑ **Additional Information:**

In addition to SUMIF, the formulas of COUNTIF, and AVERAGEIF *(please see below for definitions)* can also be accomplished with Pivot Tables, which are introduced in the next chapter. However, sometimes it is quicker to use one of these formulas when your sample size is small or you're simply providing these results in an email, IM (instant message), or text.

COUNTIF: Counts the number of times a values appears in a range of cells based on the criteria you identify.

AVERAGEIF: Returns the average value (number) in a range of cells based on the criteria you identify.

(PART 2) - CHAPTER 7
INTRODUCTION TO PIVOT TABLES

Feature:

- Pivot Tables

Definition:

- By using built-in filters and functions, Pivot Tables allow you to quickly organize and summarize large amounts of data. Various types of analysis can then be completed without needing to manually enter formulas into the spreadsheet you're analyzing.

Scenario:

You may be tasked with analyzing significant amounts of data, perhaps consisting of several thousand or hundreds of thousands of records, or you may have to reconcile information from many different sources and forms, such as assimilating material from:

1. Reports generated by another application, such as a legacy system
2. Data imported into Excel® via a query from a database or other application
3. Data copied or cut, and pasted into Excel® from the web or other types of screen scraping activities

One of the easiest ways to perform high level analysis on this information is to use Pivot Tables. The following examples will demonstrate five types of analysis that can be performed on large amounts of data using the Microsoft® Excel® Pivot Table feature. In the following examples we will:

1. Determine the total sales by region and quarter
2. Create a chart that displays the sales by region and quarter
3. Show the individual fruit sales by region and quarter
4. Identify what the percentage of individual fruit sales are by quarter and what the overall percentage of total sales are for each region
5. Rank each sales person, including their total & average sales

Sample data for examples 1- 5 above, due to space limitations ***the entire data set is not displayed****:*

To download a free copy of the Excel® file used in this scenario please go to:
http://bentonexcelbooks.my-free.website/sample-data-files

select the file for ***Chapter 7 (Pivot Tables)*** *in the* ***'The Microsoft Excel Step-By-Step Training Guide Book Bundle'*** *section*

	A	B	C	D	E	F	G	H	I
1	REGION	SALES PERSON FIRST NAME	SALES PERSON LAST NAME	SALES PERSON ID	QUARTER	APPLES	ORANGES	MANGOS	TOTAL
2	Central	bob	TAYLOR	1174	1	1,810	2,039	1,771	**5,620**
3	Central	helen	SMITH	833	1	102	354	59	**516**
4	Central	jill	JOHNSON	200	1	93	322	54	**469**
5	Central	sally	MORTON	500	1	595	824	556	**1,975**
6	Central	sam	BECKER	800	1	863	1,092	824	**2,779**
7	East	Abbey	Williams	690	1	346	237	260	**843**
8	East	John	Dower	255	1	260	178	195	**633**
9	East	John	Wilson	300	1	286	196	215	**696**
10	East	Mary	Nelson	600	1	315	215	236	**766**
11	East	Sarah	Taylor	900	1	381	261	285	**927**
12	West	Alex	Steller	1000	1	163	212	127	**502**
13	West	Billy	Winchester	1156	1	179	234	140	**552**
14	West	Helen	Simpson	817	1	148	193	116	**457**
15	West	Jack	Smith	100	1	111	145	87	**343**
16	West	Joe	Tanner	400	1	122	160	96	**377**
17	West	Peter	Graham	700	1	134	175	105	**415**
18	Central	bob	TAYLOR	1174	2	113	390	65	**567**
19	Central	helen	SMITH	833	2	1,006	1,393	940	**3,338**
20	Central	jill	JOHNSON	200	2	774	1,071	723	**2,568**
21	Central	sally	MORTON	500	2	1,295	1,638	1,236	**4,169**
22	Central	sam	BECKER	800	2	2,806	3,160	2,745	**8,711**
23	East	Abbey	Williams	690	2	1,674	1,494	1,531	**4,699**
24	East	John	Dower	255	2	762	680	697	**2,139**

Detailed Example How To Use The Feature:

Let's first determine the '**Total Sales by Region**' and then we will build upon this by adding the **'Quarterly Sales by Region'**:

1. In this example, **cells A1:I65** were selected
2. From the toolbar select **INSERT : PivotTable**

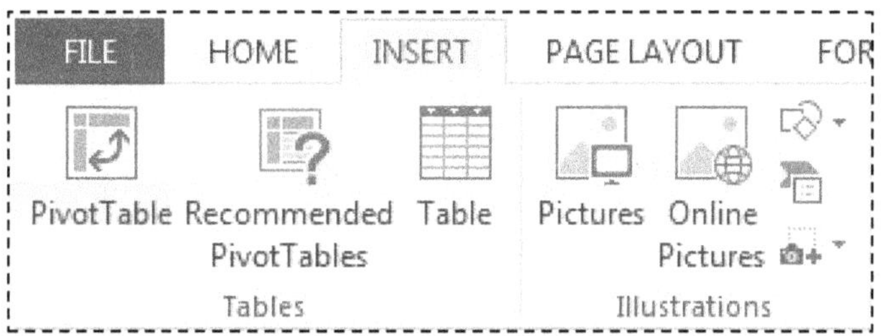

The following dialogue box should appear:

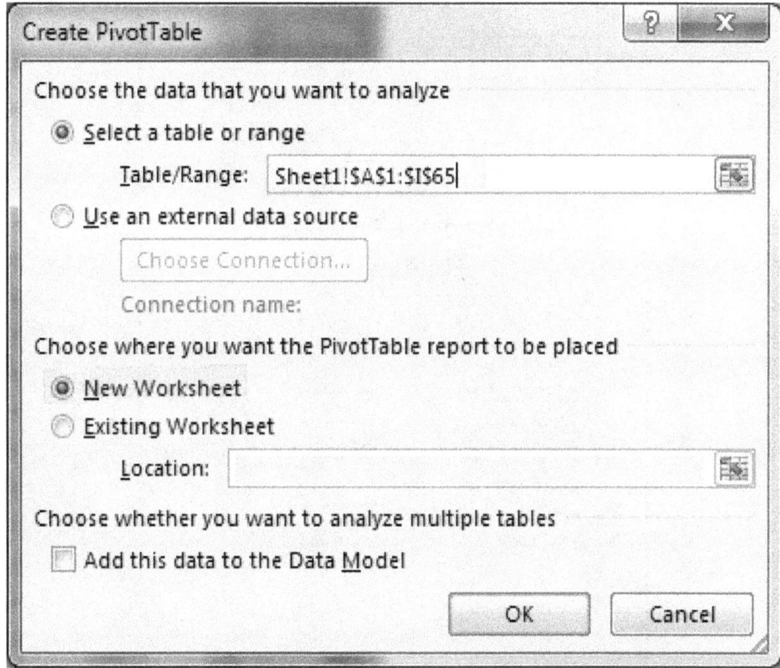

3. For this demonstration, the '**New Worksheet**' radio button has been selected
4. Click the '**OK**' button

A new tab will be created and looks similar to the following *(due to display limitations the below screenshot is split, showing the left & right sides of your screen separately)*:

Left side of your screen:

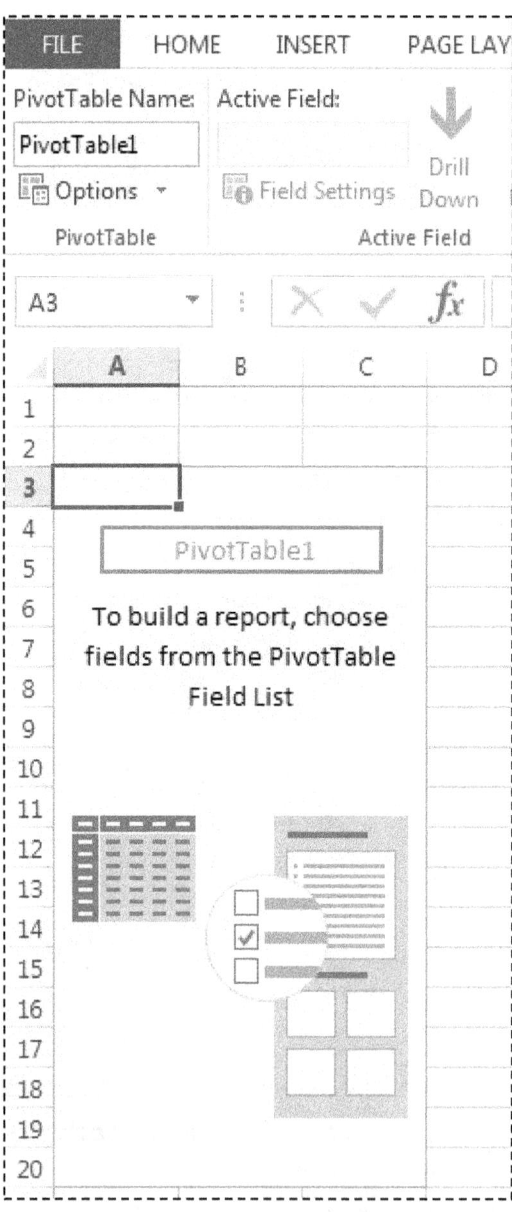

Right side of your screen:

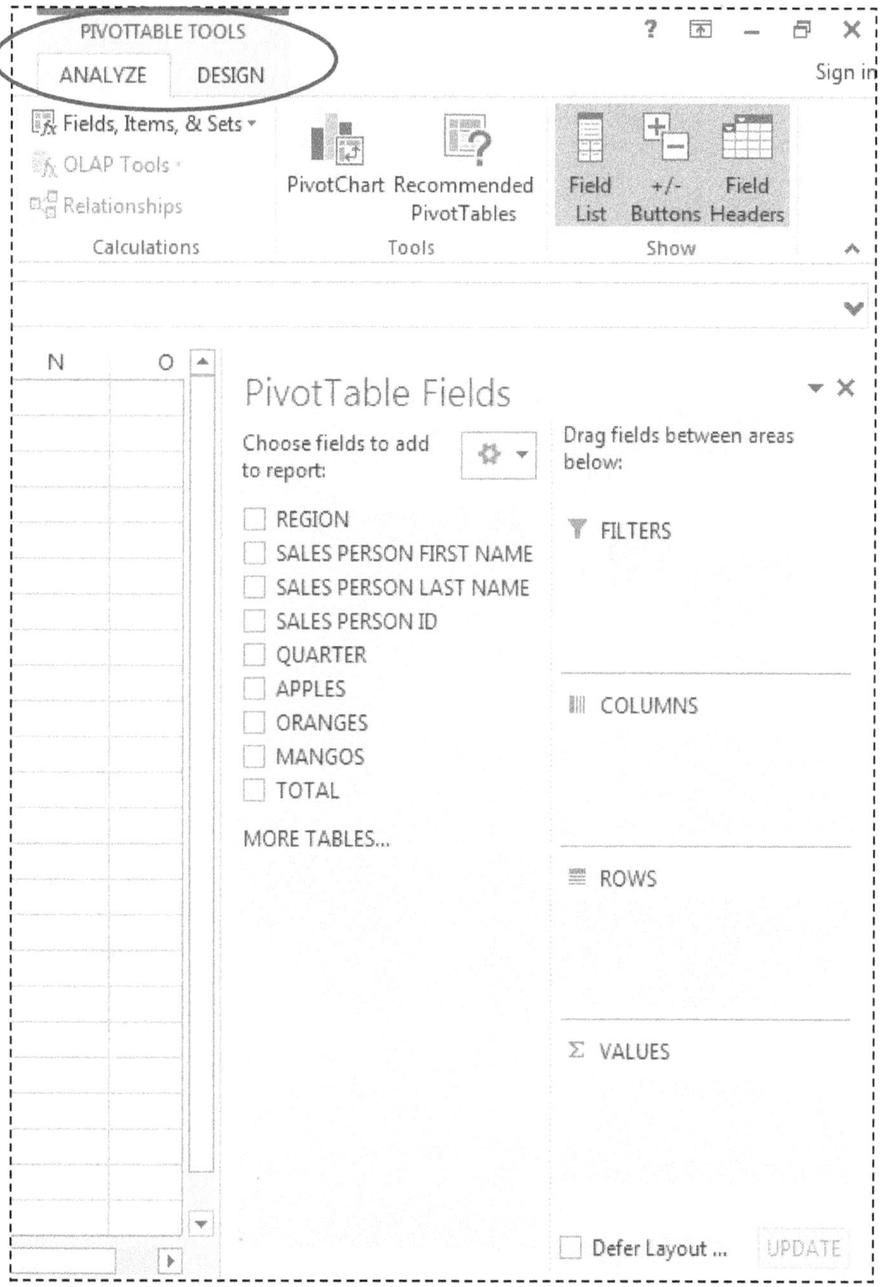

5. Click the **'REGION'** and **'TOTAL' PivotTable Fields** check boxes

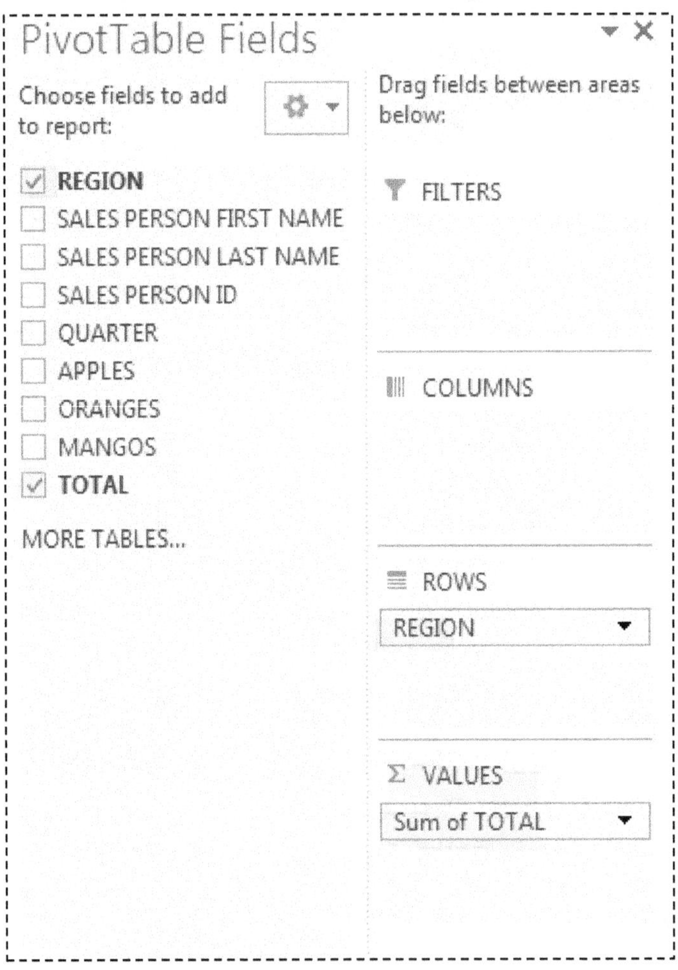

The following should be displayed on the left side of your screen
Note: the format is not very easy to read.

	A	B
1		
2		
3	**Row Labels**	**Sum of TOTAL**
4	Central	138571.3795
5	East	145587.9689
6	West	196786.7115
7	**Grand Total**	**480946.0598**

6. We can change the column labels and format of the numbers. In the below example:
    a. Cell label **'A3'** was changed to **'REGION'**
    b. Cell label **'B3'** was changed to **'TOTAL SALES'**
    c. The dollar sales total format was changed to currency with zero decimal places

Below is the formatted example:

	A	B
1		
2		
3	**REGION**	**TOTALS SALES**
4	Central	$ 138,571
5	East	$ 145,588
6	West	$ 196,787
7	**Grand Total**	**$ 480,946**

7. Now let's add the **'QUARTER'** by clicking the check box labeled **'QUARTER'** from the **PivotTable Fields** list. *Note: you may also drag the field 'QUARTER' over to the '**COLUMNS**' section of the PivotTable Fields list.*

We now have **'QUARTER'** added to the summary

8. The label for cell **'B3'** was changed to **'BY QUARTER**'
9. The labels for cells **'B4'**, **'C4'**, **'D4'**, & **'E4**' were changed by adding the abbreviation '**QTR**' in front of each quarter number

***Before** formatting:*

	A	B	C	D	E	F
1						
2						
3	TOTALS SALES	Column Labels				
4	REGION	1	2	3	4	Grand Total
5	Central	$ 11,359	$19,352	$ 34,097	$ 73,763	$ 138,571
6	East	$ 3,865	$19,343	$ 38,811	$ 83,569	$ 145,588
7	West	$ 2,646	$23,586	$ 42,590	$127,964	$ 196,787
8	**Grand Total**	**$ 17,870**	**$62,281**	**$115,499**	**$285,296**	**$ 480,946**

***After** formatting:*

3	TOTALS SALES	BY QUARTER				
4	REGION	QTR 1	QTR 2	QTR 3	QTR 4	Grand Total
5	Central	$ 11,359	$19,352	$ 34,097	$ 73,763	$ 138,571
6	East	$ 3,865	$19,343	$ 38,811	$ 83,569	$ 145,588
7	West	$ 2,646	$23,586	$ 42,590	$127,964	$ 196,787
8	**Grand Total**	**$ 17,870**	**$62,281**	**$115,499**	**$285,296**	**$ 480,946**

Now that we have determined the '**Total Sales by Region**' and the '**Quarterly Sales by Region,'** let's add a chart to the summary

1. From the PIVOTTABLE TOOLS toolbar select the tab **ANALYZE : PivotChart**

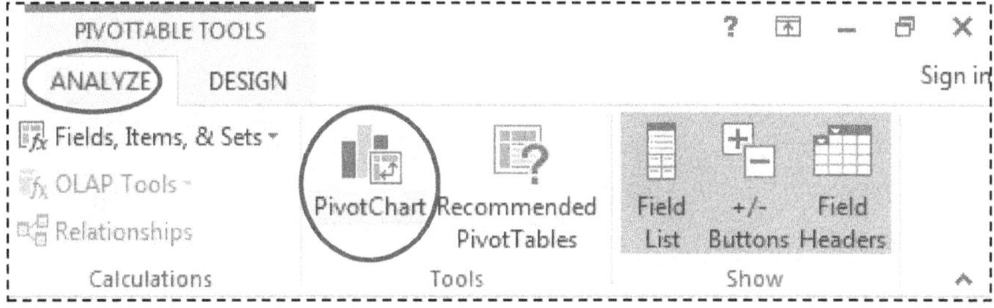

Note: *If you do not see the PIVOTTABLE TOOLS option on your toolbar, click any PivotTable cell. This toolbar option only appears when a PivotTable field is active.*

The following dialogue box should appear:

Insert Chart
All Charts
Recent
Templates
Column
Line
Pie
Bar
Area
X Y (Scatter)
Stock
Surface
Radar
Combo
Clustered Column
OK
Cancel

2. Click the **'OK'** button

A chart similar to the below should now be displayed:

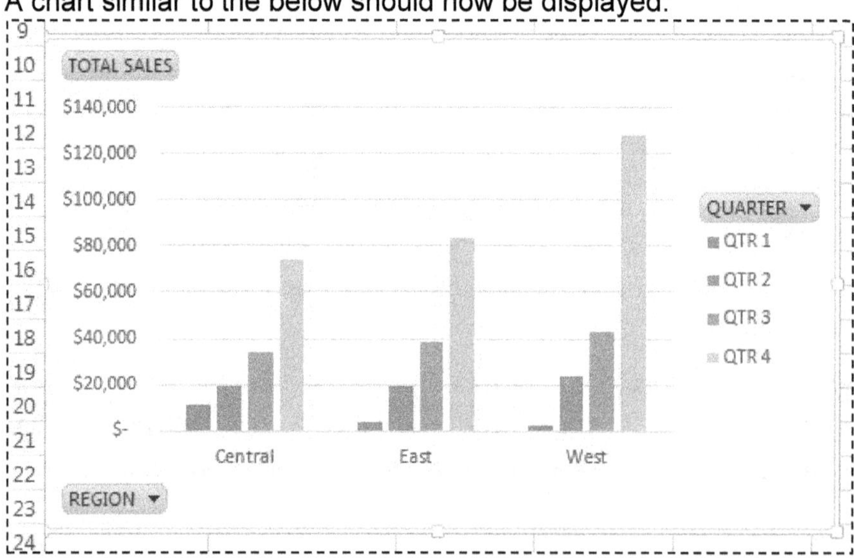

Note: for the remainder of this chapter's Pivot Table examples we do not need the chart. Please delete the chart by clicking on the chart and pressing the delete button on your keyboard.

Next, we'll extend our analysis by adding the individual fruit sales to our summary.

1. Drag the **'QUARTER'** field from the **'COLUMNS'** section to the **'ROWS'** section.

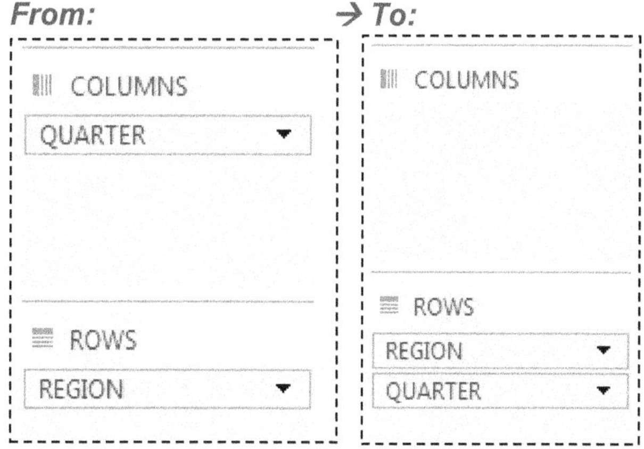

The PivotTable Fields box should now appear as follows:

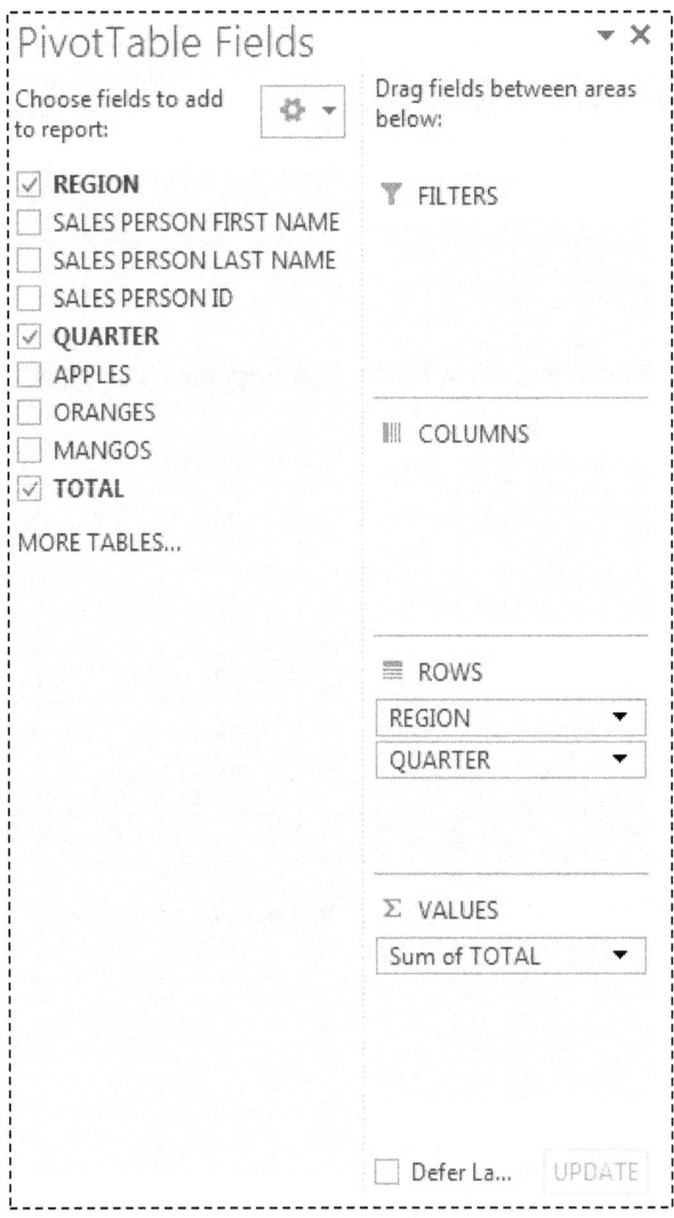
PivotTable Fields
Choose fields to add to report:
REGION
SALES PERSON FIRST NAME
SALES PERSON LAST NAME
SALES PERSON ID
QUARTER
APPLES
ORANGES
MANGOS
TOTAL
MORE TABLES...
Drag fields between areas below:
FILTERS
COLUMNS
ROWS
REGION
QUARTER
VALUES
Sum of TOTAL
Defer La...
UPDATE

2. Drag the fields **'APPLES'**, '**ORANGES**', & **'MANGOS'** to the **'VALUES'** section of the **PivotTables Fields** list

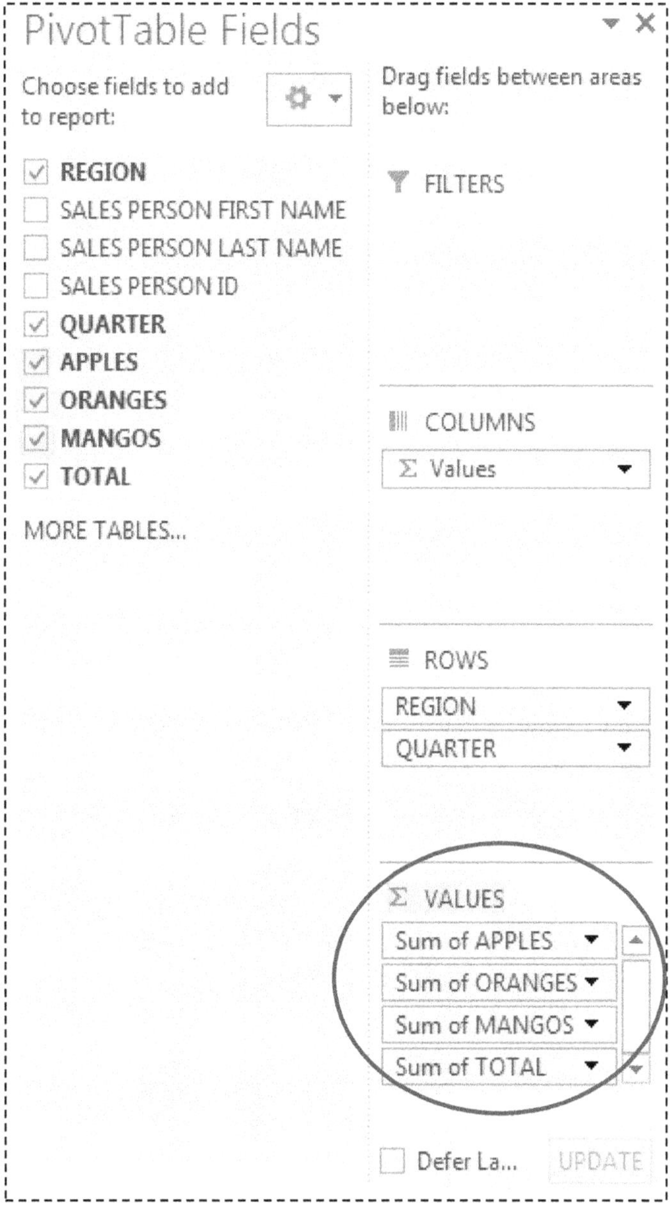

The results should look similar to the following:

	A	B	C	D	E
1					
2					
3	**REGION**	**TOTAL APPLES**	**TOTAL ORANGES**	**TOTAL MANGOS**	**TOTAL SALES**
4	**⊟Central**	**$ 43,481**	**$ 53,278**	**$ 41,812**	**$ 138,571**
5	QTR 1	$ 3,463	$ 4,631	$ 3,264	$ 11,359
6	QTR 2	$ 5,992	$ 7,652	$ 5,709	$ 19,352
7	QTR 3	$ 10,634	$ 13,280	$ 10,183	$ 34,097
8	QTR 4	$ 23,392	$ 27,715	$ 22,656	$ 73,763
9	**⊟East**	**$ 50,626**	**$ 47,117**	**$ 47,845**	**$ 145,588**
10	QTR 1	$ 1,587	$ 1,087	$ 1,190	$ 3,865
11	QTR 2	$ 6,891	$ 6,149	$ 6,303	$ 19,343
12	QTR 3	$ 13,583	$ 12,502	$ 12,726	$ 38,811
13	QTR 4	$ 28,564	$ 27,380	$ 27,625	$ 83,569
14	**⊟West**	**$ 69,750**	**$ 65,259**	**$ 61,778**	**$ 196,787**
15	QTR 1	$ 856	$ 1,119	$ 671	$ 2,646
16	QTR 2	$ 7,819	$ 8,253	$ 7,513	$ 23,586
17	QTR 3	$ 15,335	$ 14,074	$ 13,182	$ 42,590
18	QTR 4	$ 45,739	$ 41,813	$ 40,411	$ 127,964
19	**Grand Total**	**$ 163,857**	**$ 165,655**	**$ 151,435**	**$ 480,946**

We covered some of the basic types of analysis that we can do with Pivot Tables, now let's go a few steps further by answering the following questions.

- What is the percentage of Individual Fruit Sales by Quarter?
- What is the percentage of Total Sales for each Region?

1. Uncheck (deselect) the **'TOTAL SALES'** & **'REGION'** boxes from the Pivot 'Field List'

	Row Labels	Sum of APPLES	Sum of ORANGES	Sum of MANGOS	Sum of TOTAL
3	Row Labels	Sum of APPLES	Sum of ORANGES	Sum of MANGOS	Sum of TOTAL
4	**Central**	**$ 43,481**	**$ 53,278**	**$ 41,812**	**$ 138,571**
5	1	$ 3,463	$ 4,631	$ 3,264	$ 11,359
6	2	$ 5,992	$ 7,652	$ 5,709	$ 19,352
7	3	$ 10,634	$ 13,280	$ 10,183	$ 34,097
8	4	$ 23,392	$ 27,715	$ 22,656	$ 73,763
9	**East**	**$ 50,626**	**$ 47,117**	**$ 47,845**	**$ 145,588**
10	1	$ 1,587	$ 1,087	$ 1,190	$ 3,865
11	2	$ 6,891	$ 6,149	$ 6,303	$ 19,343
12	3	$ 13,583	$ 12,502	$ 12,726	$ 38,811
13	4	$ 28,564	$ 27,380	$ 27,625	$ 83,569
14	**West**	**$ 69,750**	**$ 65,259**	**$ 61,778**	**$ 196,787**
15	1	$ 856	$ 1,119	$ 671	$ 2,646
16	2	$ 7,819	$ 8,253	$ 7,513	$ 23,586
17	3	$ 15,335	$ 14,074	$ 13,182	$ 42,590
18	4	$ 45,739	$ 41,813	$ 40,411	$ 127,964
19	**Grand Total**	**$ 163,857**	**$ 165,655**	**$ 151,435**	**$ 480,946**

Only the following fields should be selected:

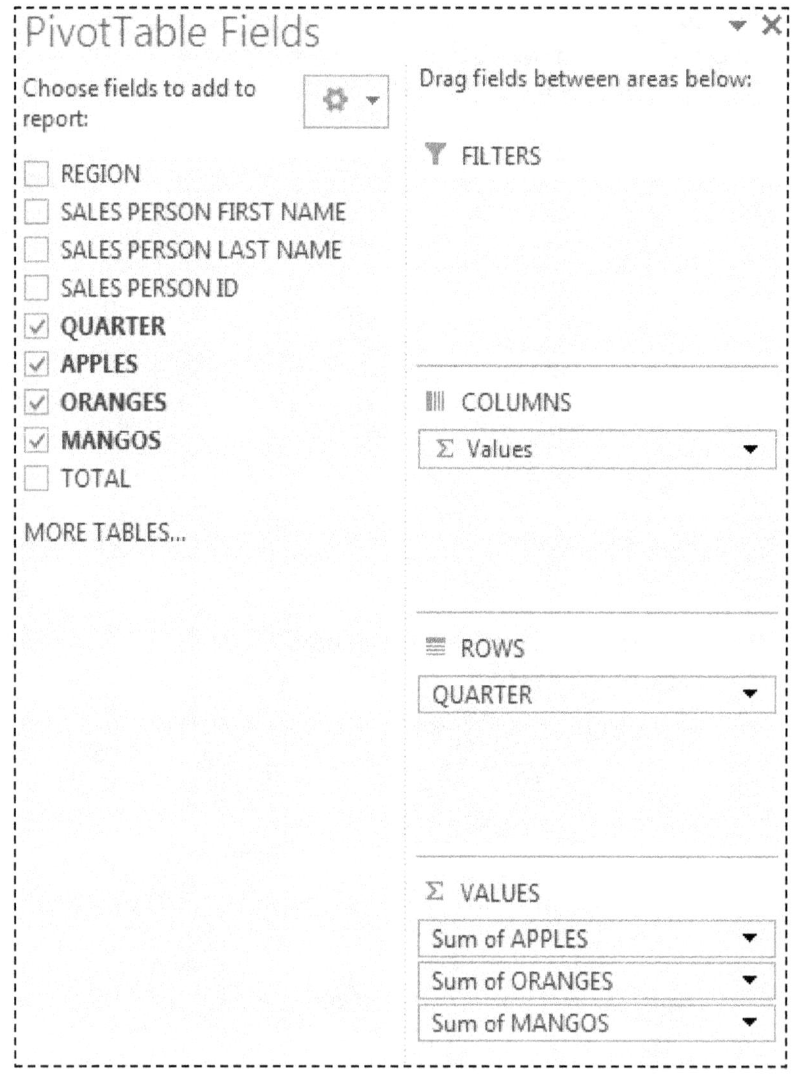
PivotTable Fields
Choose fields to add to report:
REGION
SALES PERSON FIRST NAME
SALES PERSON LAST NAME
SALES PERSON ID
QUARTER
APPLES
ORANGES
MANGOS
TOTAL
MORE TABLES...
Drag fields between areas below:
FILTERS
COLUMNS
Σ Values
ROWS
QUARTER
Σ VALUES
Sum of APPLES
Sum of ORANGES
Sum of MANGOS

2. Click on the **'Sum of APPLES'** drop-down box and select **'Value Field Settings...'**.

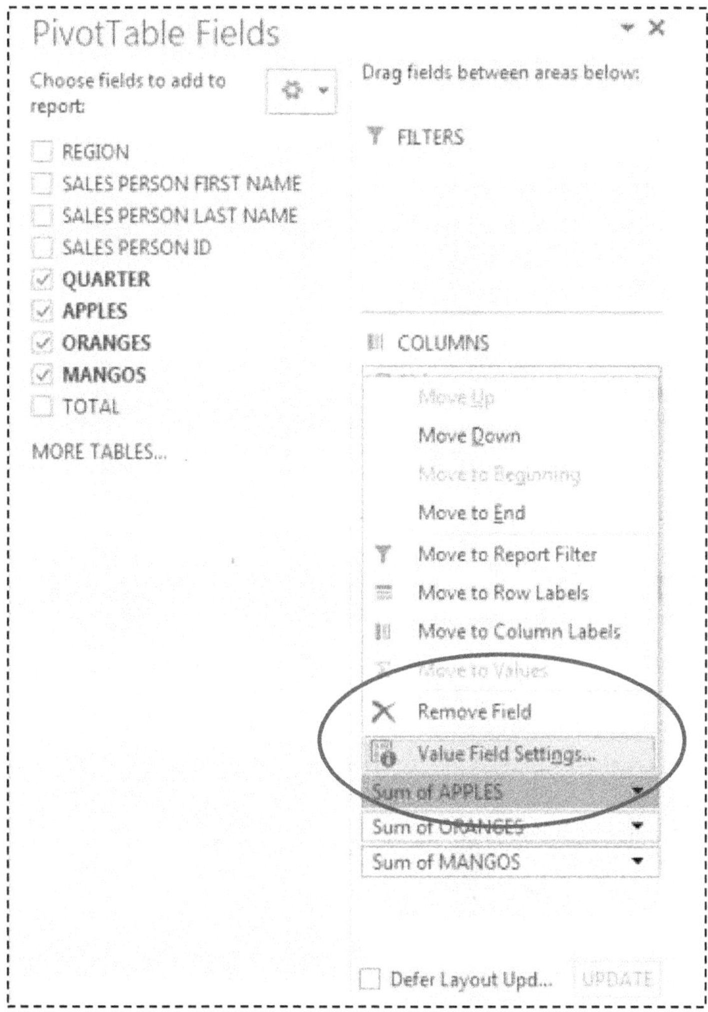

The following dialogue box should appear:

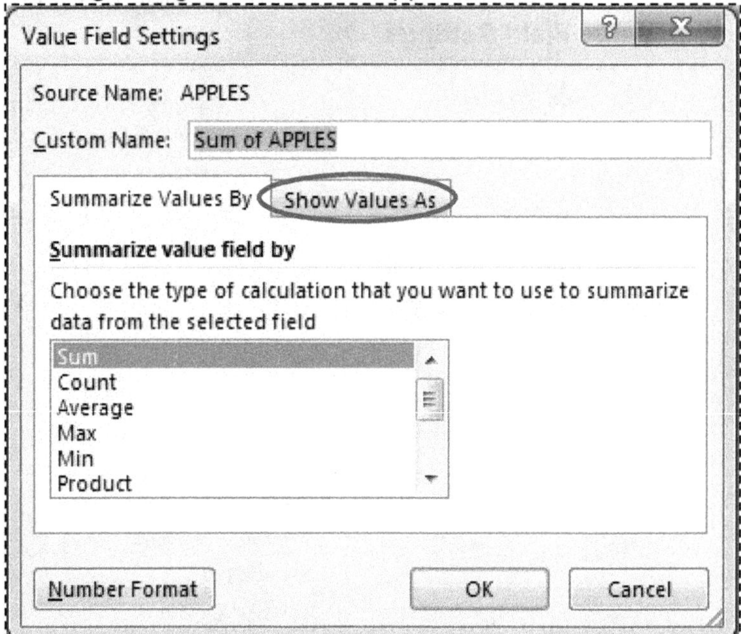

3. Select the tab **'Show Values As'**

4. From the '**Show values as**' drop-down list select **'% of Grand Total'**
5. Click the **'OK'** button

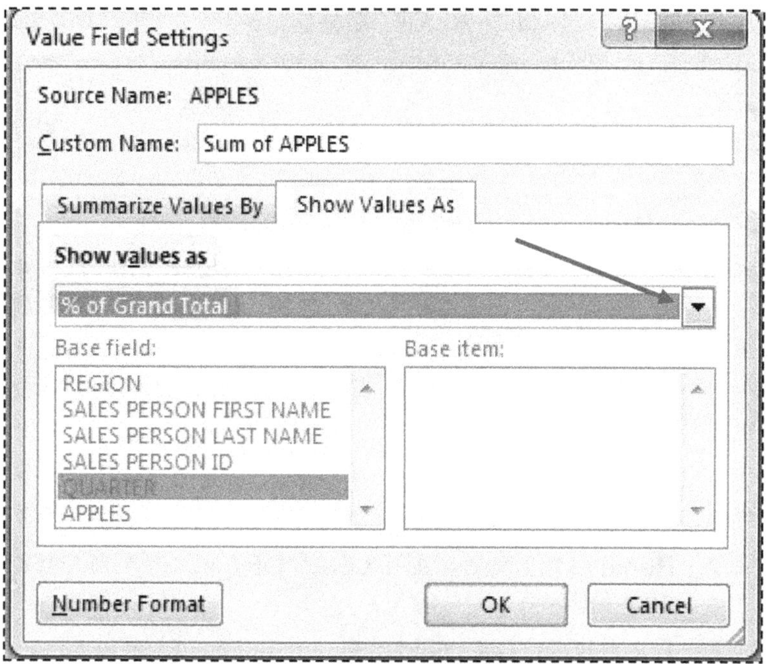

6. Repeat the process for **'Sum of ORANGES'** and **'Sum of MANGOS'**

The Totals by fruit have been changed to a percentage. **<u>Note:</u> the column labels have been changed and the number of decimal places reduced for the percentages**

3	QUARTER	% of APPLES	% of ORANGES	% of MANGOS
4	QTR 1	4%	4%	3%
5	QTR 2	13%	13%	13%
6	QTR 3	24%	24%	24%
7	QTR 4	60%	59%	60%
8	**Grand Total**	**100%**	**100%**	**100%**

<u>Please note</u>: In Excel®, often the percentages when summed together may exceed or not equal 100%, this is due to rounding the percentages either up or down.

We've now answered the question, what are the percentage of Individual Fruit Sales by Quarter

---

To determine the percentage of Total Sales for each Region

7. Remove the fields **'APPLES,'** **'ORANGES,'** **'MANGOS,'** and **'QUARTER'**
8. Add the **'TOTAL'** field

See the below **PivotTable Fields** list:

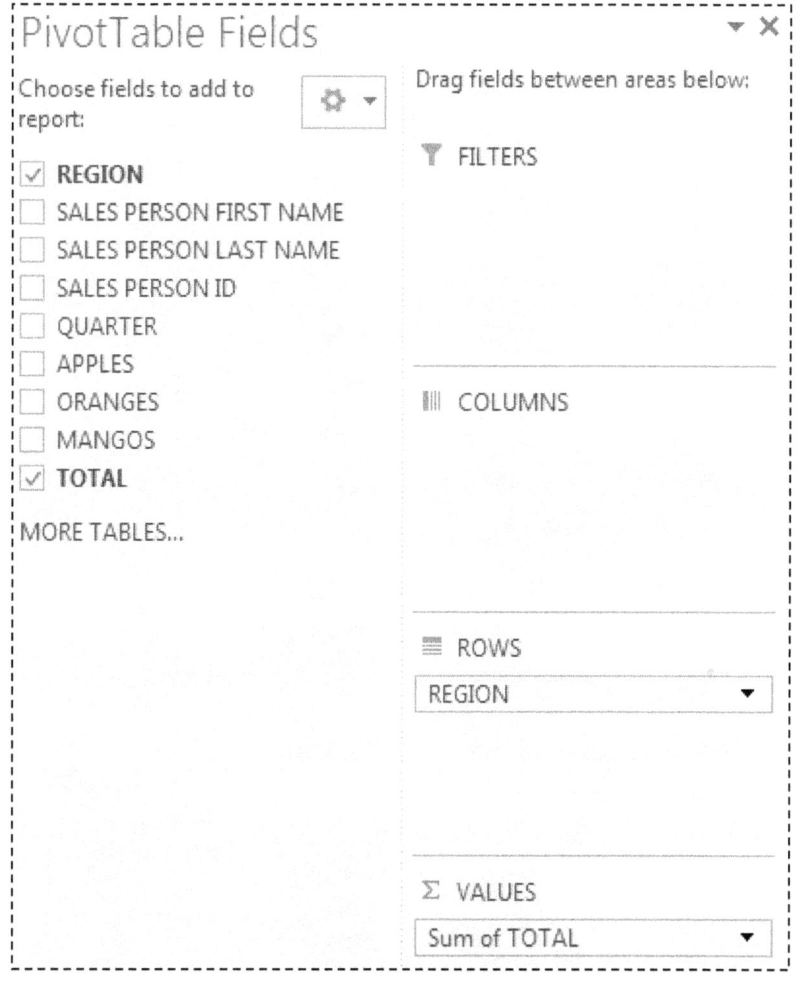
PivotTable Fields
Choose fields to add to report:
REGION
SALES PERSON FIRST NAME
SALES PERSON LAST NAME
SALES PERSON ID
QUARTER
APPLES
ORANGES
MANGOS
TOTAL
MORE TABLES...
Drag fields between areas below:
FILTERS
COLUMNS
ROWS
REGION
VALUES
Sum of TOTAL

9. Click on the **'Sum of TOTAL'** drop-down box and select **'Value Field Settings...'**.

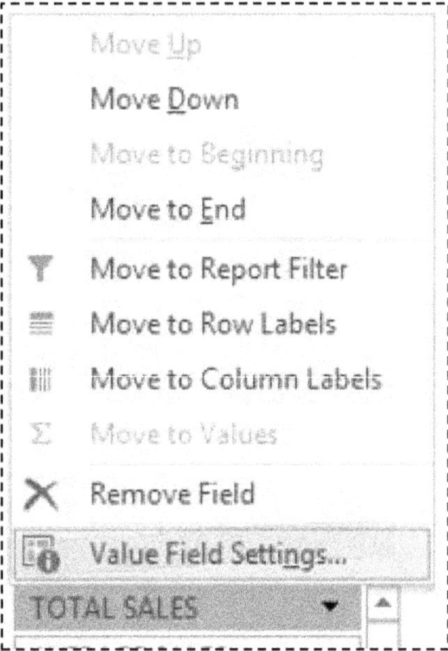

The following dialogue box should appear:

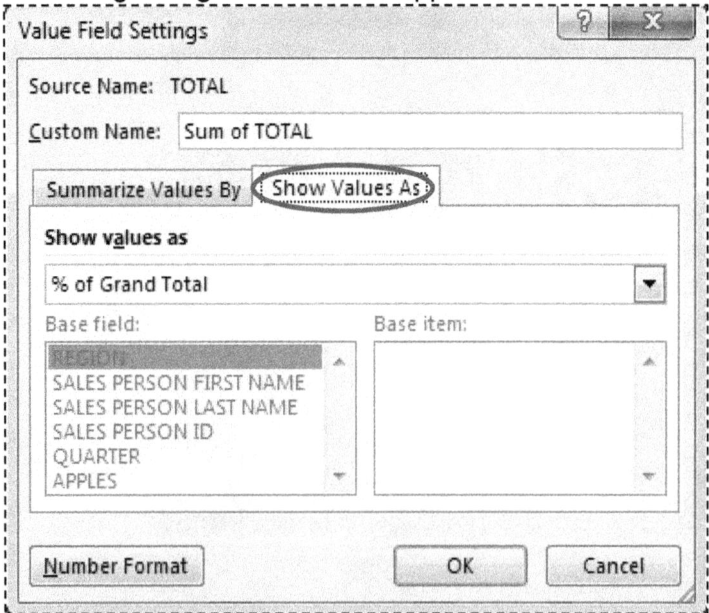

10. Select the tab **'Show Values As'**
11. From the '**Show values as'** drop-down list select **'% of Grand Total'**
12. Click the **'OK'** button

We've now determined the percentage of Total Sales for each Region.

3	REGION	Sum of TOTAL
4	Central	28.81%
5	East	30.27%
6	West	40.92%
7	**Grand Total**	**100.00%**

All of the previous Pivot Table examples focused on *summary level* types of analysis, now let's take a look at some individual results by:

- Ranking each Sales Person, including their Total & Average Sales

We'll create a new Pivot Table using similar sample data as above.

1. Begin by selecting the **'SALES PERSON ID'** and adding the **'TOTAL'** field ***three*** times to the '**VALUES'** section.

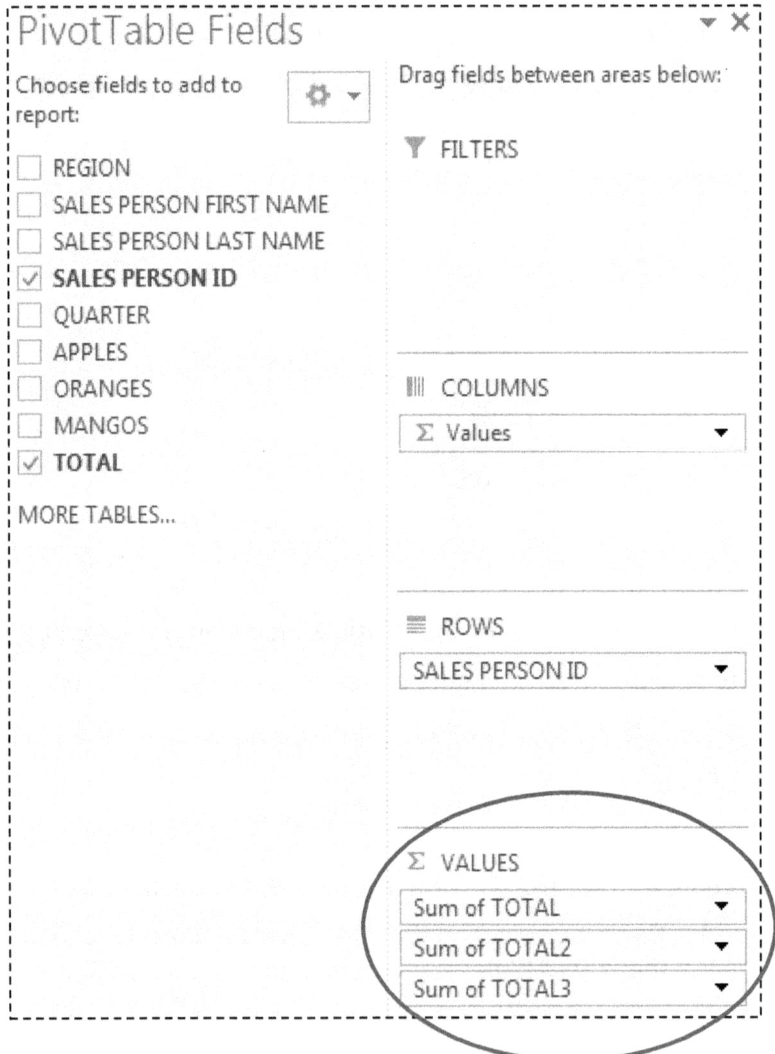
PivotTable Fields
Choose fields to add to report:
REGION
SALES PERSON FIRST NAME
SALES PERSON LAST NAME
SALES PERSON ID
QUARTER
APPLES
ORANGES
MANGOS
TOTAL
MORE TABLES...
Drag fields between areas below:
FILTERS
COLUMNS
Σ Values
ROWS
SALES PERSON ID
Σ VALUES
Sum of TOTAL
Sum of TOTAL2
Sum of TOTAL3

The spreadsheet will look similar to the below. *Note: all three of the '**Sum of TOTAL**' columns are currently the same. We will be changing them in the following steps.*

	A	B	C	D
1				
2				
3	**Row Labels**	**Sum of TOTAL**	**Sum of TOTAL2**	**Sum of TOTAL3**
4	100	10339	10339	10339
5	200	30217.4275	30217.4275	30217.4275
6	255	11499	11499	11499
7	300	16856.7	16856.7	16856.7
8	400	15276.2	15276.2	15276.2
9	500	20332.2129	20332.2129	20332.2129
10	600	24898.65	24898.65	24898.65
11	690	37013.424	37013.424	37013.424
12	700	22708.425	22708.425	22708.425
13	800	17755.0365	17755.0365	17755.0365
14	817	33931.63025	33931.63025	33931.63025
15	833	45671.45013	45671.45013	45671.45013
16	900	55320.19485	55320.19485	55320.19485
17	1000	50925.33004	50925.33004	50925.33004
18	1156	63606.12616	63606.12616	63606.12616
19	1174	24595.2525	24595.2525	24595.2525
20	**Grand Total**	**480946.0598**	**480946.0598**	**480946.0598**

2. Change the label for cell '**A3'** to **'SALES PERSON ID'**
3. Change the label for cell '**B3'** to **'TOTAL SALES'**
4. Change the label for cell '**C3'** to **'AVERAGE SALES'**
5. Change the label for cell '**D3'** to **'RANK'**
6. Change the formatting for columns **'B'** & **'C'** to currency with zero decimal places

7. In the **PivotTable Fields** list, in the **'VALUES'** section, click the drop-down box for **'AVERAGE SALES'**
8. Select the **'Value Field Settings...'**option

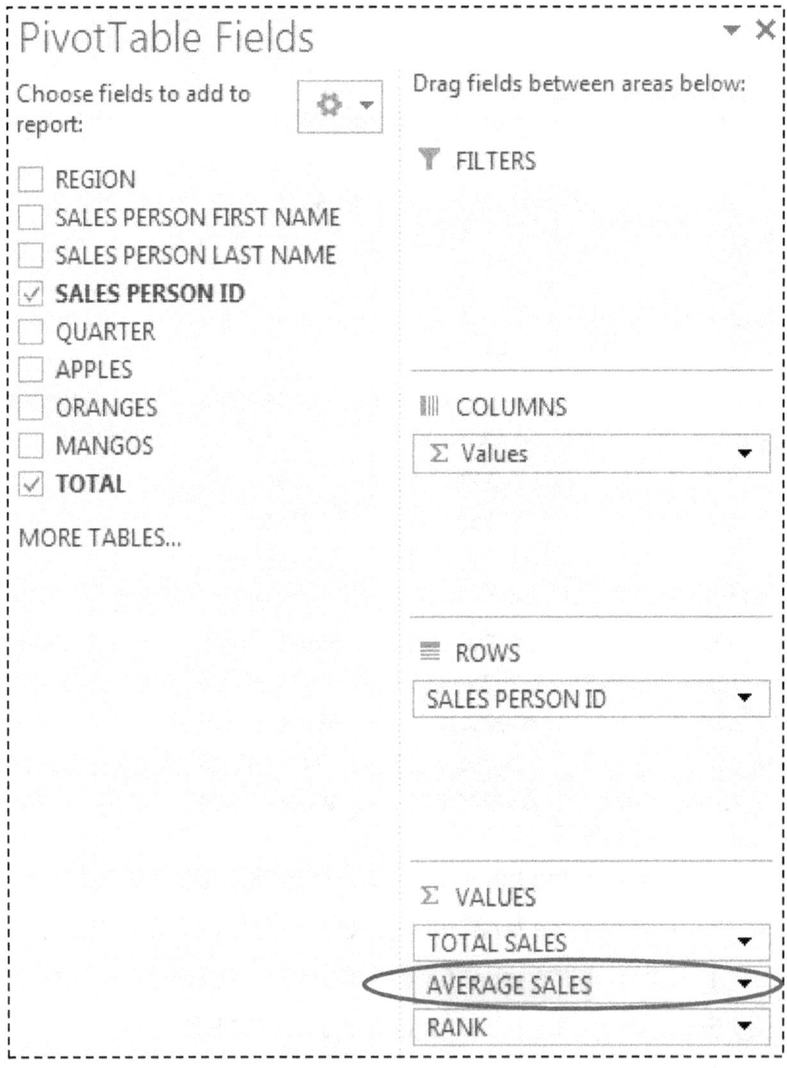

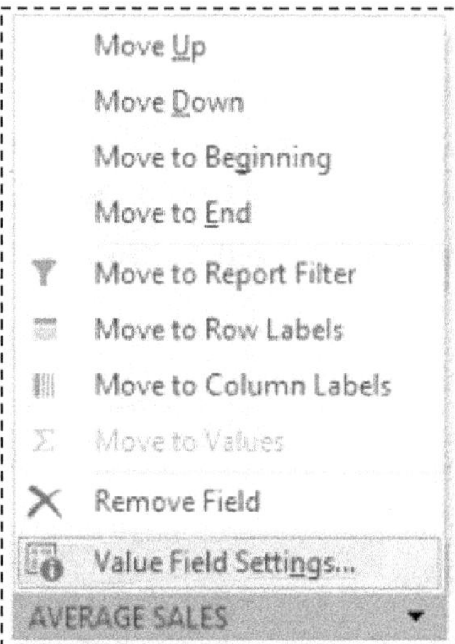

The following dialogue box should appear:

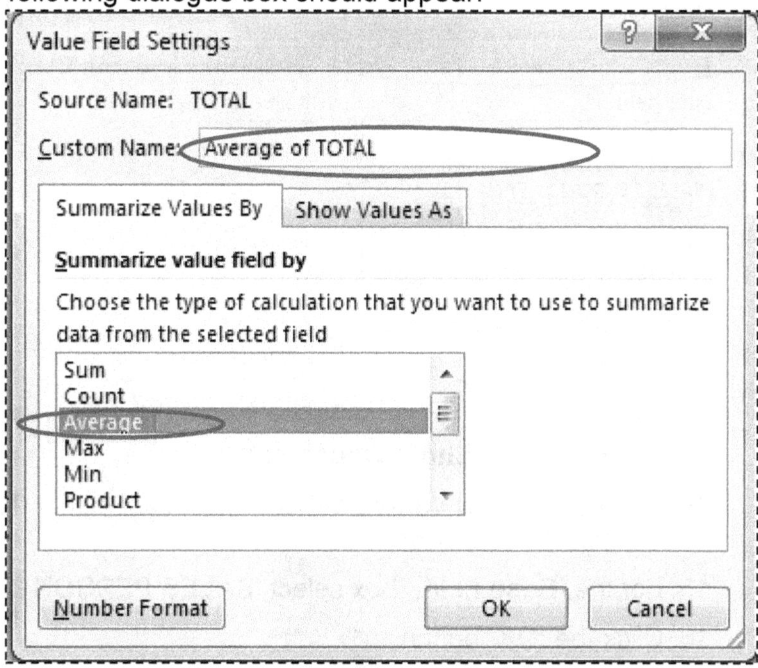

9. From the '**Summarize value field by'** list select **'Average'**. *Note: this will change the* ***'Custom Name:'*** *to* ***'Average of TOTAL',*** *change back to* **'AVERAGE SALES'**
10. Click the **'OK'** button

Next, change the field **'RANK'**

11. In the **PivotTable Fields** list, in the **'VALUES'** section, select the drop-down box for **'RANK'**
12. Select the **'Value Field Settings…'**option

The following dialogue box should appear:

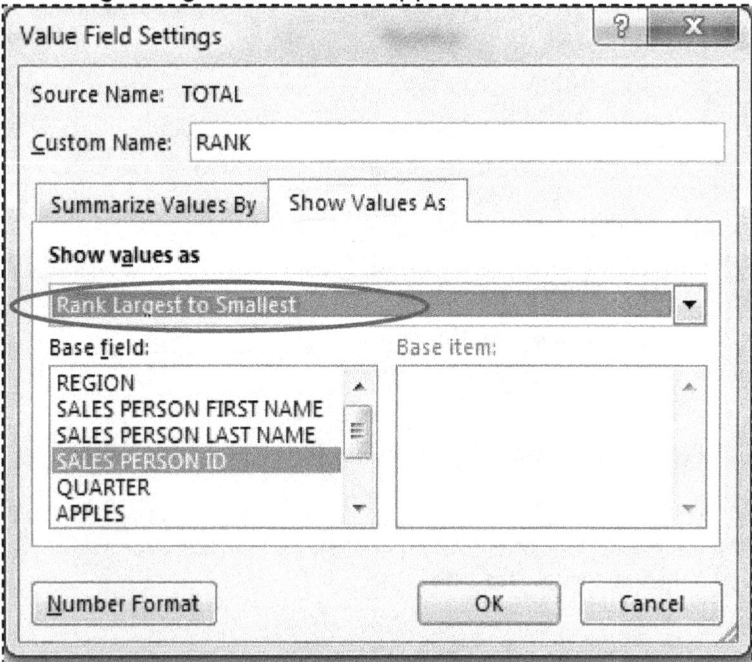

13. Select the tab **'Show Values As'**
14. From the '**Show values as'** drop-down list select **'Rank Largest to Smallest'**
15. For the **'Base field:'** box select **'SALES PERSON ID'**
16. Click the **'OK'** button

The results should look similar to the following:

3	SALES PERSON ID	TOTAL SALES	AVERAGE SALES	RANK
4	100	$ 10,339	$ 2,585	16
5	200	$ 30,217	$ 7,554	7
6	255	$ 11,499	$ 2,875	15
7	300	$ 16,857	$ 4,214	13
8	400	$ 15,276	$ 3,819	14
9	500	$ 20,332	$ 5,083	11
10	600	$ 24,899	$ 6,225	8
11	690	$ 37,013	$ 9,253	5
12	700	$ 22,708	$ 5,677	10
13	800	$ 17,755	$ 4,439	12
14	817	$ 33,932	$ 8,483	6
15	833	$ 45,671	$ 11,418	4
16	900	$ 55,320	$ 13,830	2
17	1000	$ 50,925	$ 12,731	3
18	1156	$ 63,606	$ 15,902	1
19	1174	$ 24,595	$ 6,149	9
20	**Grand Total**	**$ 480,946**	**$ 7,515**	

Let's improve the readability:

17. With your cursor in cell **'A3'** from the toolbar select PIVOTTABLE TOOLS and the tab **DESIGN**
18. Check the box **'Banded Rows'**

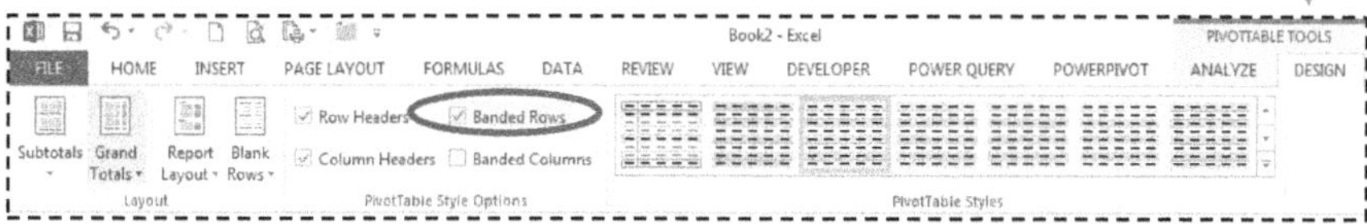

19. Place your cursor in cell **'A3'** and click the drop-down arrow
20. Select the option called **'More Sort Options…'**

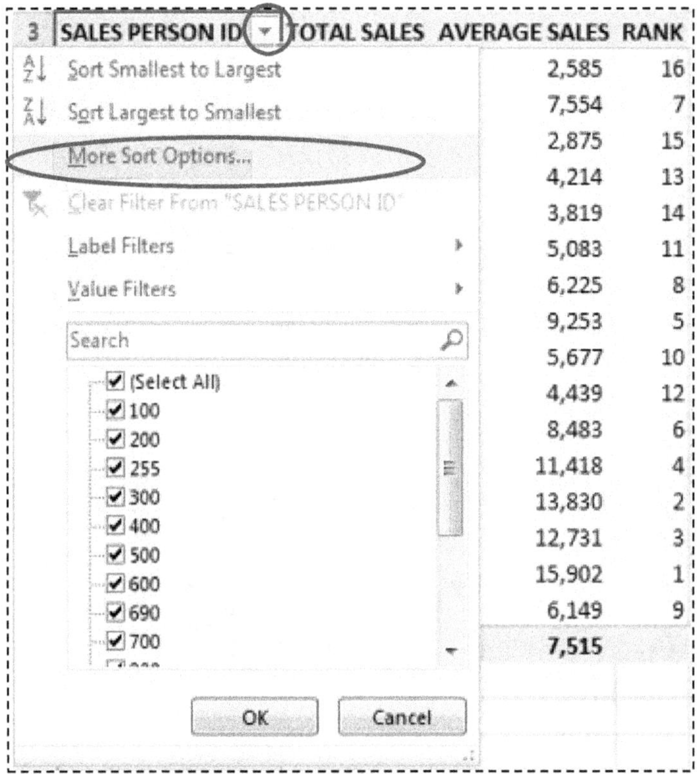

The following dialogue box will appear:

21. Select the **'Descending (Z to A) by:'** radio button
22. Select **'RANK'** from the drop-down box
23. Click the **'OK'** button

We now have a nicely formatted report that shows us each Sales Person's sales rank and their Total and Average Sales.

3	SALES PERSON ID	TOTAL SALES	AVERAGE SALES	RANK
4	1156	$ 63,606	$ 15,902	1
5	900	$ 55,320	$ 13,830	2
6	1000	$ 50,925	$ 12,731	3
7	833	$ 45,671	$ 11,418	4
8	690	$ 37,013	$ 9,253	5
9	817	$ 33,932	$ 8,483	6
10	200	$ 30,217	$ 7,554	7
11	600	$ 24,899	$ 6,225	8
12	1174	$ 24,595	$ 6,149	9
13	700	$ 22,708	$ 5,677	10
14	500	$ 20,332	$ 5,083	11
15	800	$ 17,755	$ 4,439	12
16	300	$ 16,857	$ 4,214	13
17	400	$ 15,276	$ 3,819	14
18	255	$ 11,499	$ 2,875	15
19	100	$ 10,339	$ 2,585	16
20	**Grand Total**	**$ 480,946**	**$ 7,515**	

- For advanced Pivot Table examples, please see **chapter 10**.
- For troubleshooting suggestions, please see **chapter 11**.

(PART 2) - CHAPTER 8
INTRODUCTION TO DASHBOARDS

In the previous examples, we added one Pivot Table per spreadsheet tab, in this chapter we will demonstrate how to add more than one Pivot Table to a tab, with tips on creating and formatting a basic Dashboard.

In chapter 9, we will illustrate how to update (Refresh) data once you have a Pivot Table or Dashboard formatted in a preferred layout.

Scenario:

You've been asked to create a monthly sales Dashboard that shows the following:

1. Total fruit sales by region and month
2. Individual fruits sales by region
3. Total fruit sales by region
4. A pie chart with the percent of total sales by region

The data is generated from a database query. You'll receive a new report at the start of every month of the prior month's sales results.

Detailed Example How To Use The Feature:

Sample data to create a basic Dashboard ***Note:*** *the sample contains only four months of data, but in the design we will plan for twelve months so the Dashboard can be easily updated.*

To download a free copy of the Excel® file used in this scenario please go to:
http://bentonexcelbooks.my-free.website/sample-data-files
*select the file for **Chapter 8 (Dashboards)** in the **'The Microsoft Excel Step-By-Step Training Guide Book Bundle'** section*

	A	B	C	D	E	F
1	REGION	MONTH	APPLES	ORANGES	MANGOS	TOTAL
2	Central	January	$3,463	$4,631	$3,264	**$11,359**
3	Central	February	$5,992	$7,652	$5,709	**$19,352**
4	Central	March	$10,634	$13,280	$10,183	**$34,097**
5	Central	April	$23,392	$27,715	$22,656	**$73,763**
6	East	January	$1,587	$1,087	$1,190	**$3,865**
7	East	February	$6,891	$6,149	$6,303	**$19,343**
8	East	March	$13,583	$12,502	$12,726	**$38,811**
9	East	April	$28,564	$27,380	$27,625	**$83,569**
10	West	January	$722	$943	$566	**$2,231**
11	West	February	$6,121	$6,494	$5,857	**$18,472**
12	West	March	$13,864	$12,577	$11,729	**$38,170**
13	West	April	$39,990	$36,023	$34,691	**$110,704**

1. Create a new Pivot Table, please see the beginning of chapter 7 if you do not already know how to create a Pivot Table. Please select **columns 'A' – 'F'** for your **Table/Range**.

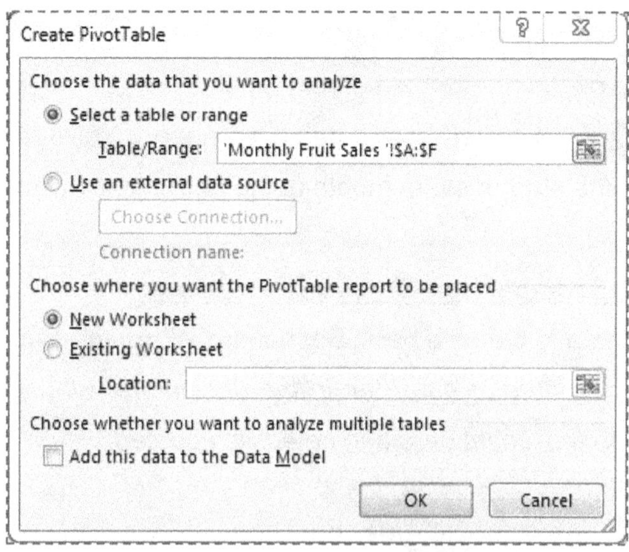

2. Rename the tab from **'Sheet2'** to **'Dashboard'**

From:

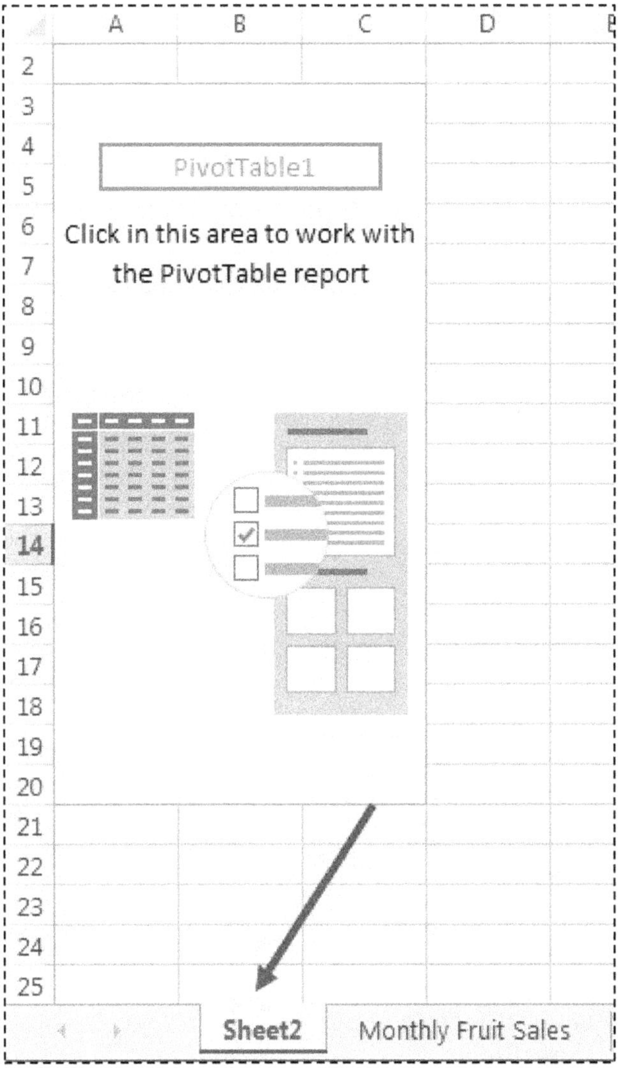

To:

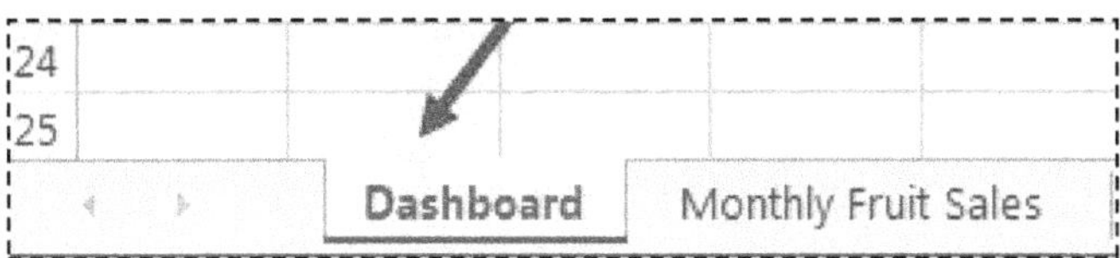

3. We'll begin by adding the Total fruit sales by region and month
4. The PivotTable Fields selected are:
    a. COLUMNS = MONTH
    b. ROWS = REGION
    c. VALUES = Sum of TOTAL

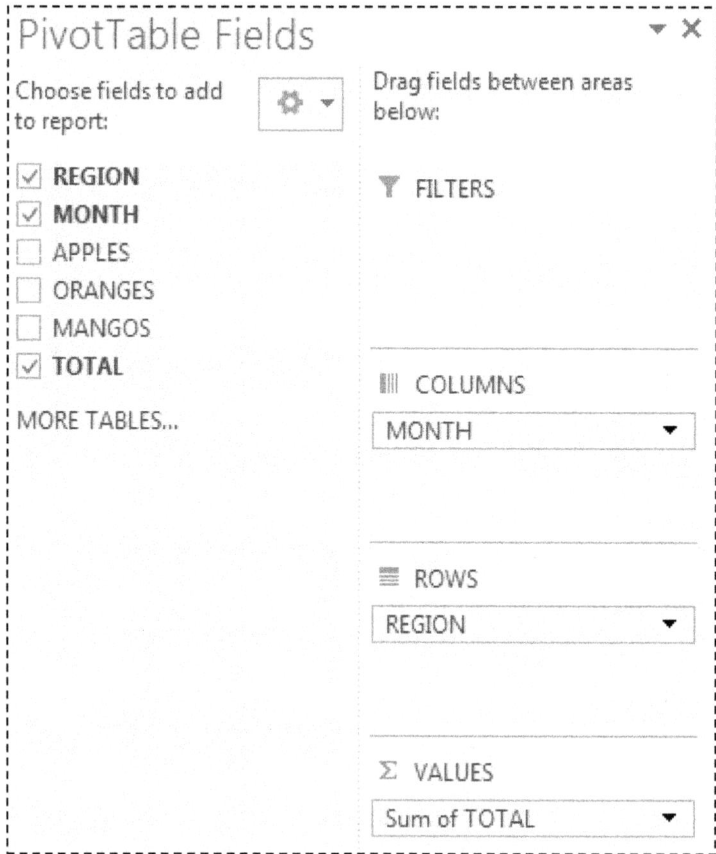

The following should be our results:

Sum of TOTAL	Column Labels					
Row Labels	January	February	March	April	(blank)	Grand Total
Central	11358.9	19352.24	34097.239	73763.00053		138571.3795
East	3864.5283	19343.1909	38810.8125	83569.43715		145587.9689
West	2231.42423	18472.41947	38170.24125	110703.5915		169577.6765
(blank)						
Grand Total	**17454.85253**	**57167.85037**	**111078.2928**	**268036.0292**		**453737.0248**

5. Next, we will add Individual fruits sales by region
6. Go back to our sample data (the tab **Monthly Fruit Sales**)
7. From the toolbar select **INSERT**: **PivotTable**
8. When you receive the **Create PivotTable** prompt, select the **'Existing Worksheet'** radio button
9. Place your cursor inside the **'Location:'** box

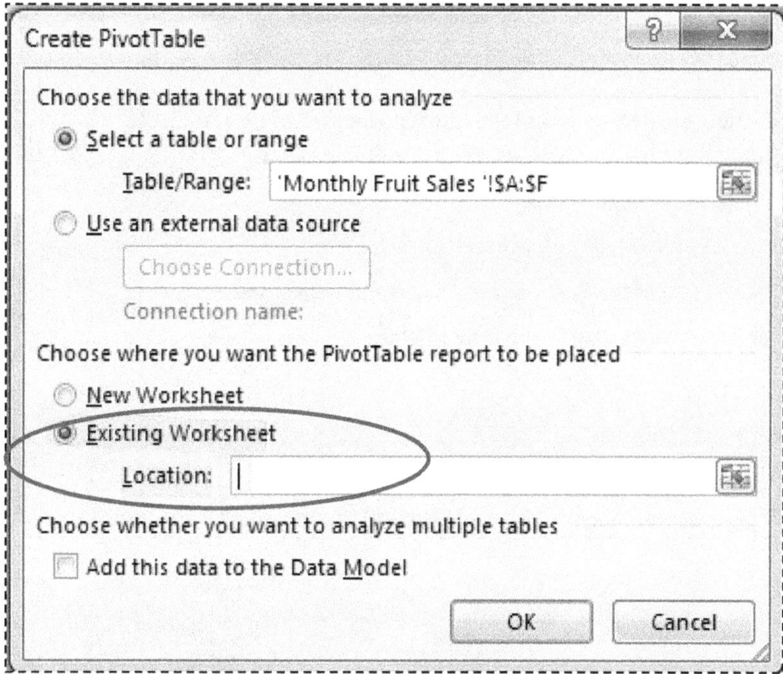

10. With your cursor still inside the **'Location:'** box click the **'Dashboard'** tab and then cell **'A11'**
11. The **'Location:'** box should now have **Dashboard!$A$11** entered

12. Click the **'OK'** button

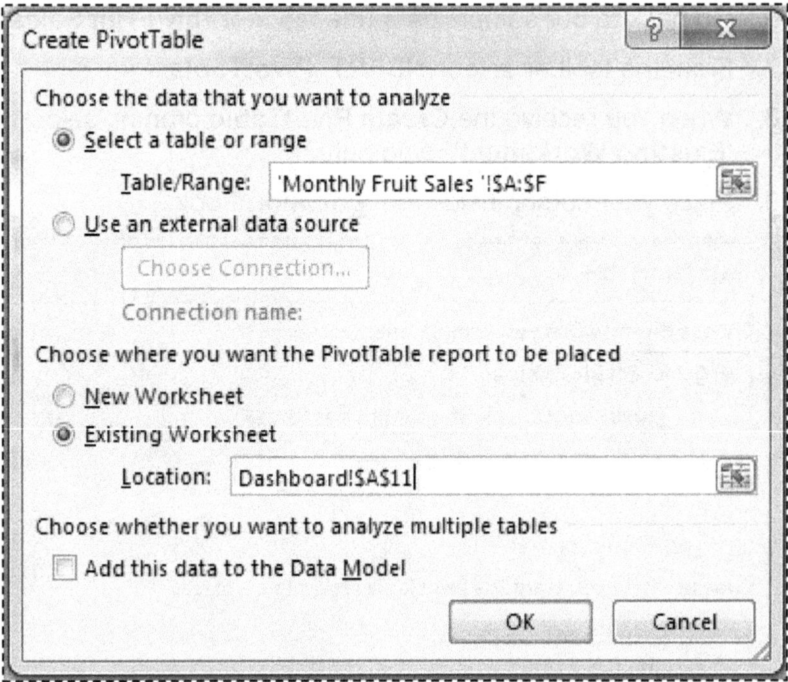

Your screen should look similar to the following:

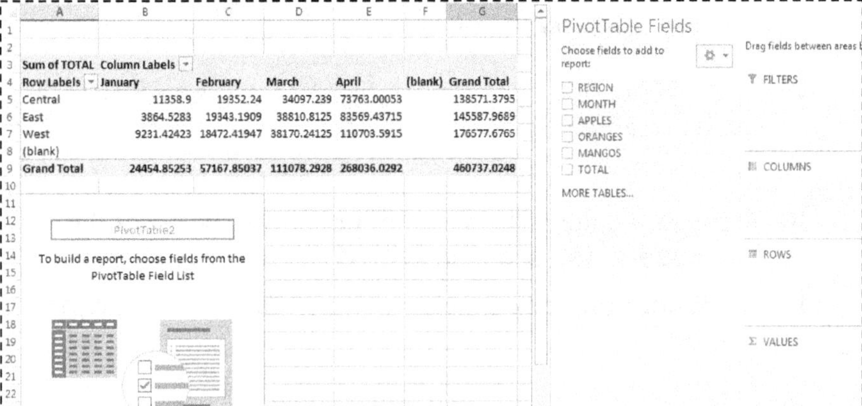

Sum of TOTAL	Column Labels					
Row Labels	January	February	March	April	(blank)	Grand Total
Central	11358.9	19352.24	34097.239	73763.00053		138571.3795
East	3864.5283	19343.1909	38810.8125	83569.43715		145587.9689
West	9231.42423	18472.41947	38170.24125	110703.5915		176577.6765
(blank)						
Grand Total	24454.85253	57167.85037	111078.2928	268036.0292		460737.0248

13. The fields selected for the *second* Pivot Table are:
    a. ROWS = REGION
    b. VALUES =
        - Sum of APPLES
        - Sum of ORANGES
        - Sum of MANGOS
        - Sum of TOTAL

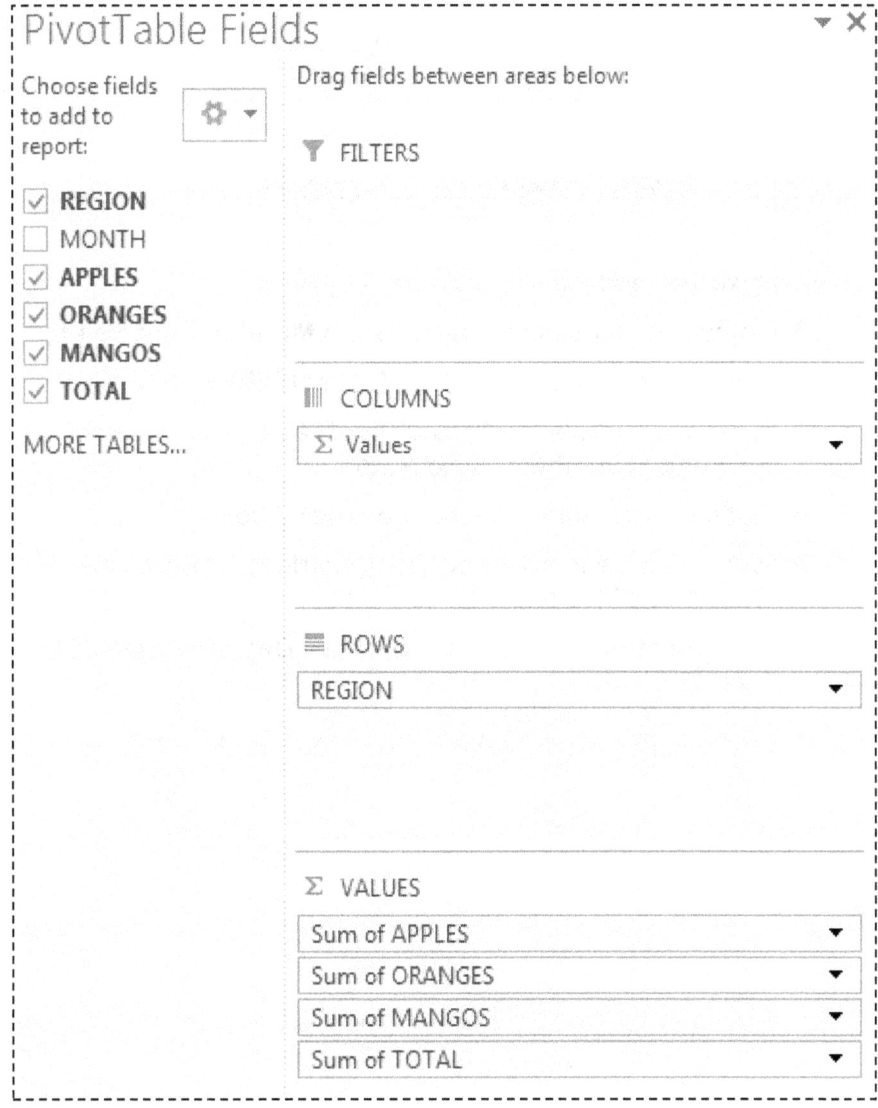

The following should be our results:

Row Labels	January	February	March	April	(blank)	Grand Total
Central	11358.9	19352.24	34097.239	73763.00053		138571.3795
East	3864.5283	19343.1909	38810.8125	83569.43715		145587.9689
West	2231.42423	18472.41947	38170.24125	110703.5915		169577.6765
(blank)						
Grand Total	**17454.85253**	**57167.85037**	**111078.2928**	**268036.0292**		**453737.0248**

Row Labels	Sum of APPLES	Sum of ORANGES	Sum of MANGOS	Sum of TOTAL
Central	43480.80136	53278.35597	41812.22219	138571.3795
East	50625.74293	47117.44827	47844.77765	145587.9689
West	60697.03378	56037.4377	52843.20497	169577.6765
(blank)				
Grand Total	**154803.5781**	**156433.2419**	**142500.2048**	**453737.0248**

14. Next, well add the total fruit sales by region
15. Go back to our sample data (the tab **Monthly Fruit Sales**)
16. From the toolbar select **INSERT**: **PivotTable**
17. When you receive the **Create PivotTable** prompt, select the **'Existing Worksheet'** radio button
18. Place your cursor inside the **'Location:'** box
19. With your cursor still inside the **'Location:'** box click the **'Dashboard'** tab and then cell **'G11'**
20. The **'Location:'** box should now have **Dashboard!$G$11** entered

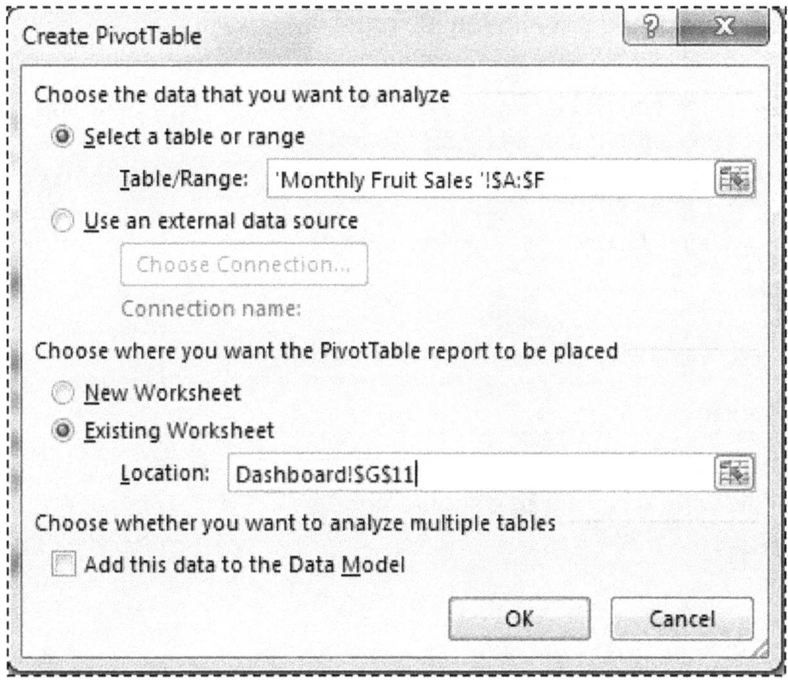

21. Click the **'OK'** button
22. The fields selected for the *third* Pivot Table are:
    a. ROWS = REGION
    b. VALUES = Sum of TOTAL

The following should be our results:

Row Labels	January	February	March	April	(blank)	Grand Total
Central	11358.9	19352.24	34097.239	73763.00053		138571.3795
East	3864.5283	19343.1909	38810.8125	83569.43715		145587.9689
West	2231.42423	18472.41947	38170.24125	110703.5915		169577.6765
(blank)						
Grand Total	**17454.85253**	**57167.85037**	**111078.2928**	**268036.0292**		**453737.0248**

Row Labels	Sum of APPLES	Sum of ORANGES	Sum of MANGOS	Sum of TOTAL
Central	43480.80136	53278.35597	41812.22219	138571.3795
East	50625.74293	47117.44827	47844.77765	145587.9689
West	60697.03378	56037.4377	52843.20497	169577.6765
(blank)				
Grand Total	**154803.5781**	**156433.2419**	**142500.2048**	**453737.0248**

Row Labels	Sum of TOTAL
Central	138571.3795
East	145587.9689
West	169577.6765
(blank)	
Grand Total	**453737.0248**

23. Lastly, we will add the pie chart with the percent of total sales by region
24. Click cell **'G12'**, From the PIVOTTABLE TOOLS toolbar select the tab **ANALYZE : PivotChart**

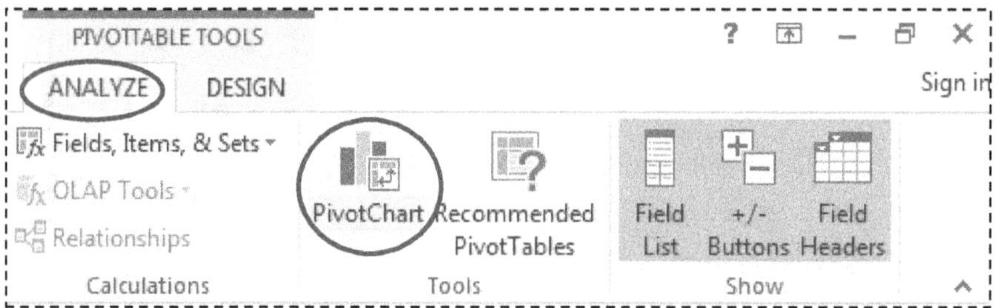

The following dialogue box should appear:

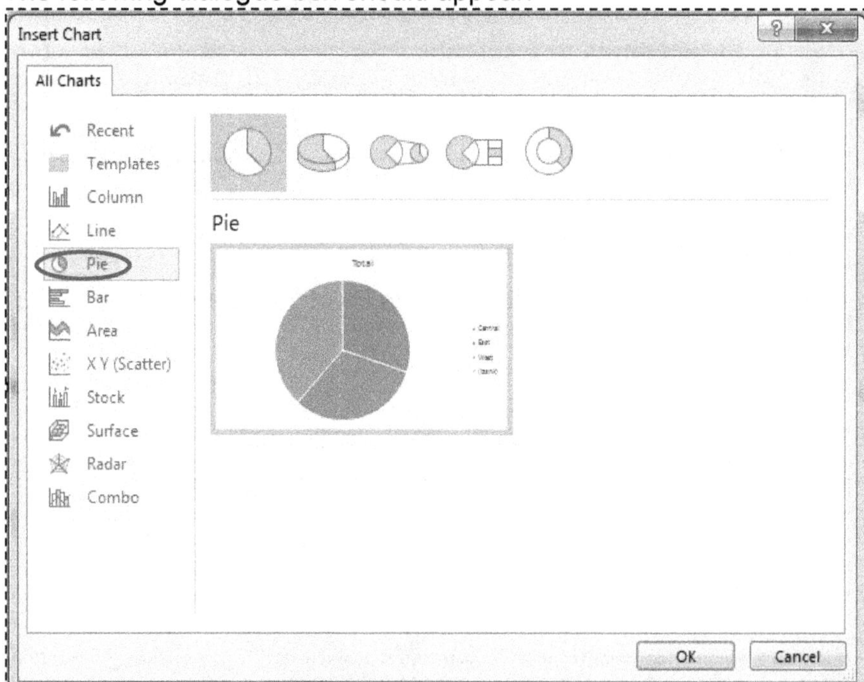

25. Select the **'Pie'** option
26. Click the **'OK'** button

The following pie chart should now be displayed *(you may need to drag you chart down near cell **'A18'**).* We will add the percentages in a later step.

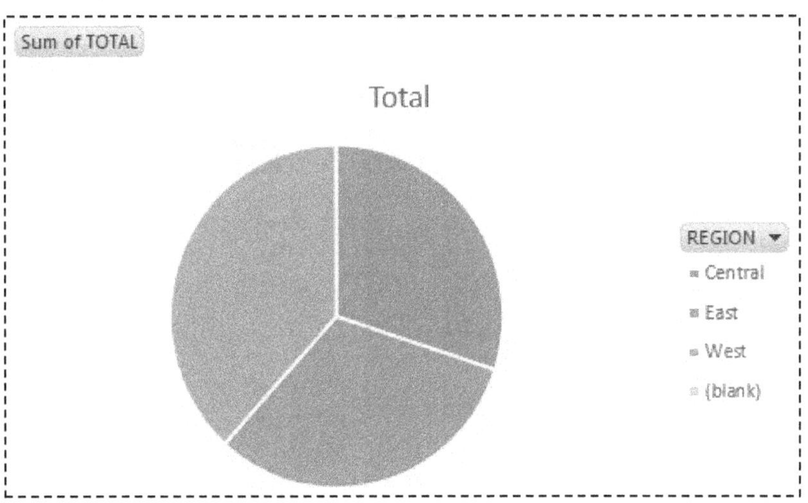

We now have our Dashboard data, but the format does not look very user friendly. Our next steps will focus on **formatting** & **presentation**.

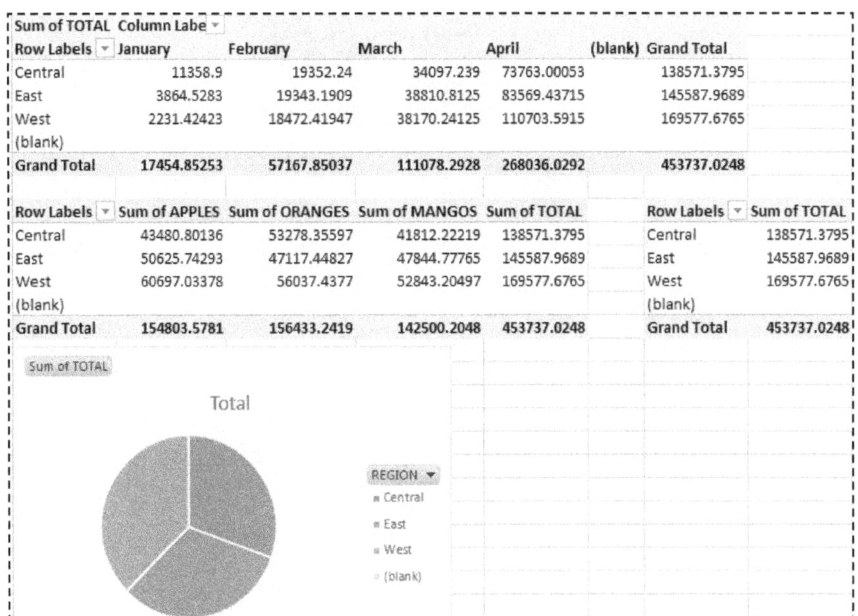

Sum of TOTAL	Column Labe					
Row Labels	January	February	March	April	(blank)	Grand Total
Central	11358.9	19352.24	34097.239	73763.00053		138571.3795
East	3864.5283	19343.1909	38810.8125	83569.43715		145587.9689
West	2231.42423	18472.41947	38170.24125	110703.5915		169577.6765
(blank)						
Grand Total	**17454.85253**	**57167.85037**	**111078.2928**	**268036.0292**		**453737.0248**

Row Labels	Sum of APPLES	Sum of ORANGES	Sum of MANGOS	Sum of TOTAL
Central	43480.80136	53278.35597	41812.22219	138571.3795
East	50625.74293	47117.44827	47844.77765	145587.9689
West	60697.03378	56037.4377	52843.20497	169577.6765
(blank)				
Grand Total	**154803.5781**	**156433.2419**	**142500.2048**	**453737.0248**

Row Labels	Sum of TOTAL
Central	138571.3795
East	145587.9689
West	169577.6765
(blank)	
Grand Total	**453737.0248**

1. We'll begin with the pie chart, click on the chart, the **'PIVOTCHART TOOLS'** toolbar should appear
2. Select the **'DESIGN'** tab
3. Click the drop-down for **'Quick Layout'**
4. Select **'Layout 1'**

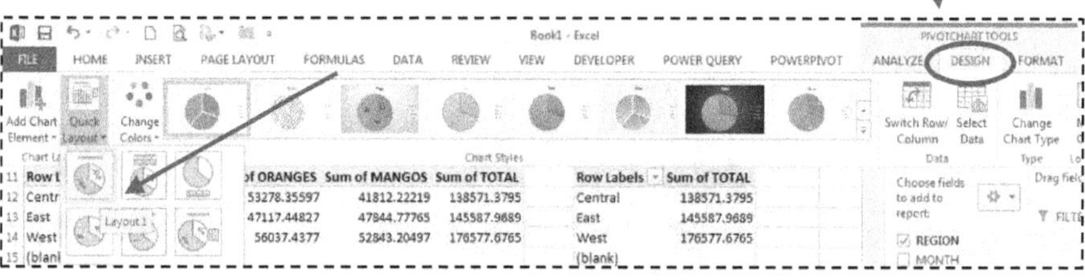

5. Change the chart title from **'TOTAL'** to **'% OF SALES BY REGION'**

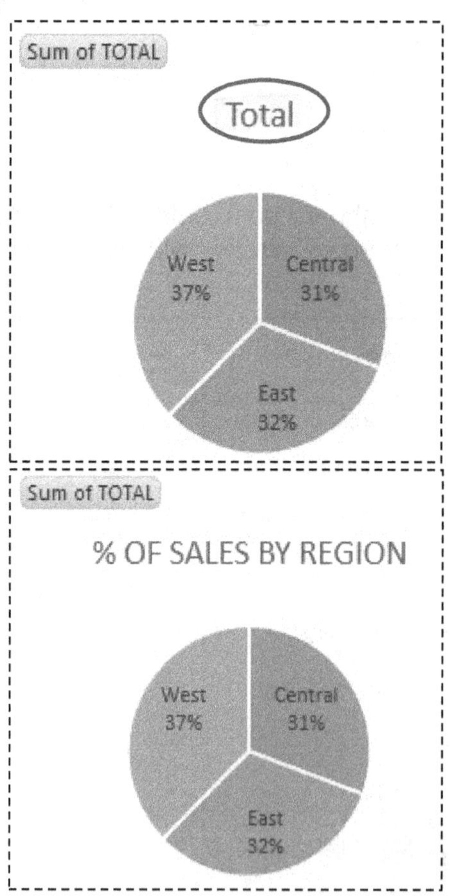

6. Change '**Row Labels'** to **'REGION'**
7. Change the '**Column Label'** to '**MONTH'**
8. Change **'Sum of TOTAL'** to **'SALES'**
9. Remove the word **'Grand'** from **'Grand Total'** and change to uppercase
10. Add the word **'SALES'** after each *fruit*
11. Remove the words **'Sum of'** before each *fruit*
12. Center the row and column labels
13. Change the format for the sales results to currency, zero decimal places

Sum of TOTAL	Column Labe					
Row Labels	January	February	March	April	(blank)	Grand Total
Central	11358.9	19352.24	34097.239	73763.00053		138571.3795
East	3864.5283	19343.1909	38810.8125	83569.43715		145587.9689
West	2231.42423	18472.41947	38170.24125	110703.5915		169577.6765
(blank)						
Grand Total	**17454.85253**	**57167.85037**	**111078.2928**	**268036.0292**		**453737.0248**

Row Labels	Sum of APPLES	Sum of ORANGES	Sum of MANGOS	Sum of TOTAL
Central	43480.80136	53278.35597	41812.22219	138571.3795
East	50625.74293	47117.44827	47844.77765	145587.9689
West	60697.03378	56037.4377	52843.20497	169577.6765
(blank)				
Grand Total	**154803.5781**	**156433.2419**	**142500.2048**	**453737.0248**

Row Labels	Sum of TOTAL
Central	138571.3795
East	145587.9689
West	169577.6765
(blank)	
Grand Total	453737.0248

After steps 6 -13 above:

SALES	MONTH					
REGION	**January**	**February**	**March**	**April**	**(blank)**	**TOTAL**
Central	$11,359	$19,352	$34,097	$73,763		$138,571
East	$3,865	$19,343	$38,811	$83,569		$145,588
West	$2,231	$18,472	$38,170	$110,704		$169,578
(blank)						
TOTAL	**$17,455**	**$57,168**	**$111,078**	**$268,036**		**$453,737**

REGION	APPLES SALES	ORANGES SALES	MANGOS SALES	SALES
Central	$43,481	$53,278	$41,812	$138,571
East	$50,626	$47,117	$47,845	$145,588
West	$60,697	$56,037	$52,843	$169,578
(blank)				
TOTAL	**$154,804**	**$156,433**	**$142,500**	**$453,737**

REGION	SALES
Central	$138,571
East	$145,588
West	$169,578
(blank)	
Total	$453,737

While the formatting changes have improved the look of the Dashboard, let's take it a few steps further.

1. From the toolbar select the **'VIEW'** tab and uncheck the **'Gridlines'** box

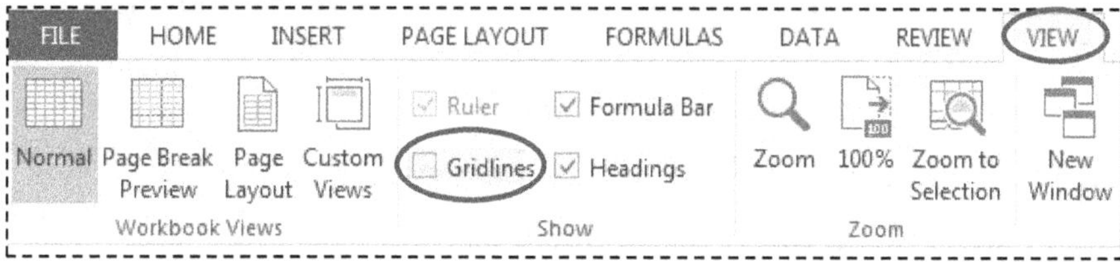

2. Click cell **'A3'**, and then from the PIVOTTABLE TOOLS toolbar select the tab **DESIGN : PivotTable Styles**

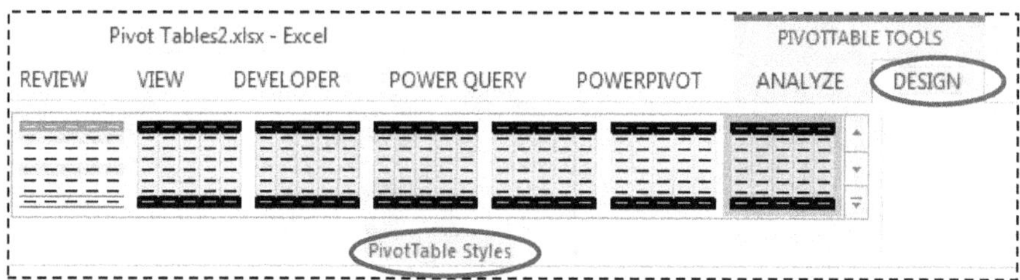

3. Select a formatted style you like
4. Repeat steps 2 & 3 for PivotTables in cells **'A11'** & '**G11**'
5. In cell **'A1'** enter **'Monthly Sales Dashboard'** and merge across columns, so it appears centered over the data
6. Increase the font size of **'A1'** to 30 and bold

The results should now look similar to the following:

Monthly Sales Dashboard

SALES REGION	MONTH January	February	March	April	(blank)	TOTAL
Central	$11,359	$19,352	$34,097	$73,763		$138,571
East	$3,865	$19,343	$38,811	$83,569		$145,588
West	$2,231	$18,472	$38,170	$110,704		$169,578
(blank)						
TOTAL	$17,455	$57,168	$111,078	$268,036		$453,737

REGION	APPLES SALES	ORANGES SALES	MANGOS SALES	SALES
Central	$43,481	$53,278	$41,812	$138,571
East	$50,626	$47,117	$47,845	$145,588
West	$60,697	$56,037	$52,843	$169,578
(blank)				
TOTAL	$154,804	$156,433	$142,500	$453,737

REGION	SALES
Central	$138,571
East	$145,588
West	$169,578
(blank)	
Total	$453,737

SALES

% OF SALES BY REGION

West 37%
Central 31%
East 32%

Almost done, lastly, let's hide the **(blank)** column and rows from display

7. Click the drop-down arrow for **'REGION'** in cell **'A4'**
8. Uncheck the **'(blank)'** check box
9. Click the **'OK'** button

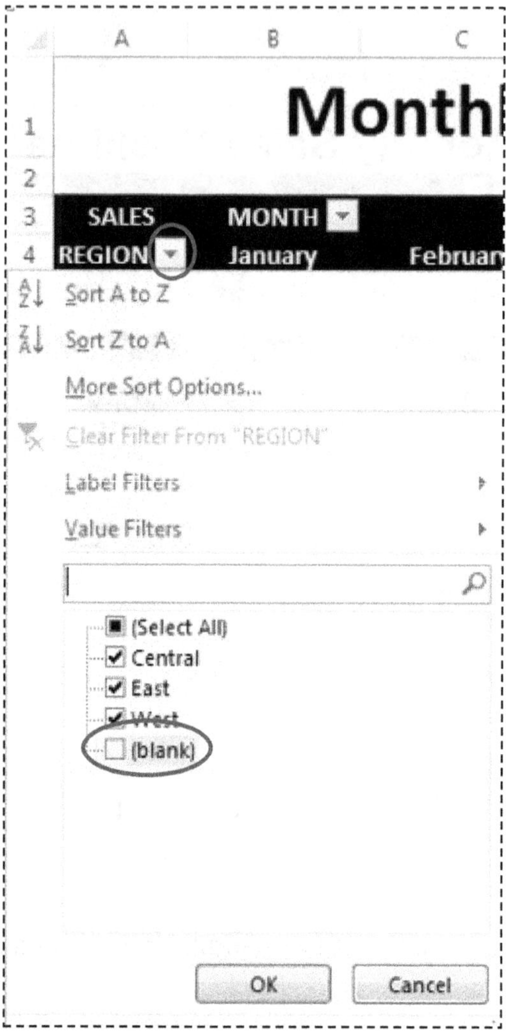

10. Repeat steps 7-9 for cells **'A11'** & **'G11'**

We now have a nicely formatted Dashboard:

Monthly Sales Dashboard

SALES REGION	MONTH January	February	March	April	TOTAL
Central	$11,359	$19,352	$34,097	$73,763	$138,571
East	$3,865	$19,343	$38,811	$83,569	$145,588
West	$2,231	$18,472	$38,170	$110,704	$169,578
TOTAL	$17,455	$57,168	$111,078	$268,036	$453,737

REGION	APPLES SALES	ORANGES SALES	MANGOS SALES	SALES
Central	$43,481	$53,278	$41,812	$138,571
East	$50,626	$47,117	$47,845	$145,588
West	$60,697	$56,037	$52,843	$169,578
TOTAL	$154,804	$156,433	$142,500	$453,737

REGION	SALES
Central	$138,571
East	$145,588
West	$169,578
Total	$453,737

SALES

% OF SALES BY REGION

West 37%
Central 31%
East 32%

☑ Additional Information:

Depending on your audience, you may want to consider *protecting* your Dashboard to prevent unauthorized users from modifying it. As well as, *hide* any data source tabs, allowing your customers to see only the Dashboard itself.

1. To *hide* the **'Monthly Fruit Sale'** tab, **right click** over the tab and select **'Hide'**
2. To *unhide* **right click** over any tab and select **'Unhide'** *(the unhide option will become active once a tab is hidden)*

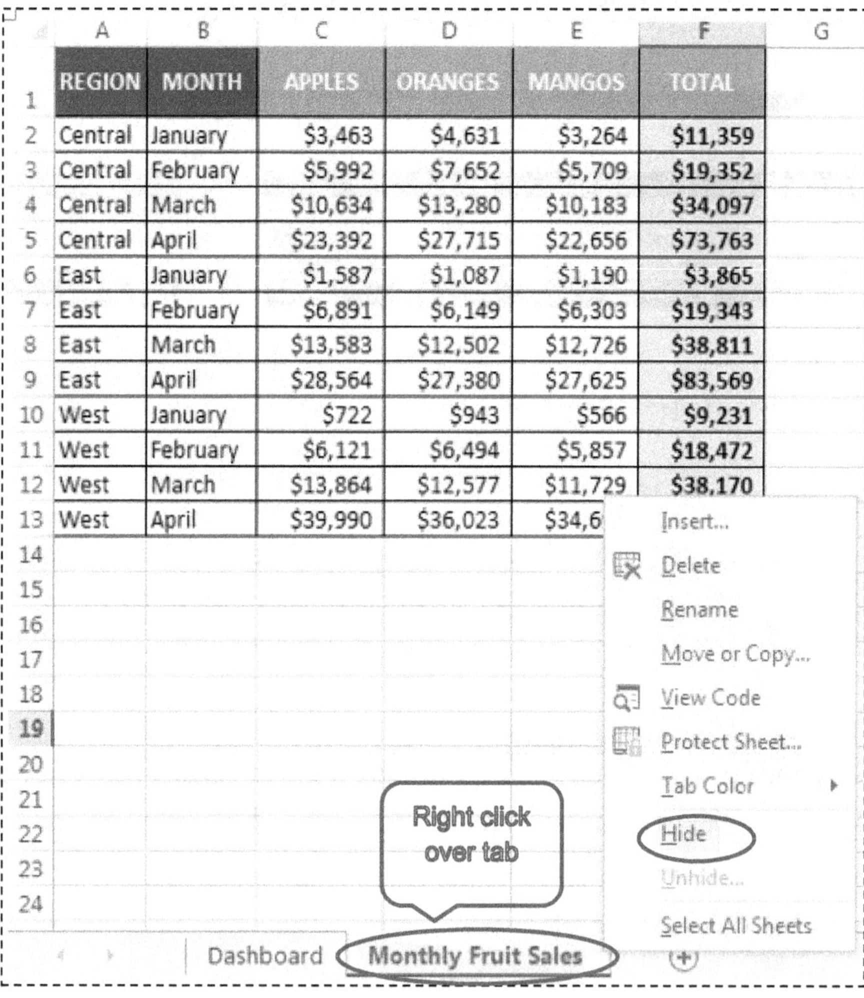

	A	B	C	D	E	F
1	REGION	MONTH	APPLES	ORANGES	MANGOS	TOTAL
2	Central	January	$3,463	$4,631	$3,264	$11,359
3	Central	February	$5,992	$7,652	$5,709	$19,352
4	Central	March	$10,634	$13,280	$10,183	$34,097
5	Central	April	$23,392	$27,715	$22,656	$73,763
6	East	January	$1,587	$1,087	$1,190	$3,865
7	East	February	$6,891	$6,149	$6,303	$19,343
8	East	March	$13,583	$12,502	$12,726	$38,811
9	East	April	$28,564	$27,380	$27,625	$83,569
10	West	January	$722	$943	$566	$9,231
11	West	February	$6,121	$6,494	$5,857	$18,472
12	West	March	$13,864	$12,577	$11,729	$38,170
13	West	April	$39,990	$36,023	$34,6	

To protect the Dashboard or any other tab:

3. From the ribbon toolbar select the **'HOME'** tab and click the **'Format'** drop-down box
4. Select **'Protect Sheet…'**

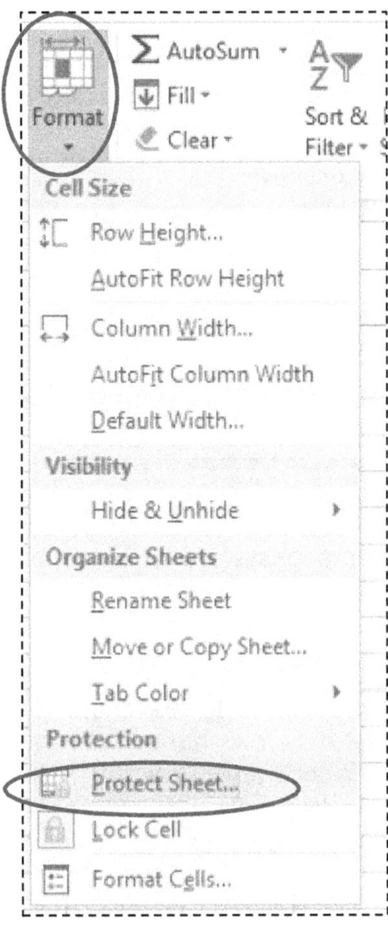

The following dialogue box will appear:

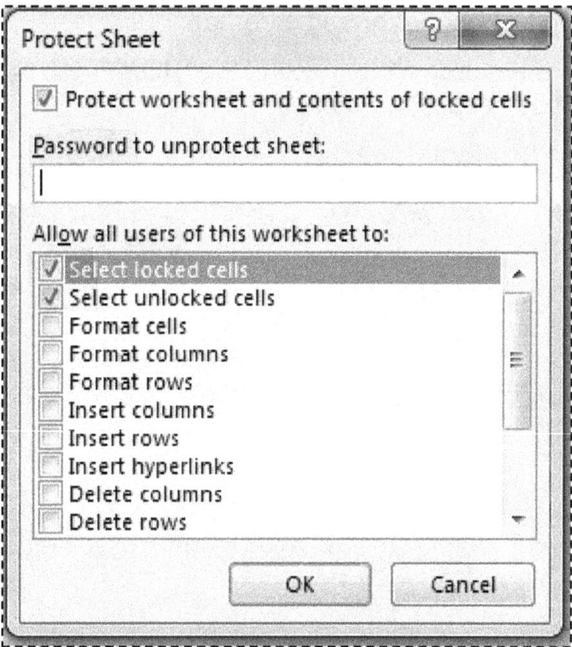

5. You may enter a password or leave blank *(if you enter a password, make sure at least one other person has access to it. They can serve as a backup resource, when you're unavailable)*
6. A good best practice is to leave the first two check boxes selected *(these will allow your customers to click on cells and scroll, but not change any content):*
    a. Select locked cells
    b. Select unlocked cells
7. Click the **'OK'** button

If a user tries to modify the sheet, they will receive the following message:

8. To **unprotect**, from the ribbon toolbar select the **'HOME'** tab and click the **'Format'** drop-down box
9. Select **'Unprotect Sheet…'** *(this option will become available if a sheet is protected)*

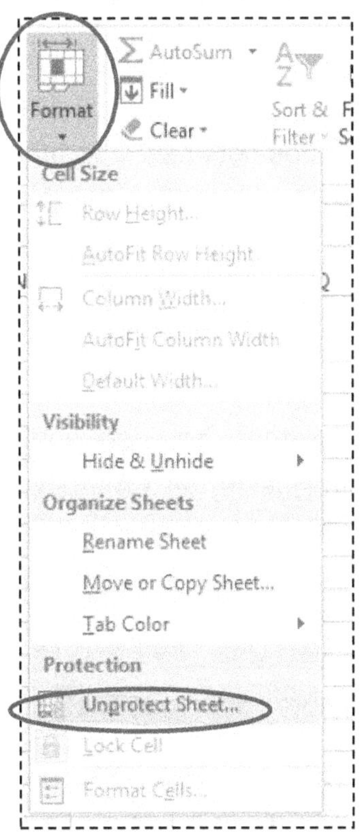

In the next chapter, we will look at how to update (Refresh) the Dashboard with new data, without having to re-create it.

(PART 2) - CHAPTER 9

UPDATING EXISTING PIVOT TABLES WITH NEW OR MODIFIED DATA

If you have already created a Pivot Table or Dashboard where the layout and format is to your liking and you receive new or modified data, you can simply **Refresh** the data in your Pivot Table(s) without having to recreate them. To do this, you must:

1. Have correctly updated your Pivot Table settings to ensure your formatting does not change with new data
2. Ensure your existing Pivot Table is reading the correct data source *AND* cell range

---

Scenario:

You've spent a lot of time creating a monthly sales Dashboard and your customers like the format. You now would like to add new data (months) to this existing Dashboard, without having to recreate all of the Pivot Tables.

Detailed Example How To Use The Feature:

First, we want to make sure your Pivot Table formatting stays intact:

1. Make sure the Dashboard tab is **'Unprotected'**

2. From the toolbar select PIVOTTABLE TOOLS and the tab **ANALYZE**
3. Under **'PivotTable Name'** click the **'Options'** drop-down box and select **'Options'**

Pivot Tables.xlsx - Excel
PIVOTTABLE TOOLS
FILE
HOME
INSERT
PAGE LAYOUT
FORMULAS
DATA
REVIEW
VIEW
DEVELOPER
POWER QUERY
POWERPIVOT
ANALYZE
DESIGN
PivotTable1
RANK
Field Settings
Options
Insert Slicer
Insert Timeline
Refresh
Change Data Source
Clear
Select
Move PivotTable
Fields, Items, & Sets
Group
Filter
Data
Actions
Calculations

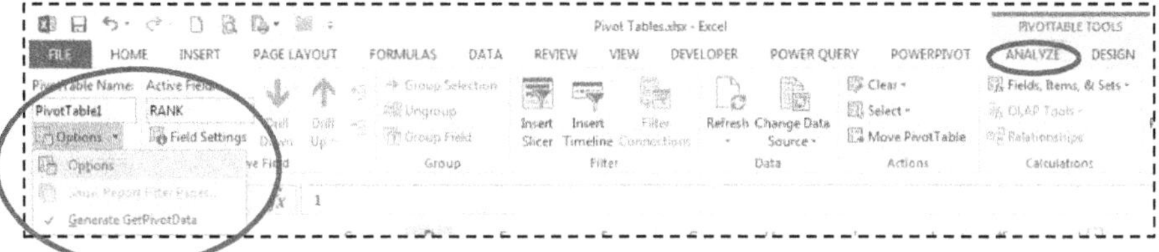

The following dialogue box will appear:

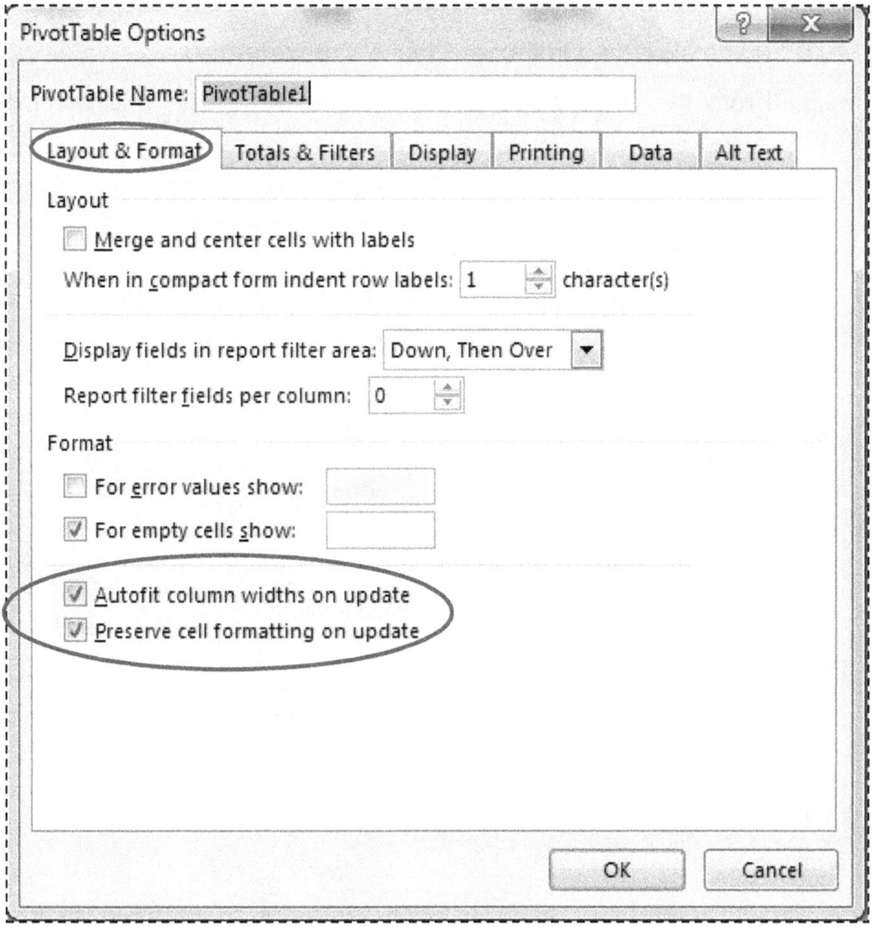

PivotTable Options
PivotTable Name: PivotTable1
Layout & Format
Totals & Filters
Display
Printing
Data
Alt Text
Layout
Merge and center cells with labels
When in compact form indent row labels: 1 character(s)
Display fields in report filter area: Down, Then Over
Report filter fields per column: 0
Format
For error values show:
For empty cells show:
Autofit column widths on update
Preserve cell formatting on update
OK
Cancel

4. Select the **'Layout & Format'** tab
5. Click the last two check boxes:
    a. **Autofit** column widths on update
    b. **Preserve** cell formatting on update
6. Click the **'OK'** button

You will need to repeat steps 2-6 for each Pivot Table you've created

---

Next, verify your Pivot Table **data source** is correct:

1. Make sure the Dashboard tab is **'Unprotected'**
2. From the toolbar select PIVOTTABLE TOOLS and the tab **ANALYZE**
3. Click the drop-down box **'Change Data Source'** and select **'Change Data Source...'**

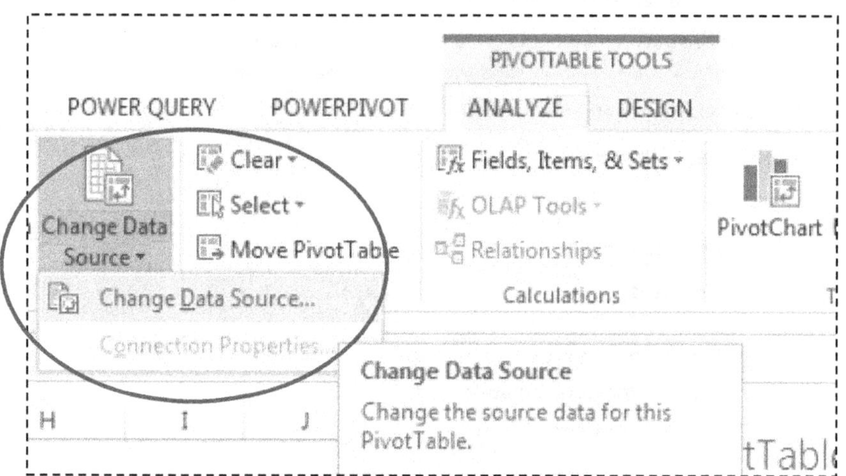

The following dialogue box will appear:

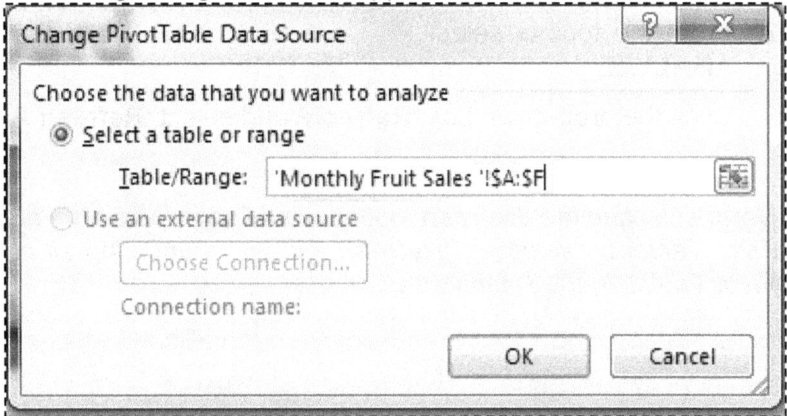

4. Verify the Table/Range is correct **_Note:_** *you will <u>not</u> receive an error message if the* ***Range*** *is incorrect, however, the new data WILL NOT APPEAR on your Pivot Table / Dashboard.*

Next, we will add new data to the Dashboard

Sample data to update (Refresh) the Pivot Table

	A	B	C	D	E	F
1	REGION	MONTH	APPLES	ORANGES	MANGOS	TOTAL
2	Central	January	$3,463	$4,631	$3,264	**$11,359**
3	Central	February	$5,992	$7,652	$5,709	**$19,352**
4	Central	March	$10,634	$13,280	$10,183	**$34,097**
5	Central	April	$23,392	$27,715	$22,656	**$73,763**
6	East	January	$1,587	$1,087	$1,190	**$3,865**
7	East	February	$6,891	$6,149	$6,303	**$19,343**
8	East	March	$13,583	$12,502	$12,726	**$38,811**
9	East	April	$28,564	$27,380	$27,625	**$83,569**
10	West	January	$722	$943	$566	**$2,231**
11	West	February	$6,121	$6,494	$5,857	**$18,472**
12	West	March	$13,864	$12,577	$11,729	**$38,170**
13	West	April	$39,990	$36,023	$34,691	**$110,704**
14	East	May	$29,964	$30,380	$28,125	**$88,469**
15	Central	May	$26,492	$29,215	$25,756	**$81,463**
16	West	May	$41,990	$38,473	$36,591	**$117,054**

1. Click cell **'A3'**
2. From the toolbar select PIVOTTABLE TOOLS and the tab **ANALYZE**
3. Click the drop-down box **'Refresh'** and select **'Refresh All'**

Note: *selecting the* ***'Refresh'*** *option would only update the* ***active*** *Pivot Table, by selecting* ***'Refresh All'*** *we're updating all of the Pivot Tables in the Dashboard.*

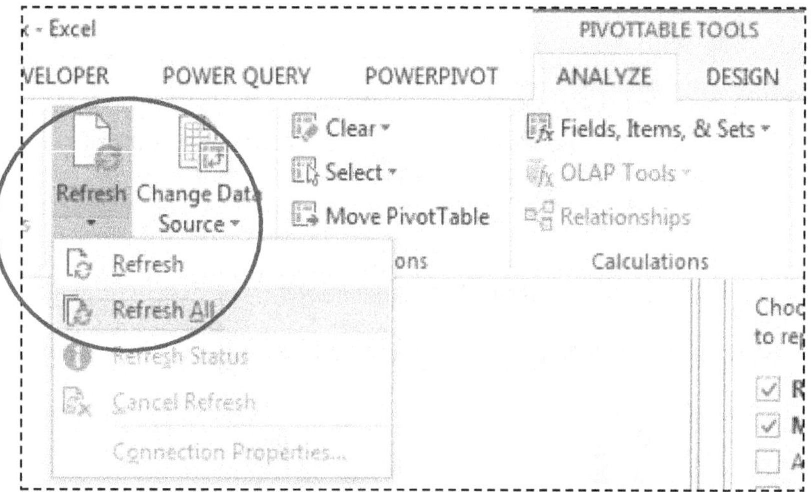

We now have the May sales data added to the Dashboard:

Monthly Sales Dashboard

SALES	MONTH					
REGION	January	February	March	April	May	TOTAL
Central	$11,359	$19,352	$34,097	$73,763	$81,463	$220,034
East	$3,865	$19,343	$38,811	$83,569	$88,469	$234,057
West	$2,231	$18,472	$38,170	$110,704	$117,054	$286,631
TOTAL	$17,455	$57,168	$111,078	$268,036	$286,986	$740,723

REGION	APPLES SALES	ORANGES SALES	MANGOS SALES	SALES
Central	$69,973	$82,494	$67,568	$220,034
East	$80,590	$77,497	$75,970	$234,057
West	$102,687	$94,510	$89,434	$286,631
TOTAL	$253,250	$254,501	$232,972	$740,723

REGION	SALES
Central	$220,034
East	$234,057
West	$286,631
Total	$740,723

SALES

% OF SALES BY REGION

West 39%
Central 30%
East 31%

In Part 4 (Text Formulas) chapters 16 & 17 we will review helpful formulas to assist in troubleshooting some common data formatting issues with Pivot Tables.

(PART 2) - CHAPTER 10

PIVOT TABLES (ADVANCED)

In chapter 7 we reviewed some basic and intermediate Pivot Table examples, now let's explore the advanced functionality of **'Grouping'** data and inserting **'Calculated Fields'**.

When you have a lot of detailed individual records such as customer demographics, sales, location data, etc. Sometimes more insight can be gained when you can cluster this data into categories or ranges. The **'Grouping'** feature allows you to complete this type of segmented analysis.

Additionally, the type of work you perform may require more complex or technical types of calculations than those included in the standard set of Pivot Table '**Value Field Settings**.' This is when being able to insert your own **'Calculated Fields'** is particularly helpful.

Scenario:

You've received a large amount of detailed customer records and need to:

- Group the number of customers by how much they spent, and include their segment's percentage to the overall sales total.

To download a free copy of the Excel® file used in this scenario please go to: *http://bentonexcelbooks.my-free.website/sample-data-files* *select the file for* ***Chapter 10 (Grouping)*** *in the* ***'The Microsoft Excel Step-By-Step Training Guide Book Bundle'*** *section.*

Detailed Example How To Use The Feature:

Sample data, due to space limitations ***the entire data set is not displayed****:*

	A	B
1	CUSTOMER ID	AMOUNT PURCHASED
2	111	$ 142
3	222	$ 153
4	333	$ 442
5	444	$ 409
6	555	$ 136
7	666	$ 147
8	777	$ 436
9	888	$ 403
10	999	$ 1,500
11	1110	$ 106
12	1221	$ 395
13	1332	$ 362
14	1443	$ 857
15	1554	$ 890
16	1665	$ 1,157
17	1776	$ 1,146
18	1887	$ 719
19	1998	$ 796
20	2109	$ 1,019
21	2220	$ 1,052
22	2331	$ 100
23	2442	$ 277
24	2553	$ 385
25	2664	$ 533
26	2775	$ 100
27	2886	$ 401
28	2997	$ 400
29	3108	$ 657
30	3219	$ 985

1. Insert a Pivot Table, please see the beginning of chapter 7 if you do not already know how to create a new Pivot Table

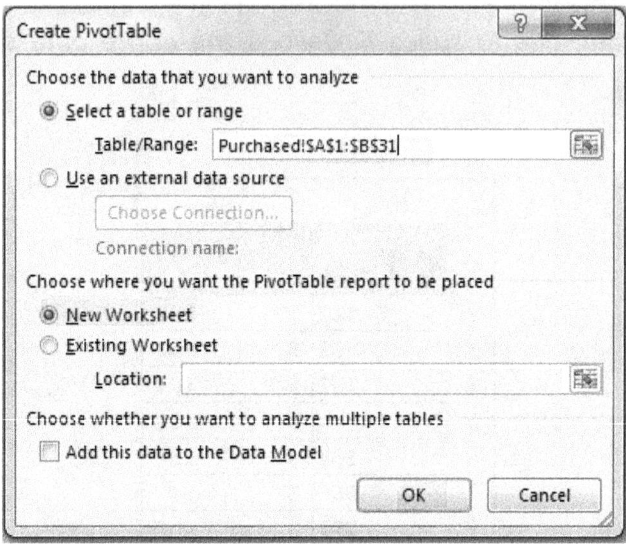

2. Select **'AMOUNT PURCHASED**' and drag under the **'ROWS'** section of the **PivotTable Fields** dialogue box

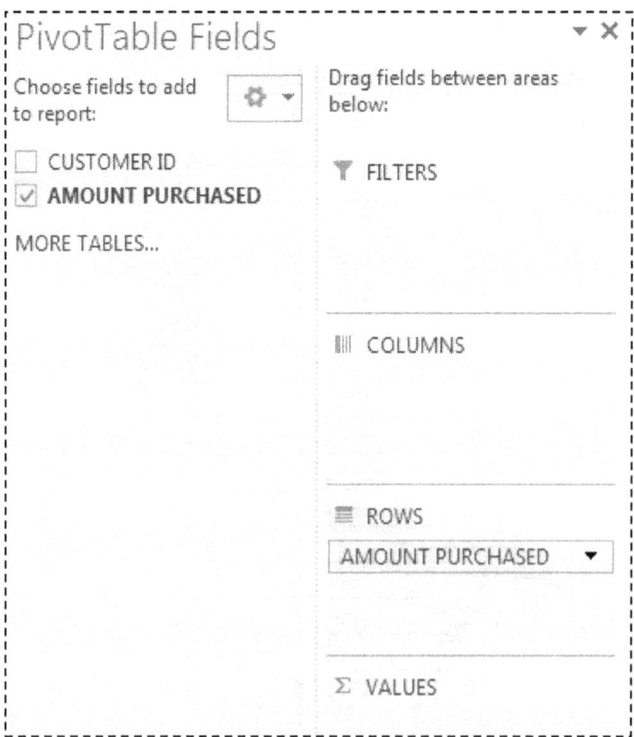

3. Select **'CUSTOMER ID'** *twice* and drag under the **'VALUES'** section of the **PivotTable Fields** dialogue box.

The following should now be displayed:

*It is **ok** that columns **'B'** & **'C'** are the same and incorrectly displaying the 'Sum of Customer ID,' we will fix this in a later step.*

	A	B	C
3	Row Labels	Sum of CUSTOMER ID	Sum of CUSTOMER ID2
4	$ 100	5106	5106
5	$ 106	1110	1110
6	$ 136	555	555
7	$ 142	111	111
8	$ 147	666	666
9	$ 153	222	222
10	$ 277	2442	2442
11	$ 362	1332	1332
12	$ 385	2553	2553
13	$ 395	1221	1221
14	$ 400	2997	2997
15	$ 401	2886	2886
16	$ 403	888	888
17	$ 409	444	444
18	$ 436	777	777
19	$ 442	333	333
20	$ 533	2664	2664
21	$ 657	3108	3108
22	$ 719	1887	1887
23	$ 752	3330	3330
24	$ 796	1998	1998
25	$ 857	1443	1443
26	$ 890	1554	1554
27	$ 985	3219	3219
28	$ 1,019	2109	2109
29	$ 1,052	2220	2220
30	$ 1,146	1776	1776
31	$ 1,157	1665	1665
32	$ 1,500	999	999
33	Grand Total	51615	51615

4. Click cell **'A4'**
5. From the toolbar select PIVOTTABLE TOOLS and the tab **ANALYZE**

6. Select **'Group Field'**

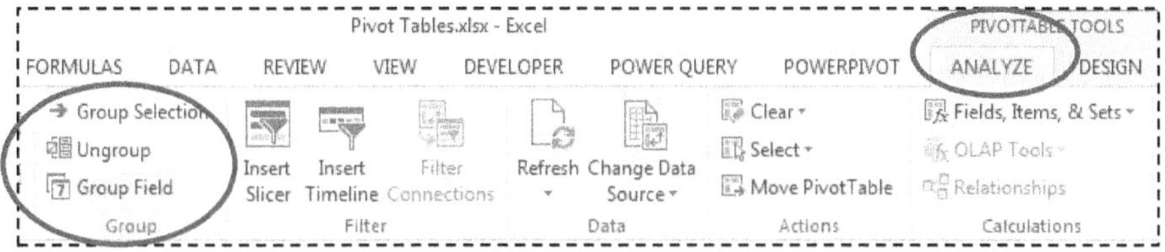

The following dialogue box will appear:

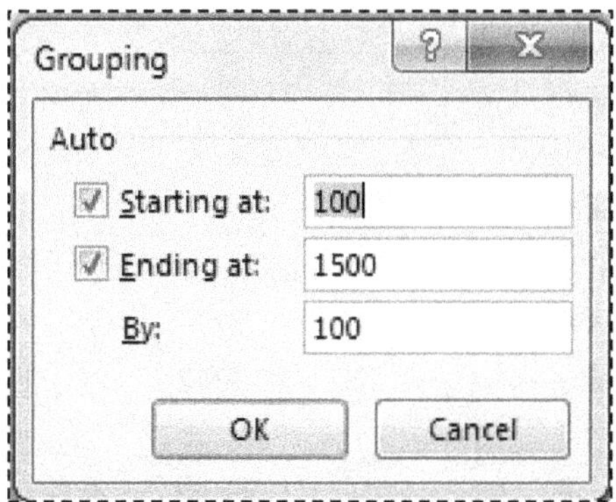

7. Click both the **'Starting at:'** and **'Ending at:'** check boxes
8. **'Starting at:'** will default to 100 (this is the *lowest value* in the dataset)
9. **'Ending at:'** will default to 1500 (this is the *highest value* in the dataset)
10. Enter 100 in the '**By:'** field *(this is the amount between group segments*)
11. Click the **'OK'** button

We've now grouped customer purchase amounts into ~$100 segments, with each bracket differential representing approximately $100:

100-199
200-299
300-399
400-499
500-599
600-699
700-799
800-899
900-999
1000-1099
1100-1199
1400-1500

3	Row Labels	Sum of CUSTOMER ID	Sum of CUSTOMER ID2
4	100-199	7770	7770
5	200-299	2442	2442
6	300-399	5106	5106
7	400-499	8325	8325
8	500-599	2664	2664
9	600-699	3108	3108
10	700-799	7215	7215
11	800-899	2997	2997
12	900-999	3219	3219
13	1000-1099	4329	4329
14	1100-1199	3441	3441
15	1400-1500	999	999
16	**Grand Total**	**51615**	**51615**

However, this table is not providing meaningful information, because it is incorrectly summing **'CUSTOMER ID'**, to fix this:

12. In the PivotTable Fields list, in the **'VALUES'** section, click the drop-down box for the *first* **'Sum of CUSTOMER ID'**
13. Select the **'Value Field Settings…'**option.

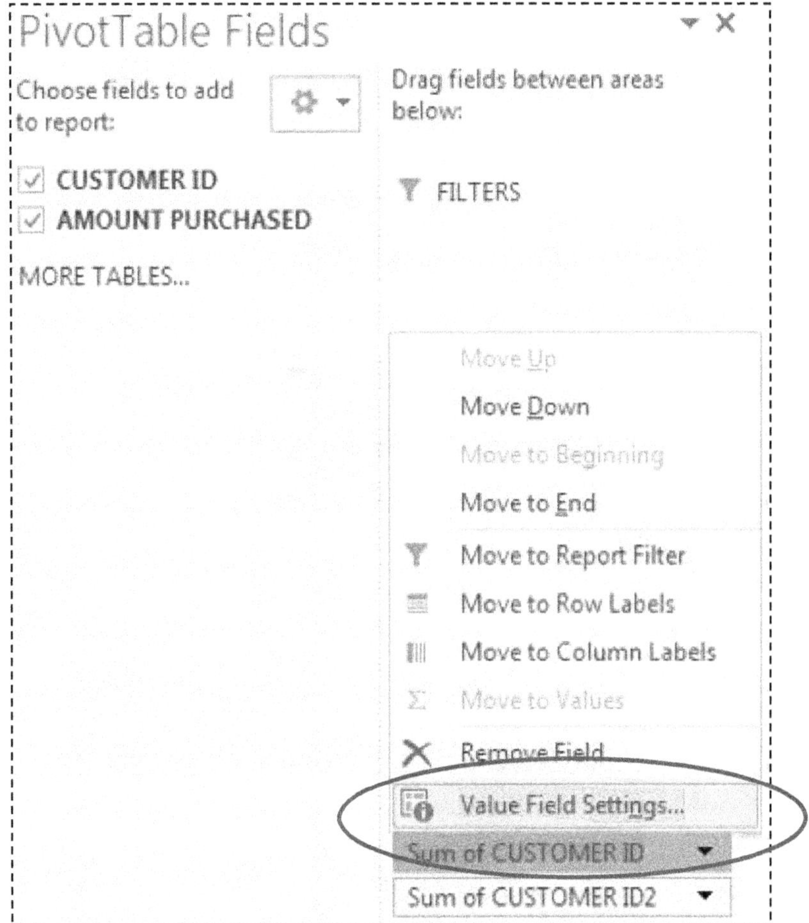
PivotTable Fields
Choose fields to add to report:
CUSTOMER ID
AMOUNT PURCHASED
MORE TABLES...
Drag fields between areas below:
FILTERS
Move Up
Move Down
Move to Beginning
Move to End
Move to Report Filter
Move to Row Labels
Move to Column Labels
Move to Values
Remove Field
Value Field Settings...
Sum of CUSTOMER ID
Sum of CUSTOMER ID2

The following dialogue box will appear:

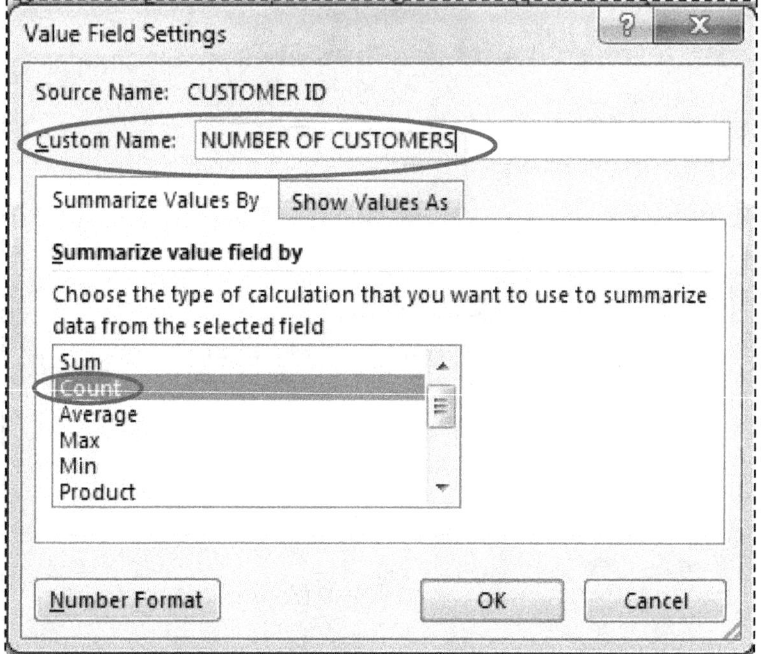

1. In the **'Custom Name:'** field change to '**NUMBER OF CUSTOMERS'**
2. In the '**Summarize value field by'** list box select **'Count'**.
3. Click the **'OK'** button

Next, we'll address the *second* **'Sum of CUSTOMER ID'** field

4. In the **PivotTable Fields** list, in the **'VALUES'** section, click the drop-down box for the *second* **'Sum of CUSTOMER ID'**
5. Select the **'Value Field Settings…'**option

The following dialogue box will appear:

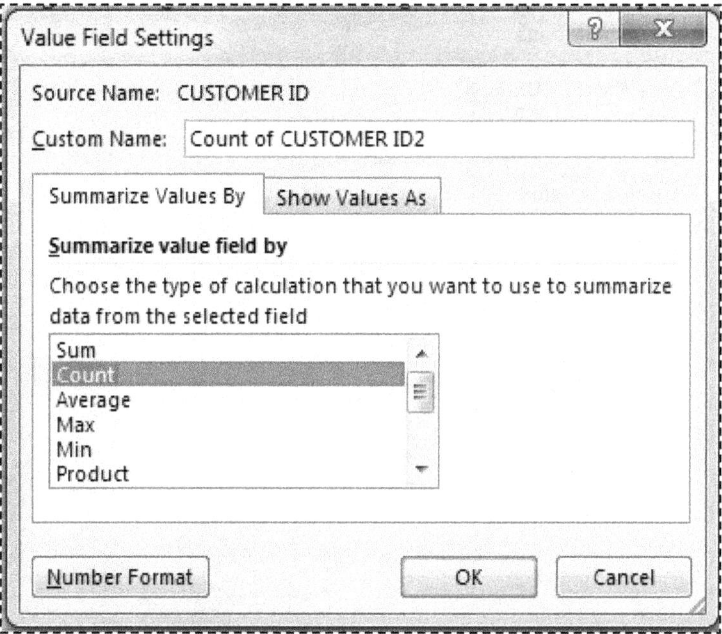

6. In the **'Custom Name:'** field change to '**% OF CUSTOMERS'**
7. In the **'Summarize value field by'** list select **'Count'**
8. Click the **'Show Values As'** tab

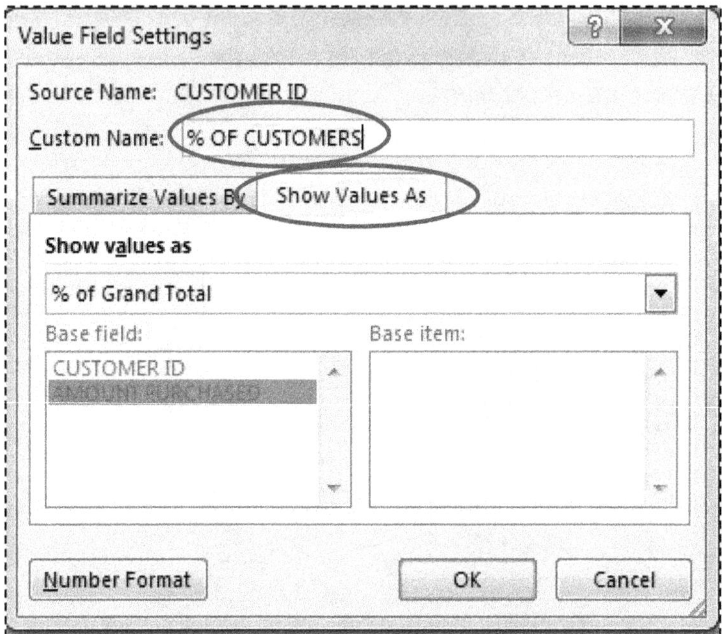

9. Click the **'Show values as'** drop-down box and select **'% of Grand Total'**
10. Click the **'OK'** button
11. Change the label in cell '**A3**' to '**AMOUNT PURCHASED**'

We now have a report that groups the number of customers by how much they spent and the segment's percentage to overall total sales.

3	AMOUNT PURCHASEI	NUMBER OF CUSTOMERS	% OF CUSTOMERS
4	100-199	7	23%
5	200-299	1	3%
6	300-399	3	10%
7	400-499	6	20%
8	500-599	1	3%
9	600-699	1	3%
10	700-799	3	10%
11	800-899	2	7%
12	900-999	1	3%
13	1000-1099	2	7%
14	1100-1199	2	7%
15	1400-1500	1	3%
16	**Grand Total**	**30**	**100%**

For our last example, we'll examine inserting calculated fields into a Pivot Table.

Scenario:

You're responsible for analyzing your company's store sales data plan vs. actual. This is something you do every month and it is the type of business, where some stores may close and others open from month-to-month. You need to report:

1. The sales dollar variance -/+ plan vs. actual
2. The percent variance -/+ plan vs. actual

Sample data:

	A	B	C
1	STORE	PLAN SALES	ACTUAL SALES
2	AAA	$ 50,000	$ 55,000
3	BBB	$ 40,000	$ 35,500
4	CCC	$ 30,000	$ 32,000
5	DDD	$ 20,000	$ 18,500
6	EEE	$ 25,000	$ 42,000

1. Create a Pivot Table, make sure to select the entire column of '**A' – 'C'** for the **Table/Range**. This is what will allow us to simply refresh the data each month, when new stores are opened and others close

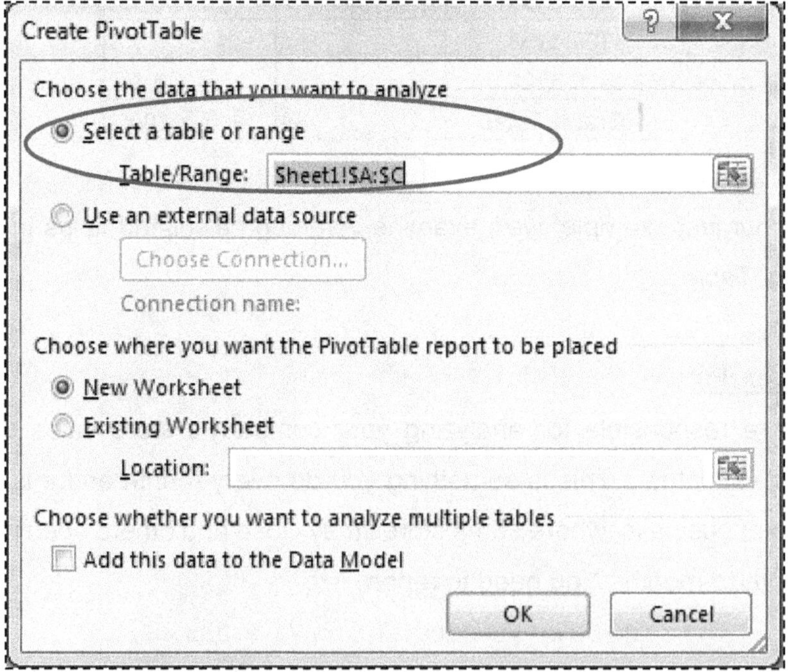

2. Select **'STORE**' and drag under the **'ROWS'** section of the **PivotTable Fields** list

3. Select **'PLAN SALES**' and drag under the **'VALUES'** section of the **PivotTable Fields** list

4. Select **'ACTUAL SALES**' and drag under the **'VALUES'** section of the **PivotTable Fields** dialogue box

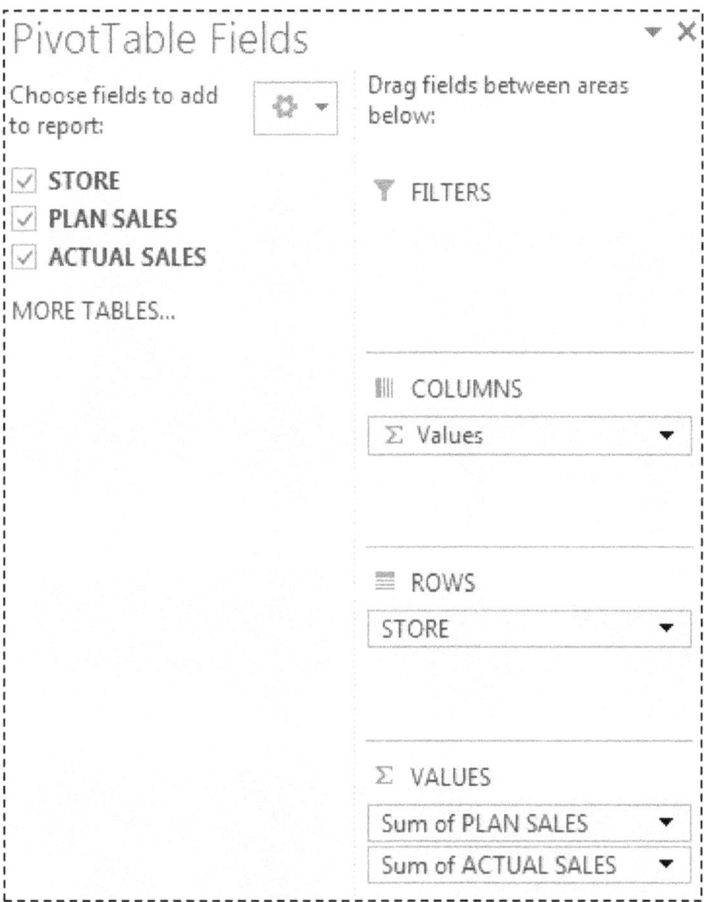

5. Change the label in cell **'A3'** to '**STORE'**
6. Change the label in cell **'B3'** to '**PLN SALES'**
7. Change the label in cell **'C3'** to '**ACT SALES'**
8. Change the formatting in cells **'B4'** – **'C9'** to currency, with no decimal places

The Pivot Table should look similar to the following:

	A	B	C
1			
2			
3	STORE	PLN SALES	ACT SALES
4	AAA	$ 50,000	$ 55,000
5	BBB	$ 40,000	$ 35,500
6	CCC	$ 30,000	$ 32,000
7	DDD	$ 20,000	$ 18,500
8	EEE	$ 25,000	$ 42,000
9	(blank)		
10	**Grand Total**	**$ 165,000**	**$ 183,000**

Next, we will add our first calculated field that shows the sales dollar variance -/+ plan vs. actual.

9. From the toolbar select PIVOTTABLE TOOLS and the tab **ANALYZE**
10. Click the **'Fields, Items & Sets'** drop-down box
11. Select **'Calculated Field...'**

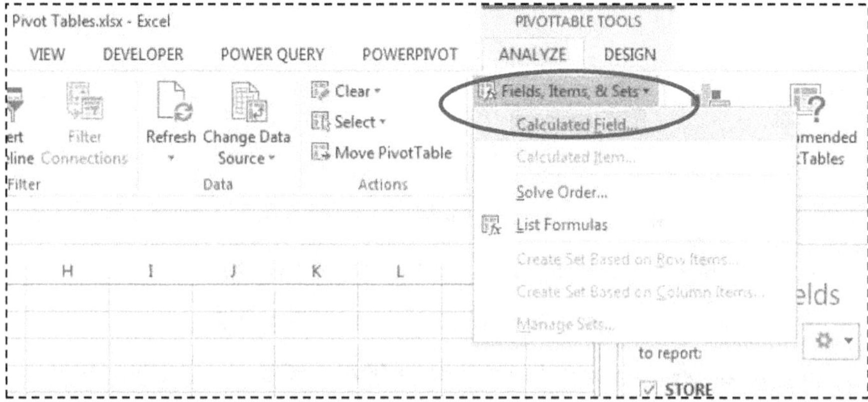

The following dialogue box will appear:

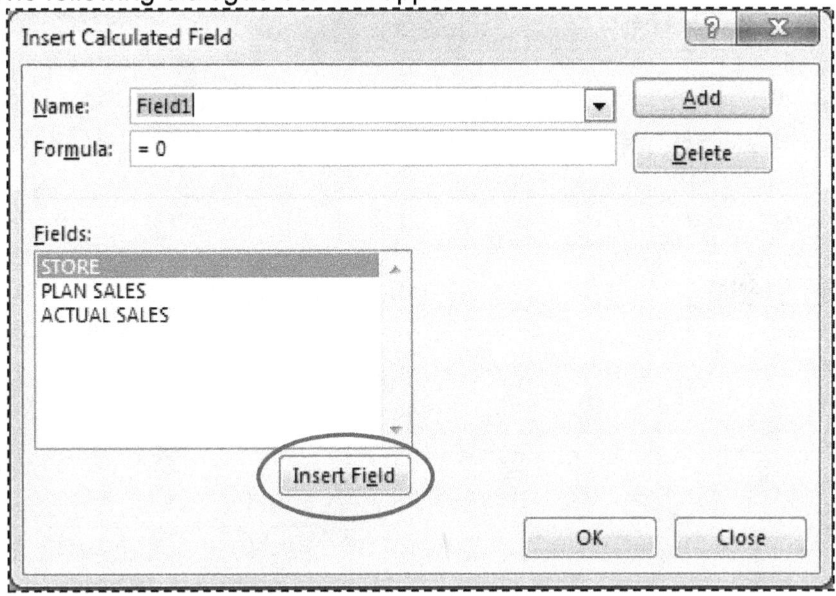

12. In the **Name:** field enter **'Dollars -/+ plan vs actual'**
13. In the **Formula:** field delete the zero '0', but leave the equal '=' sign
14. Select **'ACTUAL SALES'** from the **'Fields'** list and click the **'Insert Field'** button
15. Add the minus '-' symbol in the **Formula:** field after **'ACTUAL SALES'**
16. Select **'PLAN SALES'** from the **'Fields'** list and click the **'Insert Field'** button

This formula should now be in the **Formula:** field

```
='ACTUAL SALES' -'PLAN SALES'
```

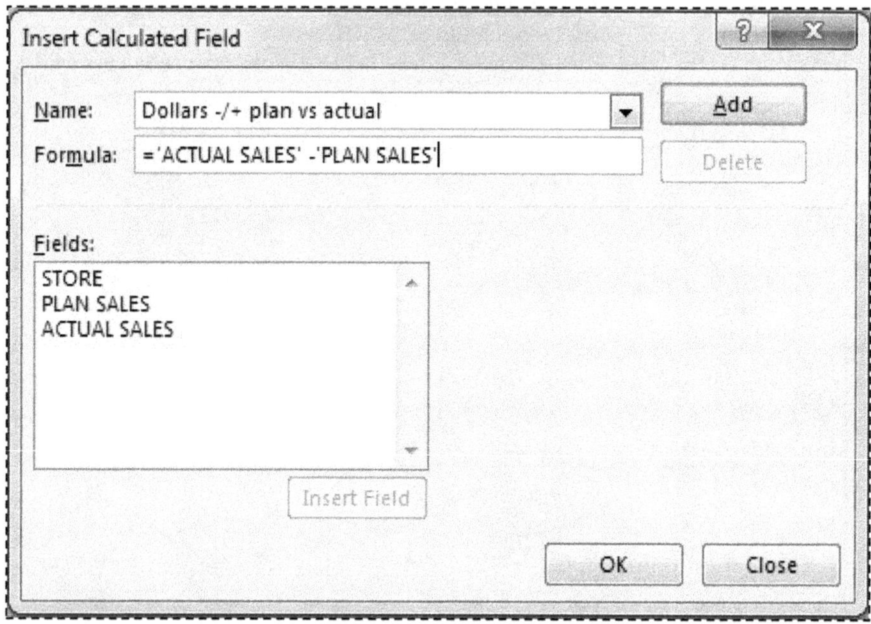

17. Click the **'OK'** button

The following field was added to our PivotTable results:

STORE	PLN SALES	ACT SALES	Sum of Dollars -/+ plan vs actual
AAA	$ 50,000	$ 55,000	$ 5,000
BBB	$ 40,000	$ 35,500	$ (4,500)
CCC	$ 30,000	$ 32,000	$ 2,000
DDD	$ 20,000	$ 18,500	$ (1,500)
EEE	$ 25,000	$ 42,000	$ 17,000
(blank)			$ -
Grand Total	**$ 165,000**	**$ 183,000**	**$ 18,000**

Now, we'll add the percent variance -/+ plan vs. actual

1. From the toolbar select PIVOTTABLE TOOLS and the tab **ANALYZE**
2. Click the **'Fields, Items & Sets'** drop-down box
3. Select **'Calculated Field...'**

The following dialogue box will appear:

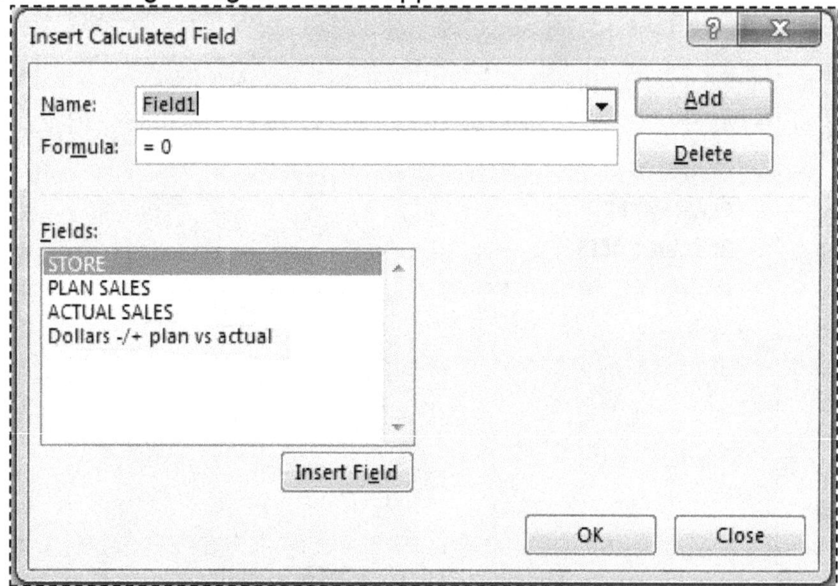

Note: *the calculated field* ***'Dollars -/+ plan vs actual'*** *has been added to our list of available* ***'Fields:'***.

4. In the **Name:** field enter **'Percent -/+ plan vs actual'**
5. In the **Formula:** field delete the zero '0', but leave the equal '=' sign
6. Add the below formula to the **Formula:** field
   `=('ACTUAL SALES'- 'PLAN SALES')/ 'PLAN SALES'`
7. Click the **'OK'** button

The following field was added to our PivotTable results: ***Note:*** *we need to change the* ***format to a percent (%)*** *in the results*

STORE	PLN SALES	ACT SALES	$ -/+ plan vs actual	Sum of Percent -/+ plan vs actual
AAA	$ 50,000	$ 55,000	$ 5,000	$ 0
BBB	$ 40,000	$ 35,500	$ (4,500)	$ (0)
CCC	$ 30,000	$ 32,000	$ 2,000	$ 0
DDD	$ 20,000	$ 18,500	$ (1,500)	$ (0)
EEE	$ 25,000	$ 42,000	$ 17,000	$ 1
(blank)			$ -	#DIV/0!
Grand Tot	**$165,000**	**$183,000**	**$ 18,000**	**$ 0**

Let's examine now how our results change when we *add* or *remove* stores. I removed store **'BBB'** and added stores **'FFF'** & **'GGG'**, notice where the **(blank)** row appears after I refresh the Pivot Table data? *Please see **chapter 9** for instructions on how to refresh Pivot Table data.*

STORE	PLN SALES	ACT SALES	$ -/+ plan vs actual	% -/+ plan vs actual
AAA	$ 50,000	$ 55,000	$ 5,000	10.0%
CCC	$ 30,000	$ 32,000	$ 2,000	6.7%
DDD	$ 20,000	$ 18,500	$ (1,500)	-7.5%
EEE	$ 25,000	$ 42,000	$ 17,000	68.0%
(blank)			$ -	#DIV/0!
FFF	$ 25,000	$ 22,000	$ (3,000)	-12.0%
GGG	$ 25,000	$ 24,000	$ (1,000)	-4.0%
Total	$175,000	$193,500	$ 18,500	10.6%

To resolve this, I'm going to change the **'STORE'** *field sorting options to **'Sort A to Z'***. This will ensure each time I refresh the data in the future, my results will always be in Ascending order.

STORE	PLN SALES	ACT SALES	$ -/+ plan vs actual	% -/+ plan vs actual
AAA	$ 50,000	$ 55,000	$ 5,000	10.0%
CCC	$ 30,000	$ 32,000	$ 2,000	6.7%
DDD	$ 20,000	$ 18,500	$ (1,500)	-7.5%
EEE	$ 25,000	$ 42,000	$ 17,000	68.0%
FFF	$ 25,000	$ 22,000	$ (3,000)	-12.0%
GGG	$ 25,000	$ 24,000	$ (1,000)	-4.0%
(blank)			$ -	#DIV/0!
Total	$175,000	$193,500	$ 18,500	10.6%

*To hide the **(blank)** row from display see page 83 for instructions.*

To remove or change a calculated field:

1. From the toolbar select PIVOTTABLE TOOLS and the tab **ANALYZE**
2. Click the **'Fields, Items & Sets'** drop-down box
3. Select **'Calculated Field...'**

The following dialogue box will appear:

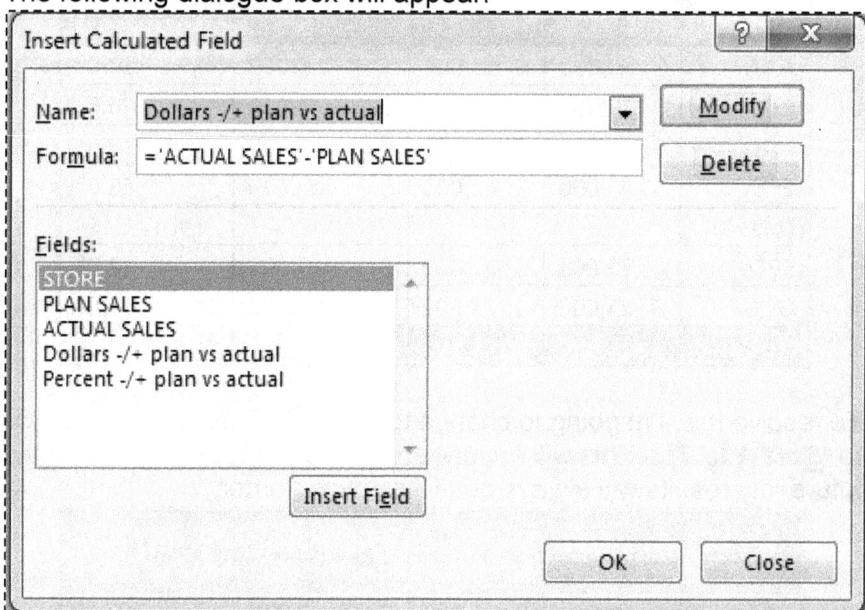

4. In the **'Name:'** drop-down box select the calculated field you would like to change or remove
5. Click appropriate button, either **'Modify'** or **'Delete'**

(PART 2) - CHAPTER 11

PIVOT TABLE ERROR MESSAGES & HOW TO RESOLVE THEM

Below are some common Pivot Table error messages with instructions on how to resolve them.

Note: *The following is not a comprehensive list of all the Pivot Table error messages, just a few of the more common ones.*

Error message:

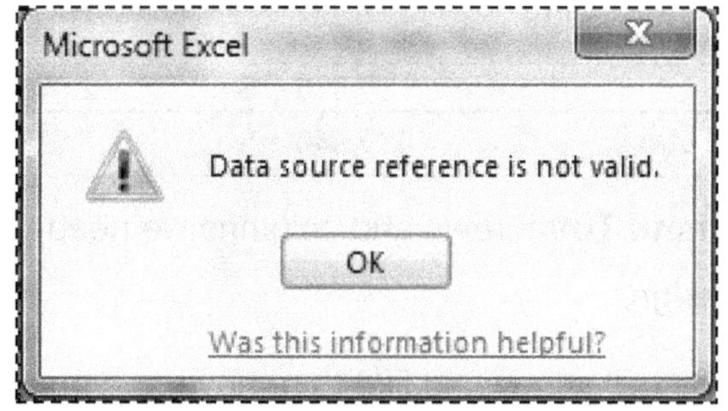

'Data source reference is not valid.'

Typically appears when you attempt to create a Pivot Table, with a **blank header row**.

	A	B	C	D	E	F	G	H	I
1									
2	REGION	SALES PERSON	SALES PERSON	SALES PERSON	QUARTER	APPLES	ORANGES	MANGOS	TOTAL
3			LAST NAME	ID					

To resolve, delete the blank row (in this case row 1) or make sure you select the correct header rows and supporting data before clicking **Insert : Pivot Table** from the toolbar.

<u>Error message</u>:

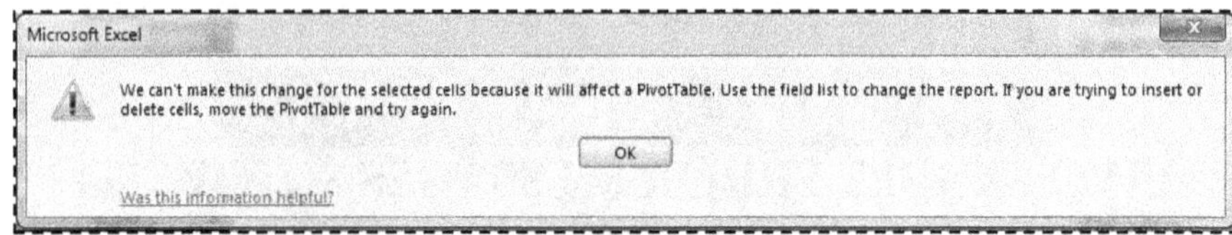

'We can't make this change for the selected cells because it will affect a PivotTable. Use the field list to change the report. If you are trying to insert or delete cells, move the PivotTable and try again.'

Often appears when you attempt to delete a calculated field, row, or column. For example, you no longer want to see the row **'Grand Total'**, unfortunately, you can't simply delete this row, you'll receive the above error message.

19	100	$	10,339	$	2,585	16
20	**Grand Total**	**$**	**480,946**	**$**	**7,515**	

To remove **'Grand Total'** rows and columns we need to change the Pivot Table design.

1. Click the cell you would like to remove and then from the toolbar select PIVOTTABLE TOOLS and the tab **DESIGN**

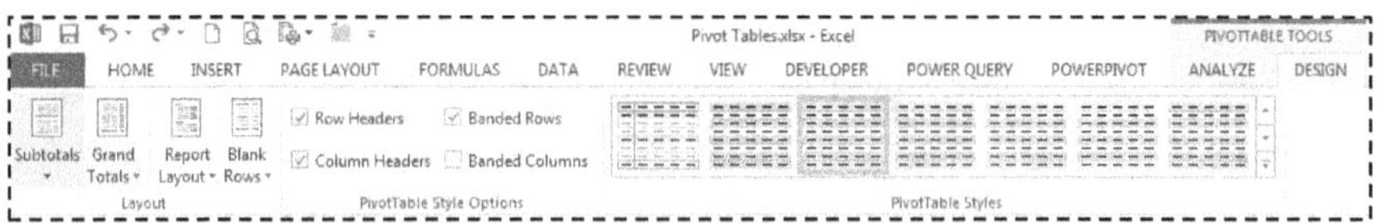

2. Click the drop-down box for **'Grand Totals'** and select your preferred option:
   a. Off for Rows and Columns
   b. On for Rows and Columns
   c. On for Rows Only
   d. On for Columns Only

For this example, we will select **'Off for Rows and Columns'**

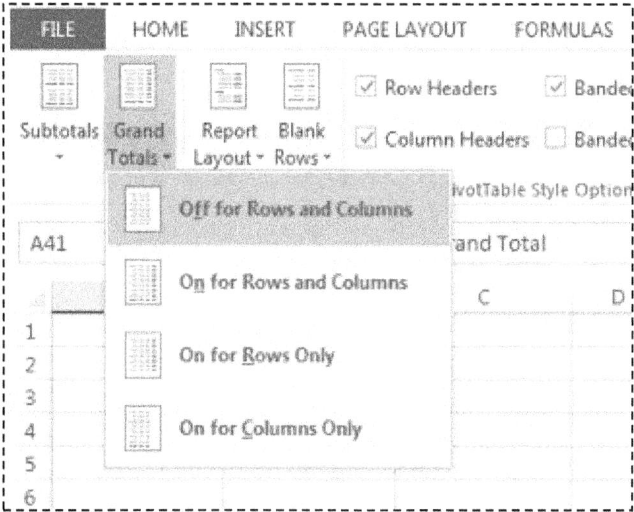

The **'Grand Total'** row has now been removed.

19	100	$ 10,339	$ 2,585	16
20				

(PART 3) - CHAPTER 12

FEATURE = DATA SORTING

Feature:

- Data Sorting

Definition:

- Allows you to change the order of rows in a spreadsheet to either ascending (A – Z alphabetical) or descending (Z-A reverse alphabetical).

Scenario:

You have a spreadsheet that contains the first and last name of sales associates. You would like to sort this list in alphabetical order by last name.

Detailed Example How To Use The Feature:

1. Begin by creating a new Excel® spreadsheet
2. Enter the following into **columns 'A' & 'B'**
   a. Cell '**A1'** enter **'FIRST NAME'** and cell **'B1'** enter **'LAST NAME'**
   b. Cell '**A2'** enter **'Helen'** and cell **'B2'** enter **'Smith'**
   c. Cell '**A3'** enter **'Jill'** and cell **'B3'** enter **'Johnson'**
   d. Cell '**A4'** enter **'Sally'** and cell **'B4'** enter **'Morton'**
   e. Cell '**A5'** enter **'John'** and cell **'B5'** enter **'Dower'**
   f. Cell '**A6'** enter **'Billy'** and cell **'B6'** enter **'Winchester'**

The spreadsheet should look similar to the following:

	A	B
1	FIRST NAME	LAST NAME
2	Helen	Smith
3	Jill	Johnson
4	Sally	Morton
5	John	Dower
6	Billy	Winchester

3. Highlight columns **'A' & 'B'**
4. From the toolbar select **Data : Sort**

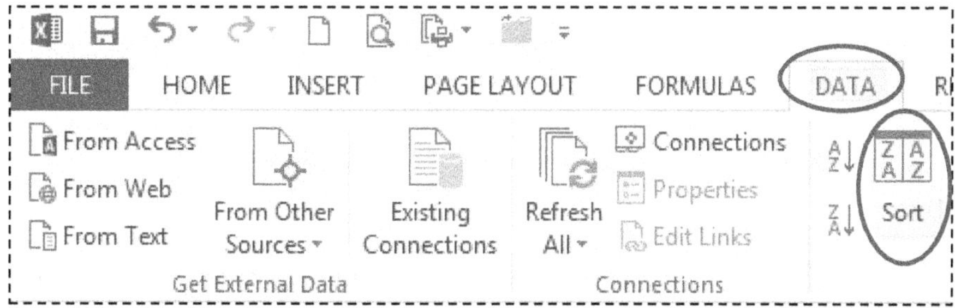

The following dialogue box should appear:

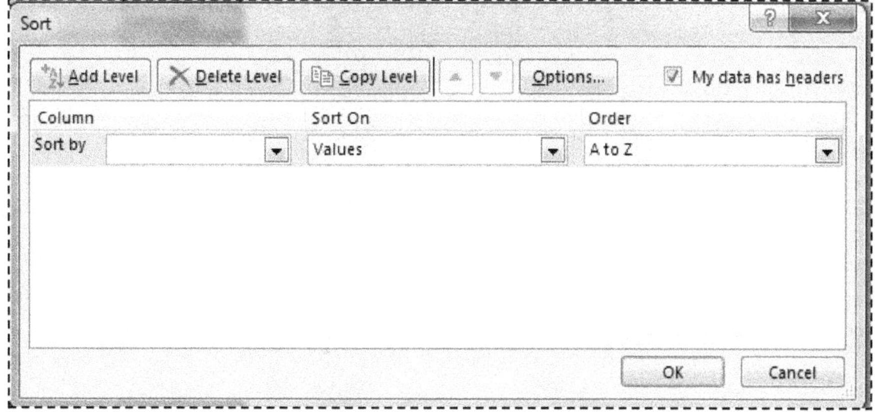

5. In the **'Sort by'** drop-down box select **'LAST NAME'** (this is the *primary* sort). For the **'Order'** drop-down box select **'A to Z'**
6. Click the **'Add Level'** button, a new row called **'Then by'** will appear
7. In the **'Then by'** drop-down box select **'FIRST NAME'** (this is the *secondary* sort). For the **'Order'** drop-down box select **'A to Z'**

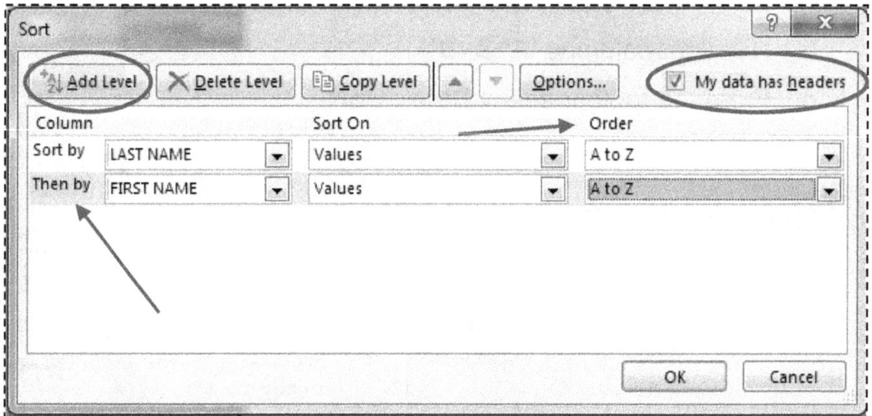

The results should look similar to the following:

	A	B
1	FIRST NAME	LAST NAME
2	John	Dower
3	Jill	Johnson
4	Sally	Morton
5	Helen	Smith
6	Billy	Winchester

You now have a list in alphabetical order by last name.

Additional Information:

NOTE: the check box **'My data has headers.'** Excel allows you to sort any range of cells. If this check box is unselected the **'Sort by'** drop-down options will appear as:

- Column A
- Column B
- Etc.

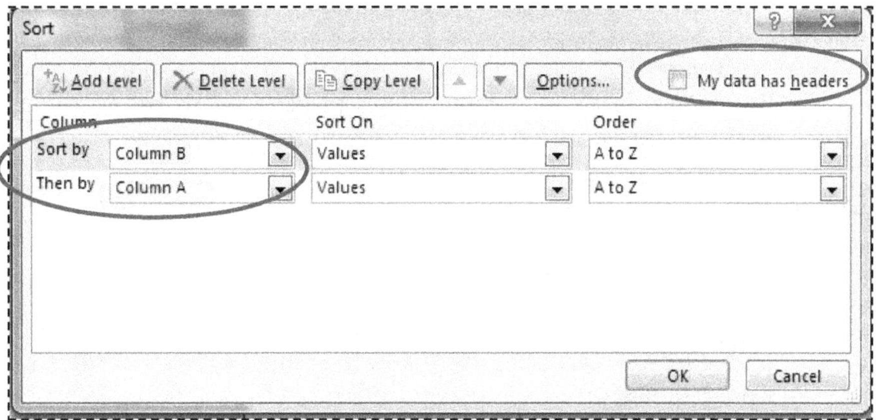

Result if **Order** (primary sort) was **descending (Z to A):**

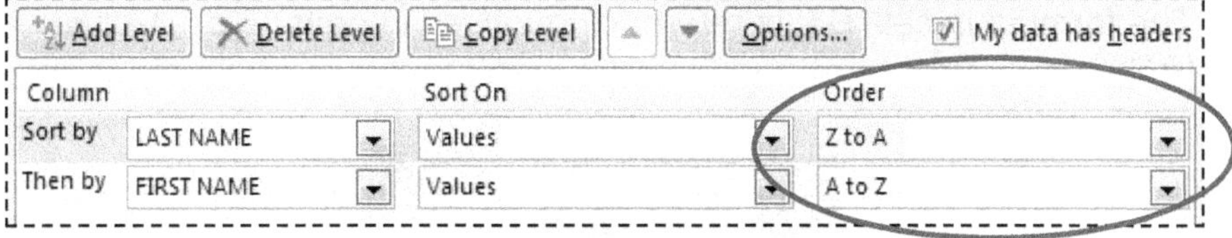

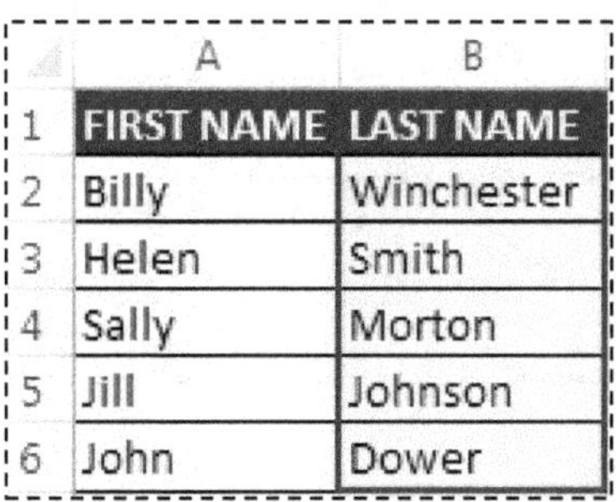

	A	B
1	FIRST NAME	LAST NAME
2	Billy	Winchester
3	Helen	Smith
4	Sally	Morton
5	Jill	Johnson
6	John	Dower

(PART 3) - CHAPTER 13

FEATURE = FORMULA TRACE

Feature:

- Formula trace is a graphical tool that can either identify all of the cells a formula is referencing *or* displays all the formulas that are dependent on a specific formula (cell).

Definition:

- **Trace Precedents:** Traces and displays graphically, with blue arrows, all of the cells a formula *is referencing*.
- **Trace Dependents:** Traces and displays graphically, with blue arrows, all of the formulas that are *dependent on* it for their calculation.

Quick Example: Trace Precedents

The formula in cell **'B3'** is *referencing values* in **cells 'A2', 'A4',** & **'A5'**:

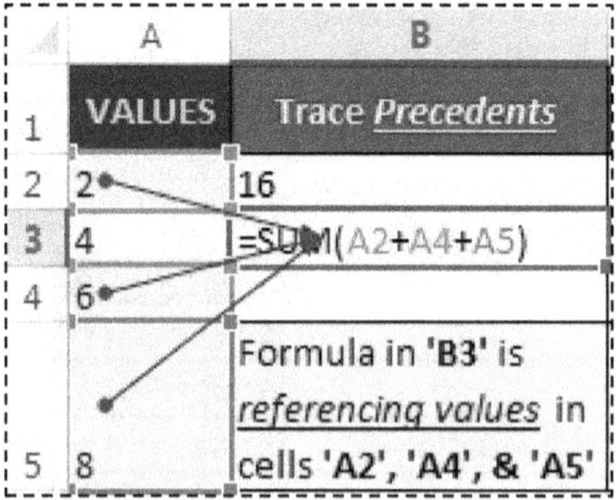

Quick Example: Trace Dependents

The formula in cell **'C3'** is *dependent* on the formula in **'B3'**:

	A	B	C
1	VALUES	Trace *Precedents*	Trace *Dependents*
2	2	16	20
3	4	=SUM(A2+A4+A5)	=B3+A3
4	6		
5	8		Formula in **'C3'** is *dependent on* the formula in **'B3'**

Scenario:

The formula trace features within Excel® are an extremely helpful tool when you need to troubleshoot or validate a formula is calculating correctly, especially when troubleshooting complex formulas referencing many cells. Let's walk through a couple of examples:

1. You've been contacted by a sales person who believes his sales are understated. He has asked you to verify his numbers are correct.
2. One of the formulas in a spreadsheet contains the error **'#VALUE'**. You've been asked to troubleshoot and fix the problem.
3. A report used by sales managers has become increasingly difficult to read. You've been asked if there are some sections that can be deleted. In order to do this without breaking (effecting) other formulas, you decide to use the Trace Dependents feature to ensure removing a particular section does not inadvertently effect other formulas.

Detailed Example How To Use The Feature:

Sample data:

	A	B	D	H	I	J
1	SALES PERSON FIRST NAME	SALES PERSON LAST NAME	QUARTER	TOTAL		B. Winchester
2	Jack	Smith	1	$ 343		63,606
3	Joe	Tanner	1	$ 377		
4	Peter	Graham	1	$ 415		
5	Helen	Simpson	1	$ 457		
6	Alex	Steller	1	$ 502		
7	Billy	Winchester	1	$ 552		
8	Jack	Smith	2	$ 1,849		
9	Joe	Tanner	2	$ 2,404		
10	Peter	Graham	2	$ 3,125		
11	Helen	Simpson	2	$ 4,062		
12	Alex	Steller	2	$ 5,281		
13	Billy	Winchester	2	$ 6,865		
14	Jack	Smith	3	$ 2,653		
15	Joe	Tanner	3	$ 3,980		
16	Peter	Graham	3	$ 5,969		
17	Alex	Steller	3	$ 13,431		
18	Billy	Winchester	3	$ 16,558		
19	Jack	Smith	4	$ 5,494		
20	Joe	Tanner	4	$ 8,516		
21	Billy	Winchester	4	$ 39,631		
22	Peter	Graham	4	$ 13,199		
23	Helen	Simpson	4	$ 8,954		
24	Alex	Steller	4	$ 31,711		

The sales person Billy Winchester has asked you to verify his sales numbers are correct for the year.

1. Place your cursor in cell **'J2'**
2. From the toolbar select **Formulas : Trace Precedents**

A similar type of graphic should appear:

J2 | fx =SUM(H7+H13+H18+H21)

	A	B	D	H	J
1	SALES PERSON FIRST NAME	SALES PERSON LAST NAME	QUARTER	TOTAL	B. Winchester
2	Jack	Smith	1	$ 343	63,606
3	Joe	Tanner	1	$ 377	
4	Peter	Graham	1	$ 415	
5	Helen	Simpson	1	$ 457	
6	Alex	Steller	1	$ 502	
7	Billy	Winchester	1	$ 552	
8	Jack	Smith	2	$ 1,849	
9	Joe	Tanner	2	$ 2,404	
10	Peter	Graham	2	$ 3,125	
11	Helen	Simpson	2	$ 4,062	
12	Alex	Steller	2	$ 5,281	
13	Billy	Winchester	2	$ 6,865	
14	Jack	Smith	3	$ 2,653	
15	Joe	Tanner	3	$ 3,980	
16	Peter	Graham	3	$ 5,969	
17	Alex	Steller	3	$ 13,431	
18	Billy	Winchester	3	$ 16,558	
19	Jack	Smith	4	$ 5,494	
20	Joe	Tanner	4	$ 8,516	
21	Billy	Winchester	4	$ 39,631	
22	Peter	Graham	4	$ 13,199	
23	Helen	Simpson	4	$ 8,954	
24	Alex	Steller	4	$ 31,711	

We've now verified the sales for Billy Winchester are correct for the year.

Now, let's look at how Trace Precedents can help us troubleshoot a formula that contains an error.

Sample data:

	A	B	C	D	E	F	G	H	I
1	SALES PERSON FIRST NAME	SALES PERSON LAST NAME	QUARTER	TOTAL		Q1	Q2	Q3	Q4
2	Peter	Graham	1	$ 415		$ 2,646	#VALUE!	$ 49,375	$ 107,505
3	Peter	Graham	2	$ 3,125					
4	Peter	Graham	3	$ 5,969					
5	Peter	Graham	4	$ 13,199					
6	Helen	Simpson	1	$ 457					
7	Helen	Simpson	2	$ 4,062					
8	Helen	Simpson	3	$ 6,785					
9	Helen	Simpson	4	$ 8,954					
10	Jack	Smith	1	$ 343					
11	Jack	Smith	2	$ 1,849					
12	Jack	Smith	3	$ 2,653					
13	Jack	Smith	4	$ 5,494					
14	Alex	Steller	1	$ 502					
15	Alex	Steller	2	$ 5,281					
16	Alex	Steller	3	$ 13,431					
17	Alex	Steller	4	$ 31,711					
18	Joe	Tanner	1	$ 377					
19	Joe	Tanner	2	$ 2403.7					
20	Joe	Tanner	3	$ 3,980					
21	Joe	Tanner	4	$ 8,516					
22	Billy	Winchester	1	$ 552					
23	Billy	Winchester	2	$ 6,865					
24	Billy	Winchester	3	$ 16,558					
25	Billy	Winchester	4	$ 39,631					

1. Place your cursor in cell **'G2'**
2. From the toolbar select **Formulas : Trace Precedents**

A similar type of graphic will be displayed. It appears someone has inadvertently typed the letter **'O'**, instead of the number zero (**0**) in cell **'D19'**.

G2 =SUM(D3+D7+D11+D15+D19+D23)

	A	B	C	D	E	F	G	H	I
1	SALES PERSON FIRST NAME	SALES PERSON LAST NAME	QUARTER	TOTAL		Q1	Q2	Q3	Q4
2	Peter	Graham	1	$ 415		$ 2[illegible]6	#VALUE!	$ 49,375	$ 107,505
3	Peter	Graham	2	$ 3,125					
4	Peter	Graham	3	$ 5,969					
5	Peter	Graham	4	$ 13,199					
6	Helen	Simpson	1	$ 457					
7	Helen	Simpson	2	$ 4,062					
8	Helen	Simpson	3	$ 6,785					
9	Helen	Simpson	4	$ 8,954					
10	Jack	Smith	1	$ 343					
11	Jack	Smith	2	$ 1,849					
12	Jack	Smith	3	$ 2,653					
13	Jack	Smith	4	$ 5,494					
14	Alex	Steller	1	$ 502					
15	Alex	Steller	2	$ 5,281					
16	Alex	Steller	3	$ 13,431					
17	Alex	Steller	4	$ 31,711					
18	Joe	Tanner	1	$ 377					
19	Joe	Tanner	2	$ 2403.7					
20	Joe	Tanner	3	$ 3,980					
21	Joe	Tanner	4	$ 8,516					
22	Billy	Winchester	1	$ 552					
23	Billy	Winchester	2	$ 6,865					
24	Billy	Winchester	3	$ 16,558					
25	Billy	Winchester	4	$ 39,631					

3. To fix, remove the letter **'O'** and replace with the number zero (**0**) in cell **'D19'**.

F	G	H	I
Q1	Q2	Q3	Q4
$ 2,646	$ 23,586	$ 49,375	$ 107,505

A report used by sales managers has become increasingly difficult to read They've asked you if the *'CURRENT YR' sales section* can be removed? You decide to use the **Trace Dependents** feature to ensure removing this particular section does not inadvertently effect other formulas.

Current report:

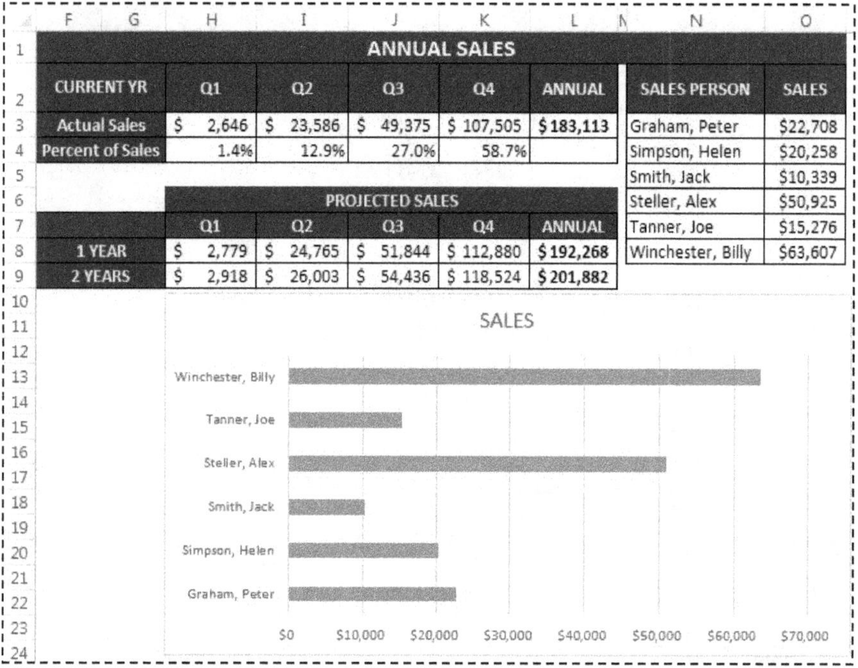

ANNUAL SALES							
CURRENT YR	Q1	Q2	Q3	Q4	ANNUAL	SALES PERSON	SALES
Actual Sales	$ 2,646	$ 23,586	$ 49,375	$ 107,505	$ 183,113	Graham, Peter	$22,708
Percent of Sales	1.4%	12.9%	27.0%	58.7%		Simpson, Helen	$20,258
						Smith, Jack	$10,339
	PROJECTED SALES					Steller, Alex	$50,925
	Q1	Q2	Q3	Q4	ANNUAL	Tanner, Joe	$15,276
1 YEAR	$ 2,779	$ 24,765	$ 51,844	$ 112,880	$ 192,268	Winchester, Billy	$63,607
2 YEARS	$ 2,918	$ 26,003	$ 54,436	$ 118,524	$ 201,882		

1. Place your cursor in cell **'H3'**
2. From the toolbar select **Formulas : Trace Dependents**

A similar type of graphic will be displayed. We can see that cells **'H4'** & **'H8'** are *dependent* on cell **'H3'** which is part of the *'CURRENT YR' sales section.* Therefore, if you were to remove this section it would adversely affect other formulas is this spreadsheet.

	F	G	H	I	J	K	L
1				ANNUAL SALES			
2	CURRENT YR		Q1	Q2	Q3	Q4	ANNUAL
3	Actual Sales		$ 2,646	$ 23,586	$ 49,375	$ 107,505	$183,113
4	Percent of Sales		1.4%	12.9%	27.0%	58.7%	
5							
6				PROJECTED SALES			
7			Q1	Q2	Q3	Q4	ANNUAL
8	1 YEAR		$ 2,779	$ 24,765	$ 51,844	$ 112,880	$192,268
9	2 YEARS		$ 2,918	$ 26,003	$ 54,436	$ 118,524	$201,882

To remove the arrows, there are two options:

A. From the toolbar select **Formulas : Remove Arrows** *or*

B. **Save** the spreadsheet

(PART 3) - CHAPTER 14
FEATURE = TEXT TO COLUMNS

Feature:

- Text To Columns

Definition:

- Allows you to parse merged data from a single cell, fixed width, delimited, or structured file into separate Excel® columns.

Scenario:

One of the things I've often had to do in my career is parse information given to me from a source that has merged data elements together. Some of the most common examples are:

1. Reports generated by another application *(often legacy systems).* These reports are typically created in a **text (.txt)** or **comma separated file (.CSV)**.
2. Data exported by a query from a database or other applications and pasted into Excel®.
3. Data copied or cut, and pasted into Excel® from the web or other types of screen scraping activities.

Detailed Example How To Use The Feature:

Let's walk through an example of data pasted into Excel®. The data elements are merged into a single cell (column **'A'**) and are separated by a comma.

Sample data:

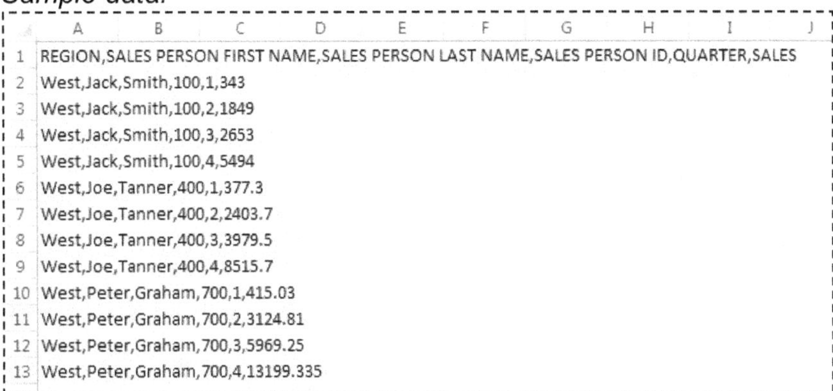

1. Click on **column 'A'**, make sure the entire column is highlighted

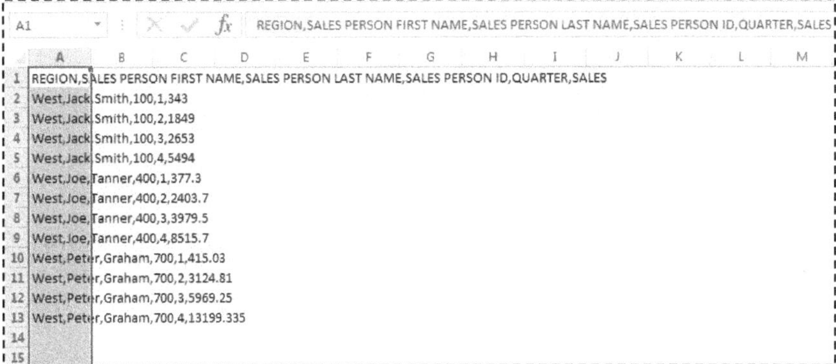

2. From the toolbar select **DATA : Text to Columns**

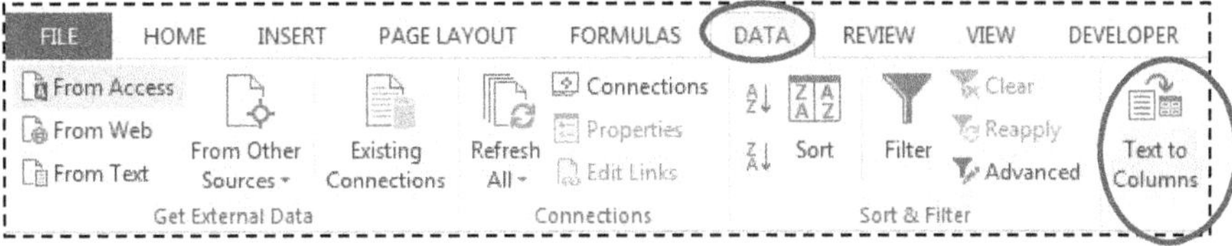

The following dialogue box / Wizard should appear:

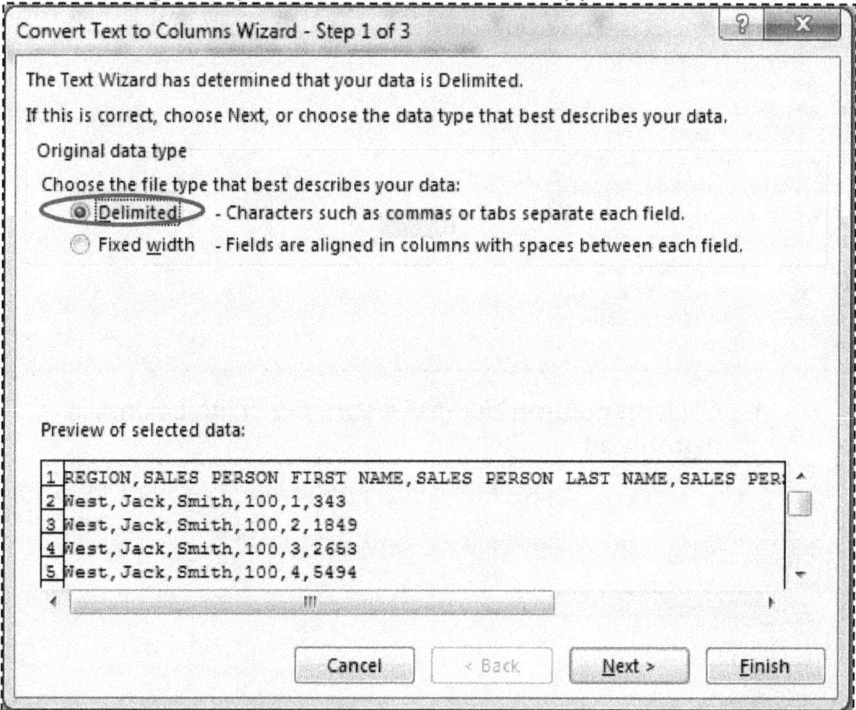

3. Select the '**Delimited**' radio button and click the '**Next>**' button

The following dialogue box should appear:

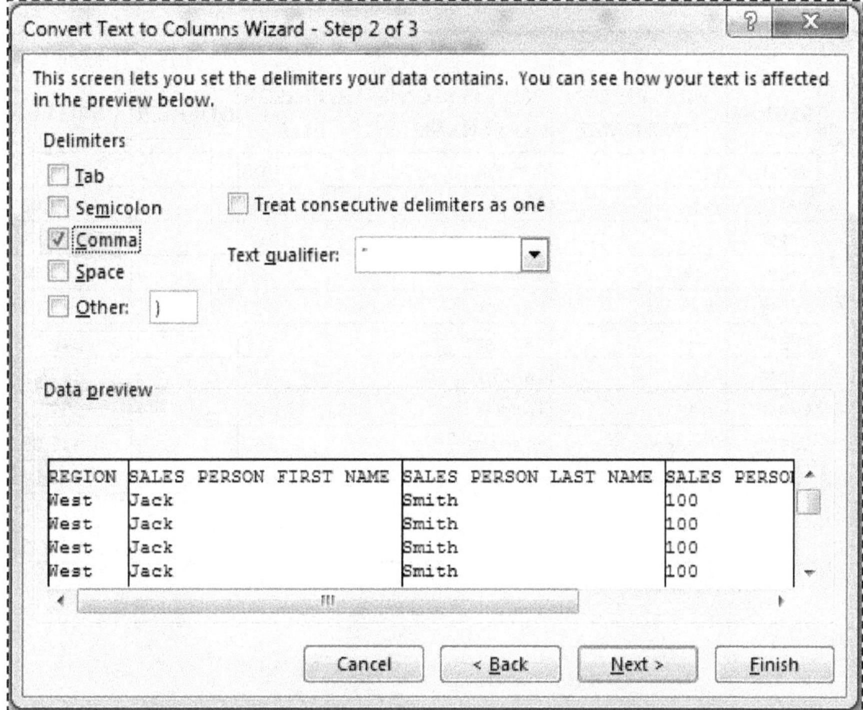

4. Select the '**Comma**' check box as your delimiter. **Note** the '**Data preview**' section. *There are now separate columns of the what was the merged data in column 'A'*
5. If the data appears to be parsed correctly, click the '**Finish**' button

The merged data is now parsed into separate columns:

	A	B	C	D	E	F
1	REGION	SALES PERSON FIRST NAME	SALES PERSON LAST NAME	SALES PERSON ID	QUARTER	SALES
2	West	Jack	Smith	100	1	343
3	West	Jack	Smith	100	2	1849
4	West	Jack	Smith	100	3	2653
5	West	Jack	Smith	100	4	5494
6	West	Joe	Tanner	400	1	377.3
7	West	Joe	Tanner	400	2	2403.7
8	West	Joe	Tanner	400	3	3979.5
9	West	Joe	Tanner	400	4	8515.7
10	West	Peter	Graham	700	1	415.03
11	West	Peter	Graham	700	2	3124.81
12	West	Peter	Graham	700	3	5969.25
13	West	Peter	Graham	700	4	13199.335

(PART 3) - CHAPTER 15

FEATURE = CONDITIONAL FORMATTING

Feature:

- Conditional Formatting

Definition:

- Using different colors for cell shading and fonts, Conditional Formatting allows you to highlight cells based on specific criteria.

- Preset options include:
  - The Top & Bottom 10 *(the number 10 can be adjusted)*
  - The Top & Bottom 10% *(this percentage can also be adjusted)*
  - Above & Below the Average

- A very useful tool to quickly identify:
  - Duplicate values
  - A reoccurring date
  - Values greater or less than a specific number
  - Equal to a specific number
  - Cells that contain specific text

Scenario:

You've been given a spreadsheet that contains the total fruit sales by quarter and sales person. You've been asked to provide the *sales people* and *quarter* in which:

- Sales are greater than $10,000
- Sales are less than $1,000

Detailed Example How To Use The Feature:

Sample data:

	A	B	C	D
1	SALES PERSON FIRST NAME	SALES PERSON LAST NAME	QUARTER	TOTAL
2	Jack	Smith	1	$ 343
3	Jack	Smith	2	$ 1,849
4	Jack	Smith	3	$ 2,653
5	Jack	Smith	4	$ 5,494
6	Joe	Tanner	1	$ 377
7	Joe	Tanner	2	$ 2,404
8	Joe	Tanner	3	$ 3,980
9	Joe	Tanner	4	$ 39,631
10	Peter	Graham	1	$ 415
11	Peter	Graham	2	$ 3,125
12	Peter	Graham	3	$ 5,969
13	Peter	Graham	4	$ 13,199
14	Helen	Simpson	1	$ 457
15	Helen	Simpson	2	$ 4,062
16	Helen	Simpson	4	$ 8,954
17	Helen	Simpson	4	$ 20,459
18	Alex	Steller	1	$ 502
19	Alex	Steller	2	$ 5,281
20	Alex	Steller	3	$ 13,431
21	Alex	Steller	4	$ 31,711
22	Billy	Winchester	1	$ 552
23	Billy	Winchester	2	$ 6,865
24	Billy	Winchester	3	$ 16,558
25	Billy	Winchester	4	$ 8,516

1. Highlight cells **'D2 – D25'**

2. From the toolbar select **HOME : Conditional Formatting**

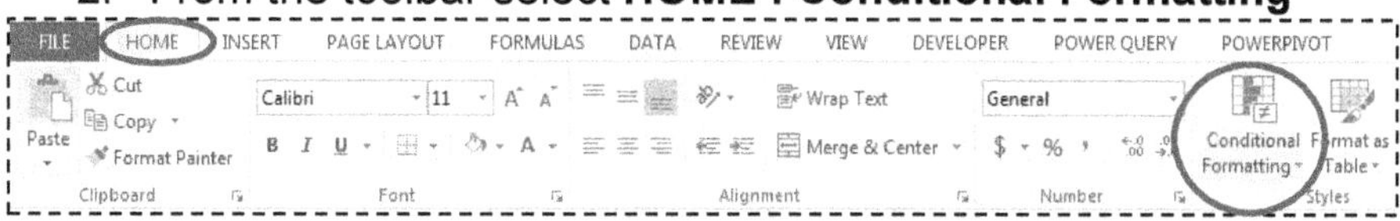

3. Select **Highlight Cells Rules > Greater Than…**

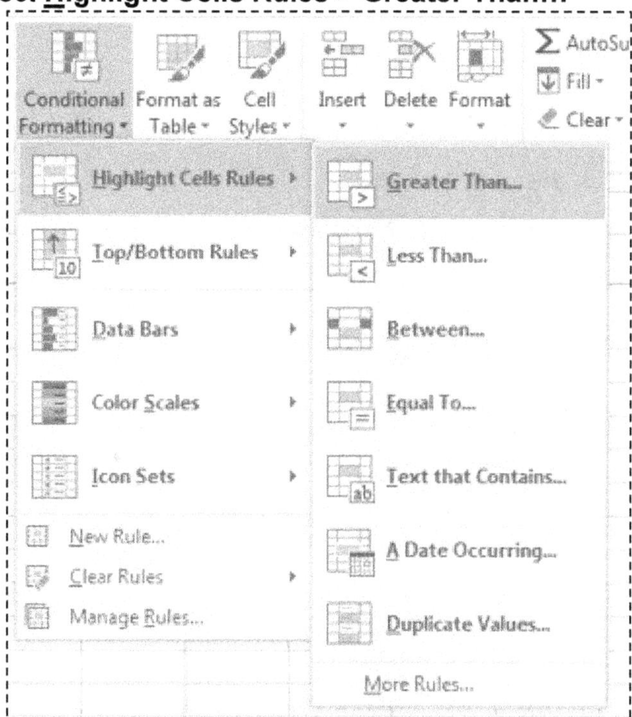

The following dialogue box should appear:

4. In the **'Format cells that are GREATER THAN':** box enter **$10,000**

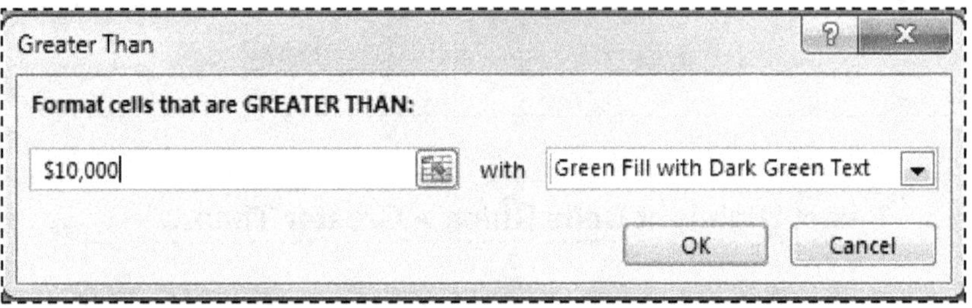

5. In the **'with'** box, click the drop-down box and select '**Green Fill with Dark Green Text'**
6. Click the '**OK**' button
7. Repeat **steps 1 & 2** above
8. This time select **Highlight Cells Rules : Less Than…**

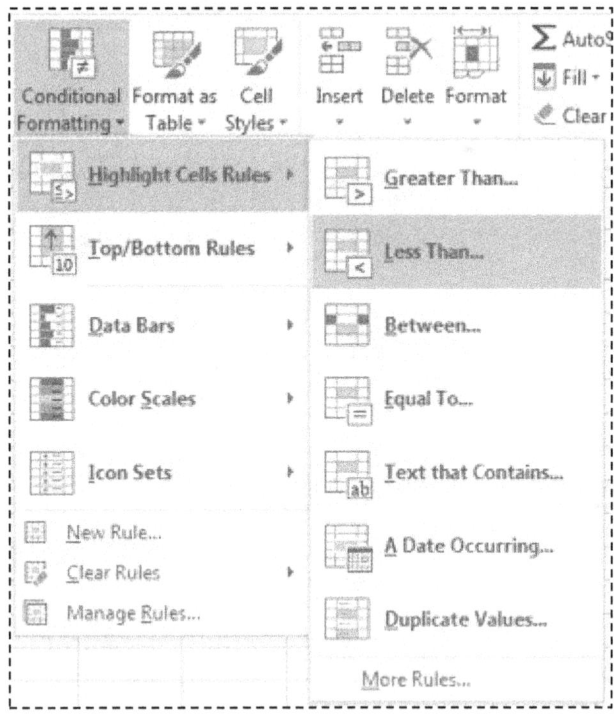

The following dialogue box should appear:

9. In the **'Format cells that are LESS THAN':** box enter **$1,000**
10. In the **'with':** box click the drop-down box and select '**Light Red Fill with Dark Red Text'**
11. Click the '**OK**' button

12. Highlight columns **'A'** – **'D'**
13. From the toolbar select **DATA : Filter**

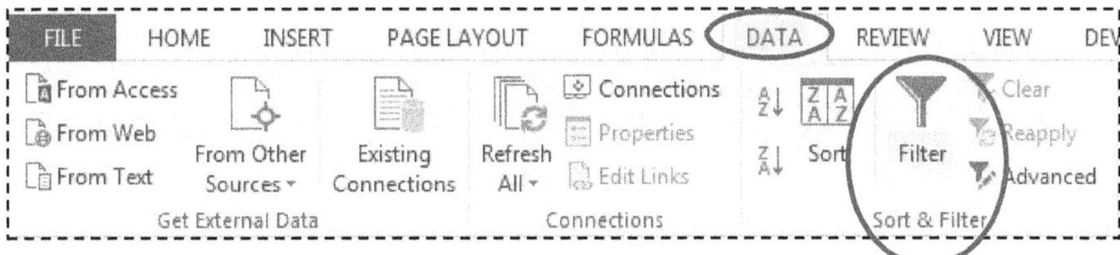

14. Click the filter drop-down arrow for **'TOTAL'** *(column 'D')*
15. Select **'Filter by Color**'
16. Select the green looking bar

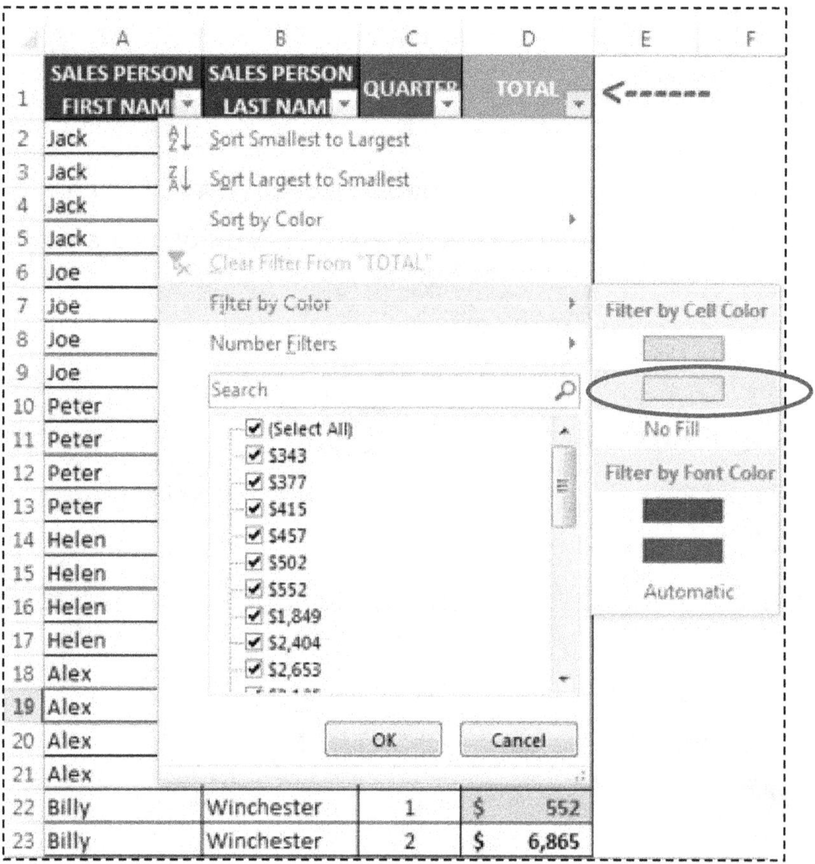

You should see something similar to the following now being displayed.

	A	B	C	D
1	SALES PERSON FIRST NAME	SALES PERSON LAST NAME	QUARTER	TOTAL
9	Joe	Tanner	4	$ 39,631
13	Peter	Graham	4	$ 13,199
17	Helen	Simpson	4	$ 20,459
20	Alex	Steller	3	$ 13,431
21	Alex	Steller	4	$ 31,711
24	Billy	Winchester	3	$ 16,558

You've now identified the quarter and sales people with sales greater than $10,000.

---

1. Click the filter drop-down arrow for **'TOTAL'** *(column 'D')*
2. Select **'Filter by Color**'
3. Select the red looking bar

You should see something similar to the following now being displayed:

	A	B	C	D
1	SALES PERSON FIRST NAME	SALES PERSON LAST NAME	QUARTER	TOTAL
2	Jack	Smith	1	$ 343
6	Joe	Tanner	1	$ 377
10	Peter	Graham	1	$ 415
14	Helen	Simpson	1	$ 457
18	Alex	Steller	1	$ 502
22	Billy	Winchester	1	$ 552

You've now identified the quarter and sales people with sales less than $1,000.

To remove the Conditional Formatting:

1. From the toolbar select **HOME : Conditional Formatting:**

2. Select '**Clear Rules**' and either option:
   a. Clear Rules from Select Cells
   b. Clear Rules from Entire Sheet

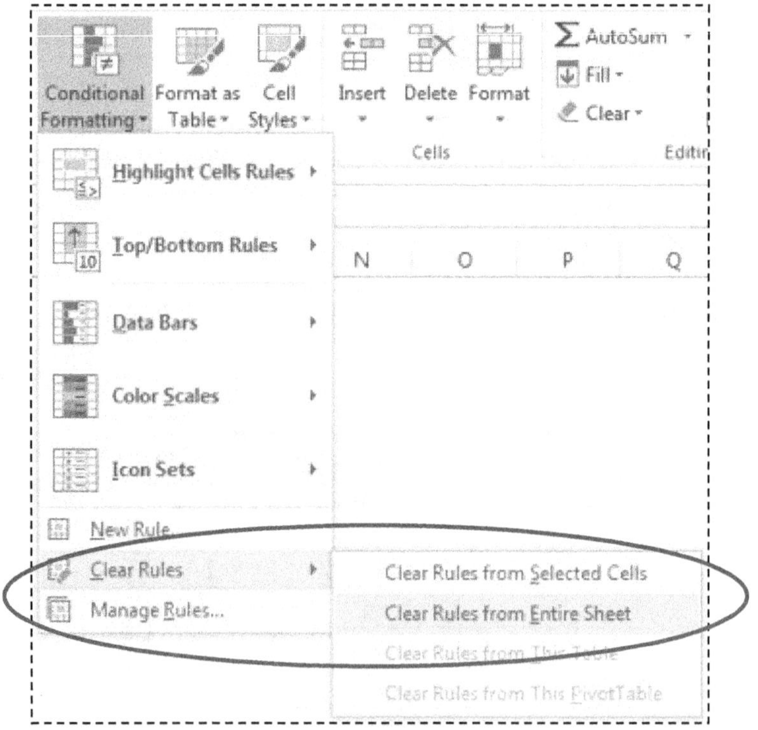

(PART 4) - CHAPTER 16

FORMULA = LEN

Formula:

- LEN

Definition:

- Counts the number characters in a cell

Quick Example:

```
Formula Syntax:
LEN(text)
text is required
```

B2 | =LEN(A2)

	A	B	C
1	FRUIT NAME	NUMBER OF CHARACTERS IN ROW 2 COLUMN 'A'	
2	Apples	6	

Scenario:

You've been given a report that was created by a Database Administrator (DBA). The DBA created the file by running a query in a database, exporting the results into a .CSV file, and then opened and re-saved the report as an Excel® file.

As the Business Analyst, you're attempting to reconcile the data using a Pivot Table. In your analysis, you've discovered cell values that *"look"* to be the same, but are being returned as two separate records in your results.

You use the LEN function to troubleshoot why you're getting two separate records in your results for what appear to be the same value.

Detailed Example How To Use The Formula:

Sample data:

	A	B
1	FRUIT NAME	FRUIT SALES
2	Apples	100
3	Kiwi	100
4	Oranges	100
5	Apples	200
6	Kiwi	200
7	Oranges	200
8	Apples	300
9	Kiwi	300
10	Oranges	300
11		

Pivot table results, the fruit '**Apples**' is listed twice and should only be listed once:

	A	B
1		
2		
3	Row Labels	Sum of FRUIT SALES
4	Apples	100
5	Apples	500
6	Kiwi	600
7	Oranges	600
8	**Grand Total**	**1800**
9		

1. You begin by sorting the results by 'Fruit Name' in Ascending order
2. Add a column, in cell '**C1**' label it "**LEN FUNCTION**"
3. Next apply the '**LEN**' function for 'Fruit Name' in row '**C2**'

	A	B	C
1	FRUIT NAME	FRUIT SALES	LEN FUNCTION
2	Apples	100	
3	Apples	200	
4	Apples	300	
5	Kiwi	100	
6	Kiwi	200	
7	Kiwi	300	
8	Oranges	100	
9	Oranges	200	
10	Oranges	300	
11			

4. From the toolbar select **Formulas : Insert Function**

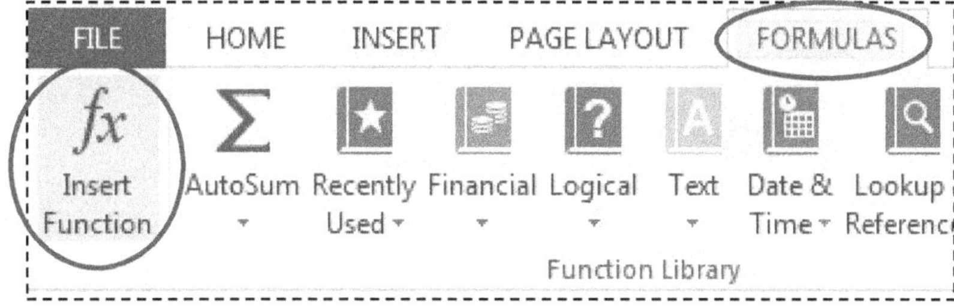

5. Type "**LEN**" in the **'Search for a function:'** dialogue box

6. Click the '**Go**' button

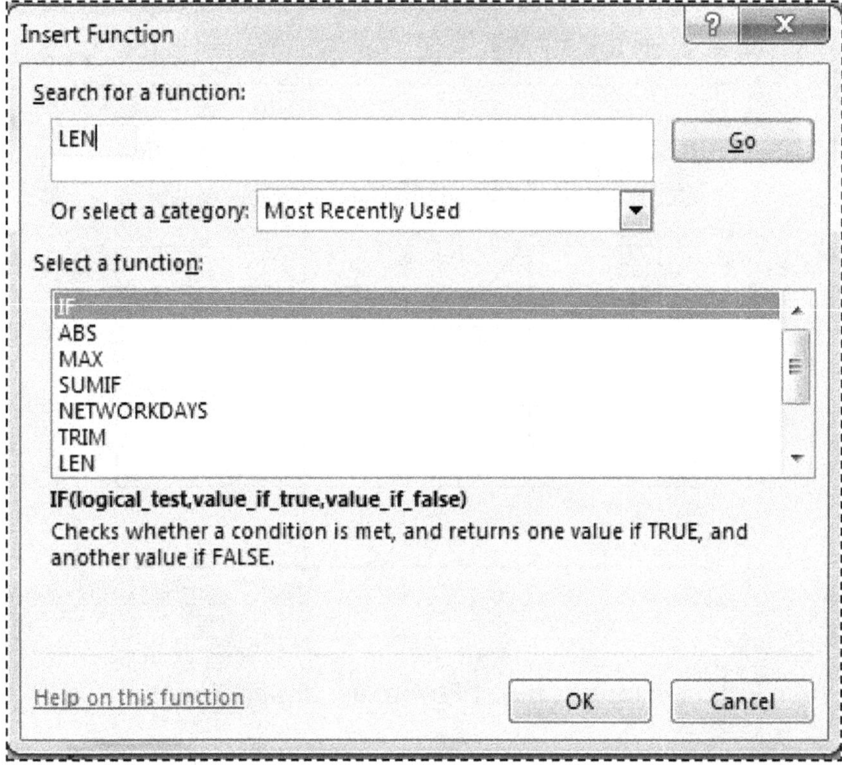

The following dialogue box should now appear:

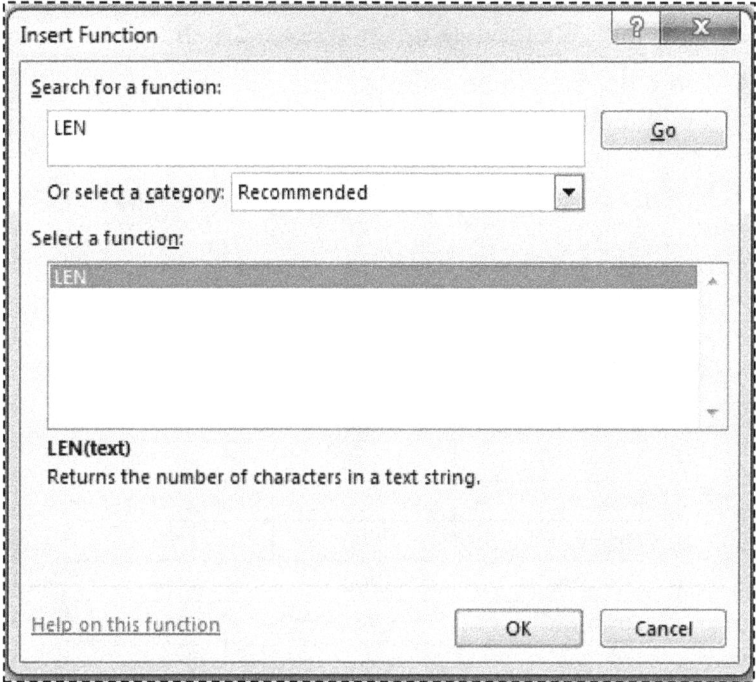

7. Click the '**OK**' button
8. Click on cell '**A2**' or enter '**A2**' in the dialogue box
9. Click 'the '**OK**' button

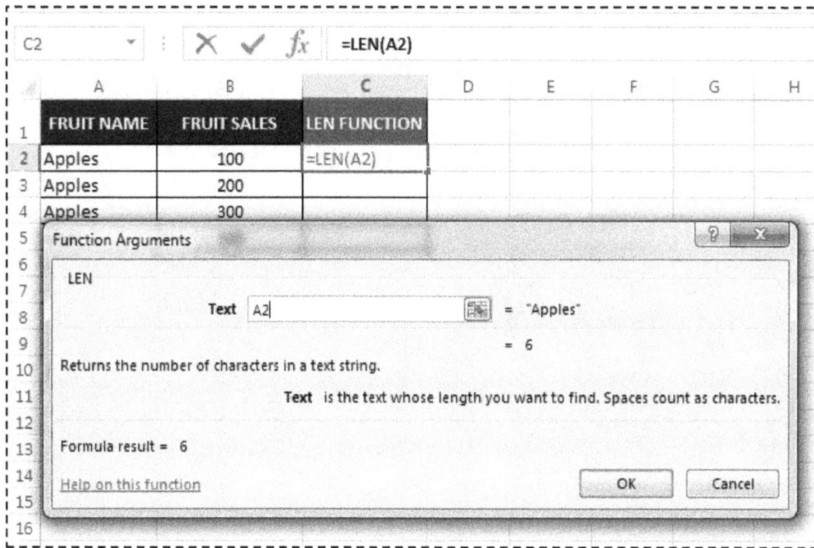

10. Copy the LEN formula down to cells '**C3**' thru '**C10**'
11. There appears to be an extra space in cells '**A3**' & '**A4'** for the fruit *'Apple*'

	A	B	C
1	FRUIT NAME	FRUIT SALES	LEN FUNCTION
2	Apples	100	6
3	Apples	200	7
4	Apples	300	7
5	Kiwi	100	4
6	Kiwi	200	4
7	Kiwi	300	4
8	Oranges	100	7
9	Oranges	200	7
10	Oranges	300	7

12. Remove the extra space in in cells '**A3**' & '**A4'** for the fruit 'Apple'
13. Save your changes
14. Re-run your Pivot Table

Results now appear correctly

3	Row Labels	Sum of FRUIT SALES
4	Apples	600
5	Kiwi	600
6	Oranges	600
7	**Grand Total**	**1800**

(PART 4) - CHAPTER 17
FORMULA = TRIM

Formula:

- TRIM

Definition:

- Removes all extraneous spaces from a cell, except for single spaces between words.

Quick Example:

```
Formula Syntax:
TRIM(text)
text is required
```

C2 =TRIM(A2)

	A	B	C	D
1	FRUIT NAME	LEN COUNT OF CHARACTERS	TRIM FUNCTION	LEN COUNT OF CHARACTERS
2	Apples, Bananas, Mangos	27	Apples, Bananas, Mangos	23
3	Apples, Bananas, Mangos	23	Apples, Bananas, Mangos	23
4				

Scenario:

You've been given an Excel® report generated by another application. Upon review you see the content in some cells contains extra spaces between and after words. In order to make the report usable for analysis and presentation you need to remove the extraneous spaces.

Detailed Example How To Use The Formula:

Sample data:

	A	B
1	FRUIT NAME	LEN COUNT OF CHARACTERS
2	Apples, Bananas, Mangos	27
3	Apples, Bananas, Mangos	23
4	Kiwi, Oranges, Strawberries	27
5	Kiwi, Oranges, Strawberries	29
6	Blueberries, Raspberries, Blackberries	38
7	Blueberries, Raspberries, Blackberries	40

1. Add a column, in cell '**C1**' label it "**TRIM FUNCTION**"
2. Next, apply the '**TRIM**' function for 'Fruit Name' in row '**C2**'

	A	B	C
1	FRUIT NAME	LEN COUNT OF CHARACTERS	TRIM FUNCTION
2	Apples, Bananas, Mangos	27	
3	Apples, Bananas, Mangos	23	
4	Kiwi, Oranges, Strawberries	27	
5	Kiwi, Oranges, Strawberries	29	
6	Blueberries, Raspberries, Blackberries	38	
7	Blueberries, Raspberries, Blackberries	40	

3. From the toolbar select **Formulas : Insert Function**

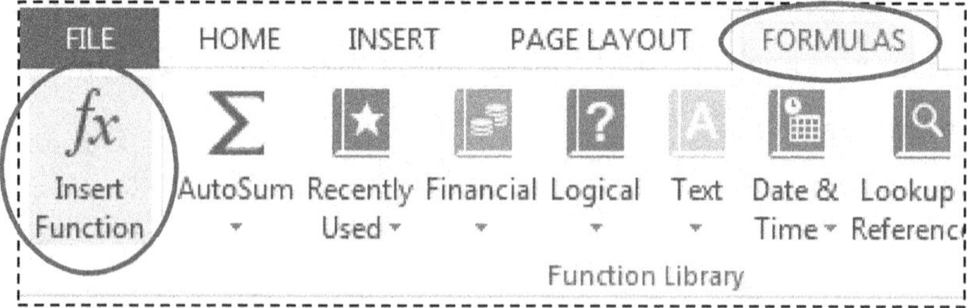

4. Type "**TRIM**" in the **'Search for a function:'** dialogue box
5. Click the '**Go**' button

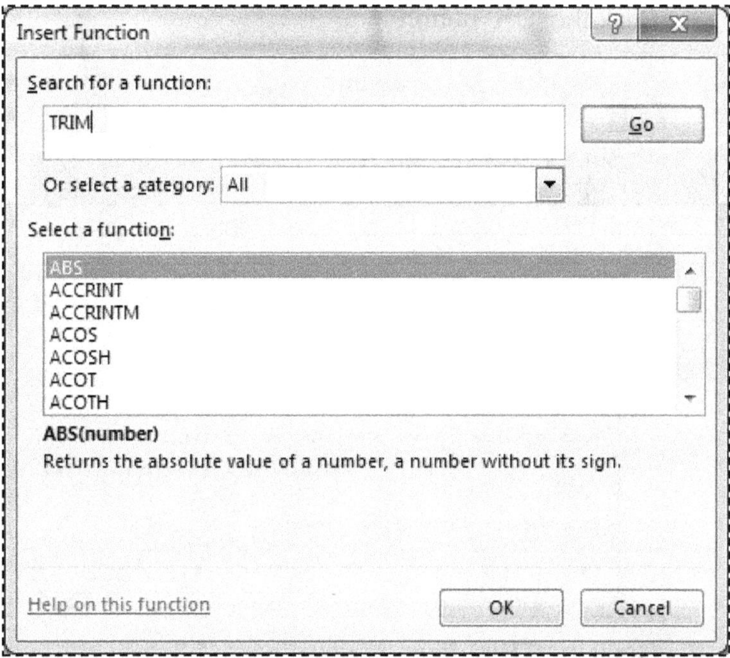

The following dialogue box should now appear:

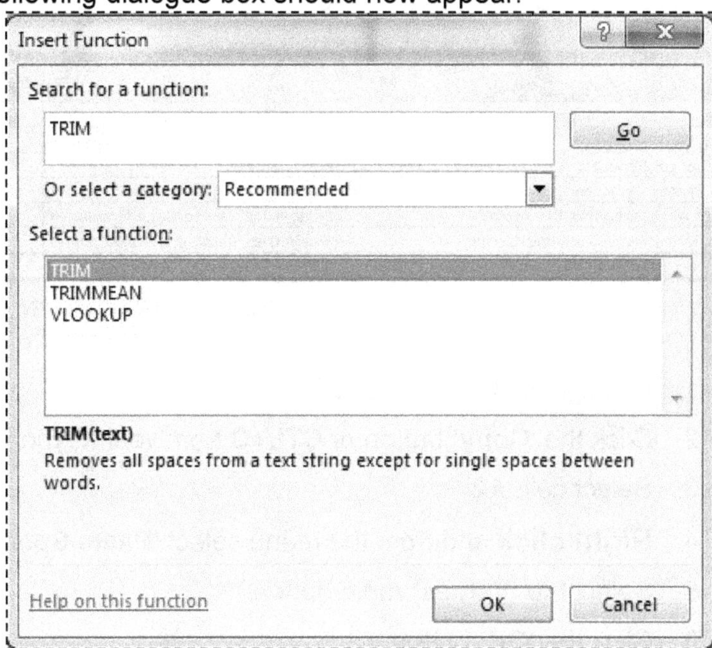

6. Click the '**OK**' button
7. Click cell '**A2**' or enter '**A2**' in the dialogue box
8. Click the '**OK**' button

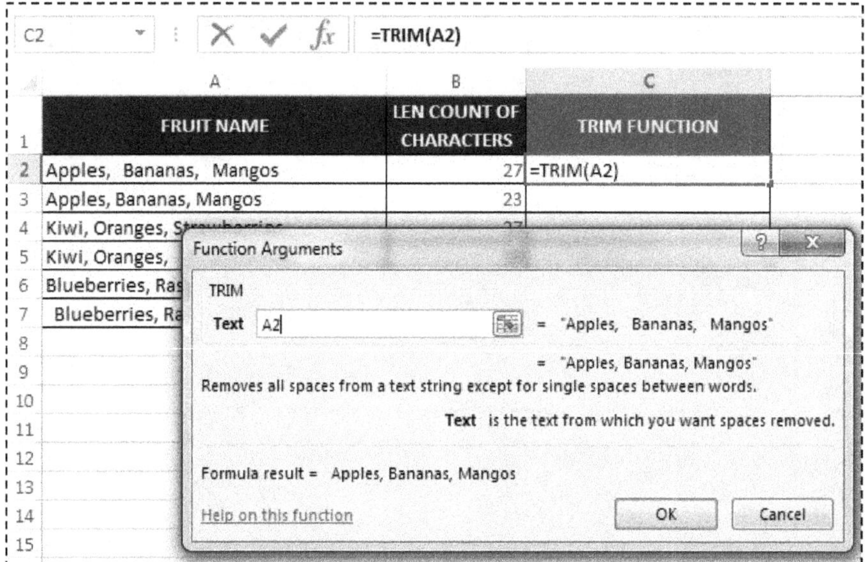

9. Copy the **TRIM** formula down cells '**C3**' thru '**C7**'

The extra spaces have been removed:

	A	B	C	D
1	FRUIT NAME	LEN COUNT OF CHARACTERS	TRIM FUNCTION	LEN COUNT OF CHARACTERS
2	Apples, Bananas, Mangos	27	Apples, Bananas, Mangos	23
3	Apples, Bananas, Mangos	23	Apples, Bananas, Mangos	23
4	Kiwi, Oranges, Strawberries	27	Kiwi, Oranges, Strawberries	27
5	Kiwi, Oranges, Strawberries	29	Kiwi, Oranges, Strawberries	27
6	Blueberries, Raspberries, Blackberries	38	Blueberries, Raspberries, Blackberries	38
7	Blueberries, Raspberries, Blackberries	40	Blueberries, Raspberries, Blackberries	38

---

*Next we'll copy and **paste as a values** the contents of **column C** and remove the columns (B, C, & D) that were used for troubleshooting.*

1. Highlight cells '**C2**' thru **'C7'**
2. Click the '**Copy'** button or **CTL+C** from your keyboard
3. Select cell **'A2'**
4. **Right click** and from the menu select **'Paste Special…'**
5. Select the **'Values'** radio button
6. Click the **'OK'** button

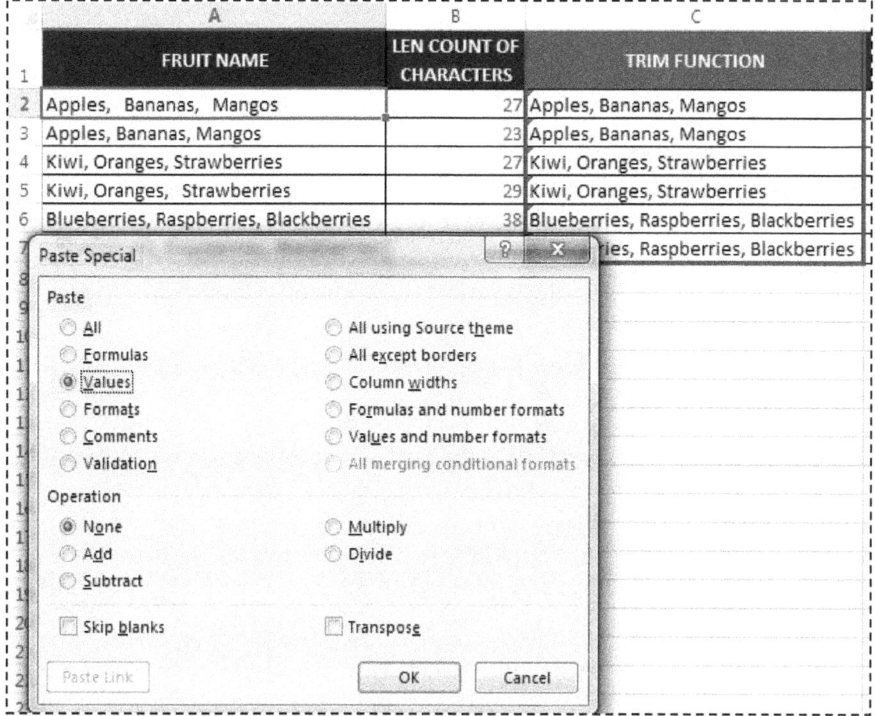

7. Highlight columns **'B'**, **'C', & 'D'**
8. **Right click** and select **'Delete'**,

The troubleshooting columns **'B'**, **'C', & 'D'** should now be removed

We have successfully removed all extraneous spaces from the values contained in **column 'A'**. Further analysis and reporting can be completed without error.

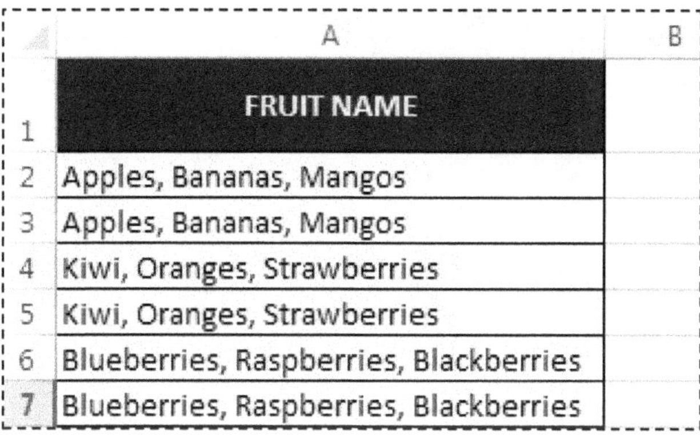

(PART 4) - CHAPTER 18

FORMULAS = PROPER, UPPER, & LOWER

Formulas:

- PROPER, UPPER, & LOWER

Definition:

- **PROPER:** Converts the text of a cell to proper (normal case). The first letter of each word is uppercase (capitalized) and all other letters of the same word are lowercase.
- **UPPER:** Converts all text characters of a cell to **uppercase** (capitalized).
- **LOWER:** Converts all text characters of a cell to **lowercase.**

Quick Examples:

Formula Syntax:	Formula Syntax:	Formula Syntax:
PROPER(text) text is required	UPPER(text) text is required	LOWER(text) text is required

	A	B	C
1	FROM--->	FORMULA	TO
2	apples	=PROPER(A2)	Apples
3	Apples	=UPPER(A3)	APPLES
4	APPLES	=LOWER(A4)	apples

Detailed Example How To Use The Formula:

Sample data:

	A	B
1	FRUIT	CASE
2	apples	
3	Apples	
4	APPLES	

1. Place your cursor in cell **'B2'**
2. From the toolbar select **FORMULAS** and the **'Text'** drop-down box
3. For this example, select **'PROPER'**

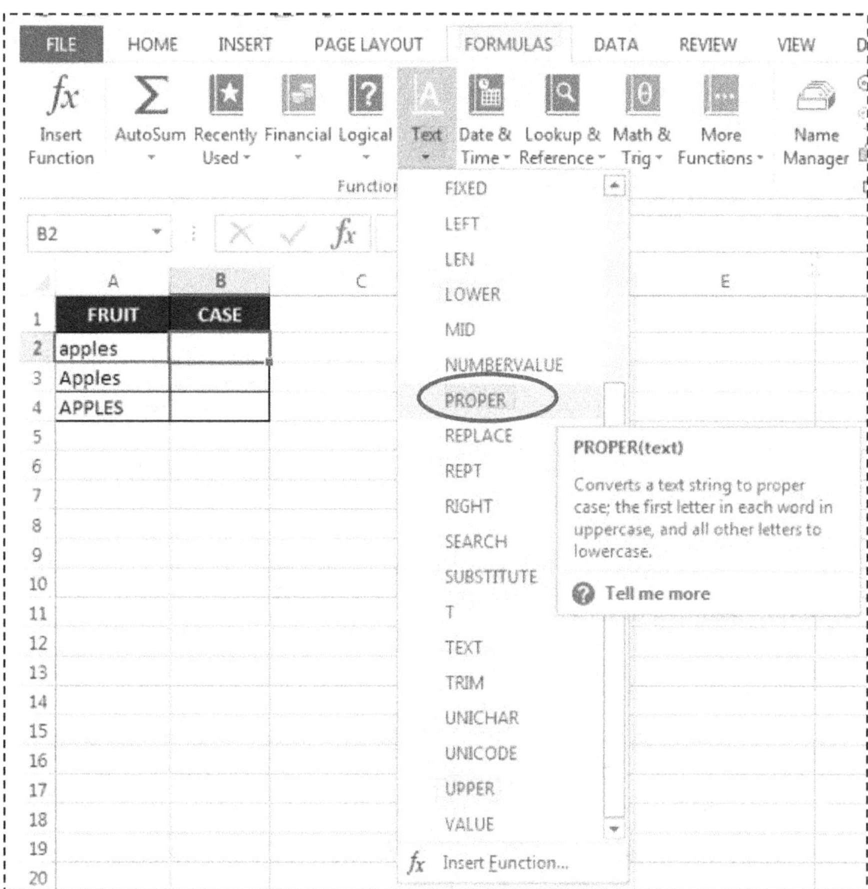

The following dialogue box should appear:

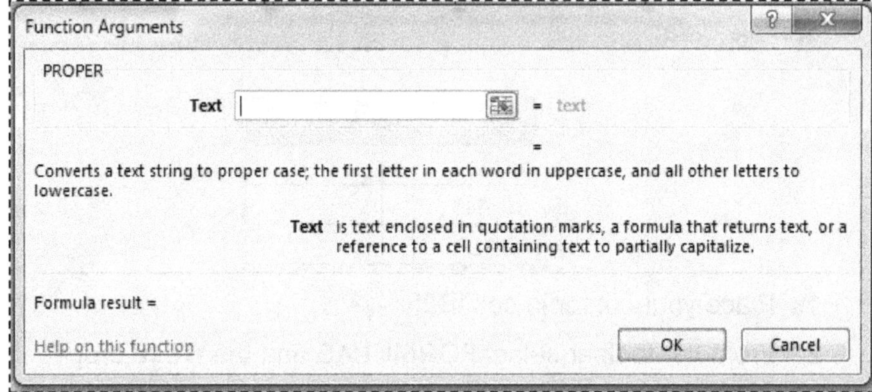

4. Click cell **'A2'** or enter **A2** in the **'Text'** box

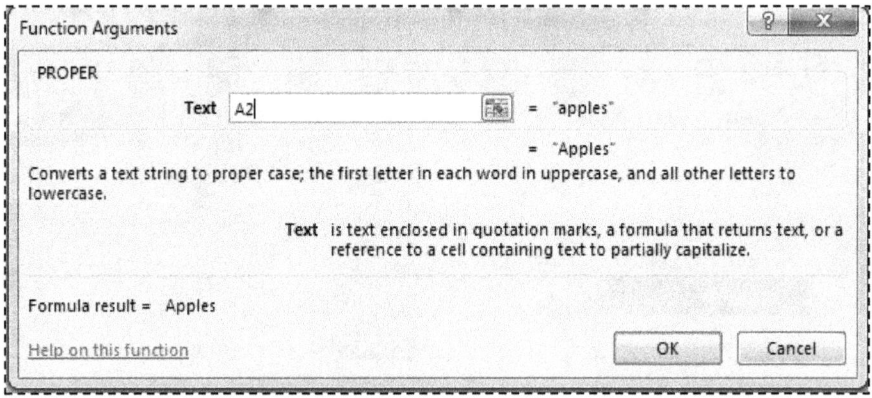

5. Click the **'OK'** button

The result should be as follows:

	A	B
1	FRUIT	CASE
2	apples	Apples
3	Apples	
4	APPLES	

You may copy the formula down to cells **'B3'** & **'B4'** or repeat the steps above and select a different option of **'UPPER'** or **'LOWER'** to practice using these formulas.

(PART 4) - CHAPTER 19

FORMULAS = CONCATENATE & MID

Formulas:

- CONCATENATE & MID

Definition:

- **CONCATENATE:** Joins two or more cells together and also allows the option to insert additional text into the merged cell.
- **MID:** Returns a specific number of characters from a text string, starting at the position you specify, based on the number of characters you stipulate.

Quick Examples:

```
Formula Syntax:
CONCATENATE(text)
text is required
```

	A	B	C	D
1	SALES PERSON FIRST NAME	SALES PERSON LAST NAME	FORMULA	Merged cells 'B2' & 'A2', Last Name, followed by a comma and space, then First Name
2	Jack	Smith	=CONCATENATE(B2,", ",A2)	Smith, Jack

```
Formula Syntax:
MID(text, start_num, num_chars)
All arguments are required
```

	A	B	C	D
1	SALES PERSON FIRST NAME	SALES PERSON LAST NAME	FORMULA	Started in positon 1 of cell 'A2' and returned the 1st character
2	Jack	Smith	=MID(A2,1,1)	J

Scenario for CONCATENATION:

You've been given a list of employees that need to be notified of a change in healthcare benefits. You've been asked to:

1. Generate an email list based on these names

Detailed Example How To Use The Formula:

Sample data:

	A	B
1	EMPLOYEE FIRST NAME	EMPLOYEE LAST NAME
2	Jack	Smith
3	Joe	Tanner
4	Peter	Graham
5	Helen	Simpson
6	Alex	Steller

1. Add a column, in cell **'C1'** label it "**EMAIL ADDRESS**"
2. Next, apply the '**CONCATENATION**' function for the Employee First & Last names to cell **'C2'**

	A	B	C
1	EMPLOYEE FIRST NAME	EMPLOYEE LAST NAME	EMAIL ADDRESS
2	Jack	Smith	
3	Joe	Tanner	
4	Peter	Graham	
5	Helen	Simpson	
6	Alex	Steller	

3. From the toolbar select **FORMULAS** and the **'Text'** drop-down box

4. Select **'CONCATENATE'**

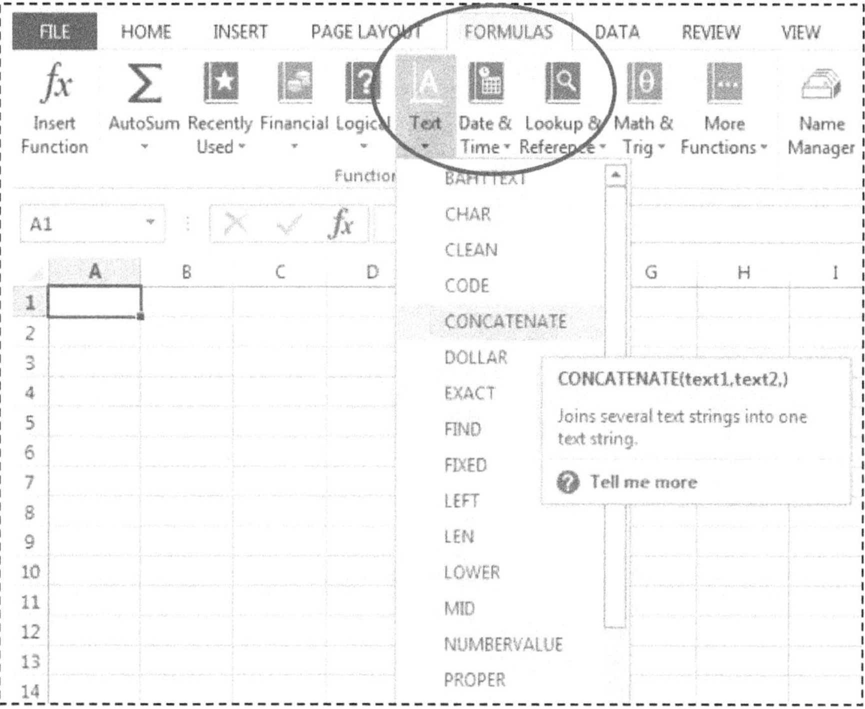

The following dialogue should now appear:

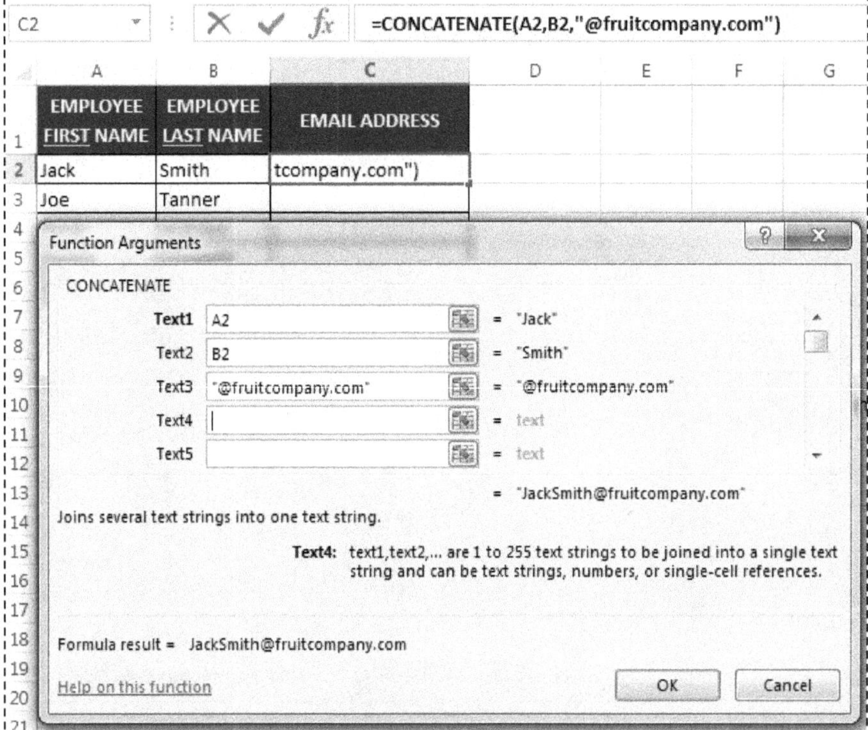

5. **Text1** box click cell '**A2**' or enter **A2**
6. **Text2** box click cell '**B2**' or enter **B2**
7. **Text3** box enter the text '**@fruitcompany.com**' *(you do not need to enter the quotation marks, these will be automatically added when using the formula wizard)*
8. Click the '**OK**' button

9. Copy the **CONCATENATE** formula down cells '**C3**' thru '**C6**'

C2 =CONCATENATE(A2,B2,"@fruitcompany.com")

	A	B	C	D	E
1	EMPLOYEE FIRST NAME	EMPLOYEE LAST NAME	EMAIL ADDRESS		
2	Jack	Smith	JackSmith@fruitcompany.com		
3	Joe	Tanner	JoeTanner@fruitcompany.com		
4	Peter	Graham	PeterGraham@fruitcompany.com		
5	Helen	Simpson	HelenSimpson@fruitcompany.com		
6	Alex	Steller	AlexSteller@fruitcompany.com		

We now have an email list.

Alternatively, we can perform the same type of functionality WITHOUT using the formula wizard for CONCATENATE. Instead, we can use the **ampersand (&) symbol**. This is how many intermediate and advanced Excel® users typically execute this command. Please see below for an example:

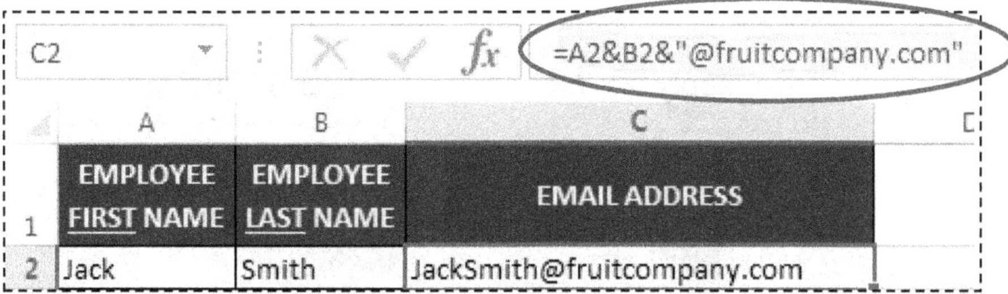

C2 =A2&B2&"@fruitcompany.com"

	A	B	C
1	EMPLOYEE FIRST NAME	EMPLOYEE LAST NAME	EMAIL ADDRESS
2	Jack	Smith	JackSmith@fruitcompany.com

Scenario for MID

You've been given a list of stores from a database that prepends each location with three zeros. You need to pull information from this list into an existing spreadsheet that does not have the leading zeros for the stores. You plan on using the MID formula to:

1. Return the store number without the three leading zeros

Detailed Example How To Use The Formula:

Sample data:

	A	B
1	STORE NUMBER	NUMBER OF EMPLOYEES
2	000111	20
3	000222	27
4	000333	31
5	000444	18
6	000555	35

1. Add a column, in cell **'C1'** label it "**MID**"
2. Next, apply the '**MID**' function for the STORE NUMBER to cell **'C2'**

	A	B	C
1	STORE NUMBER	NUMBER OF EMPLOYEES	MID
2	000111	20	
3	000222	27	
4	000333	31	
5	000444	18	
6	000555	35	

1. From the toolbar select **FORMULAS** and the **'Text'** drop-down box
2. Select **'MID'**

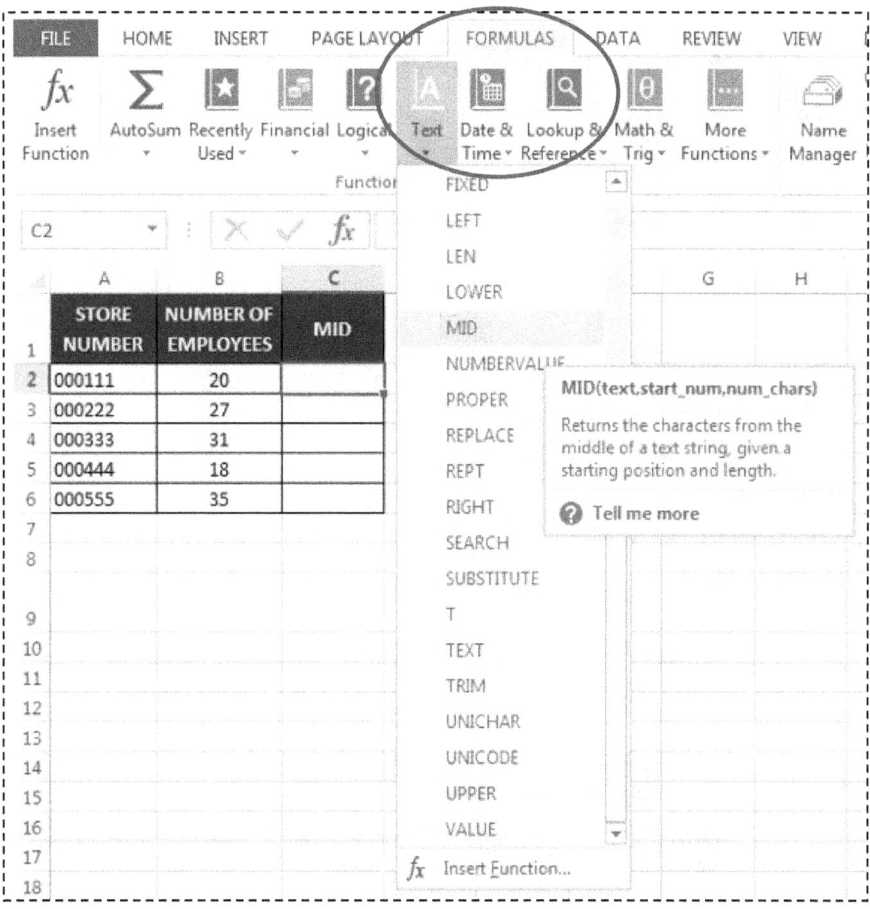

The following dialogue should now appear:

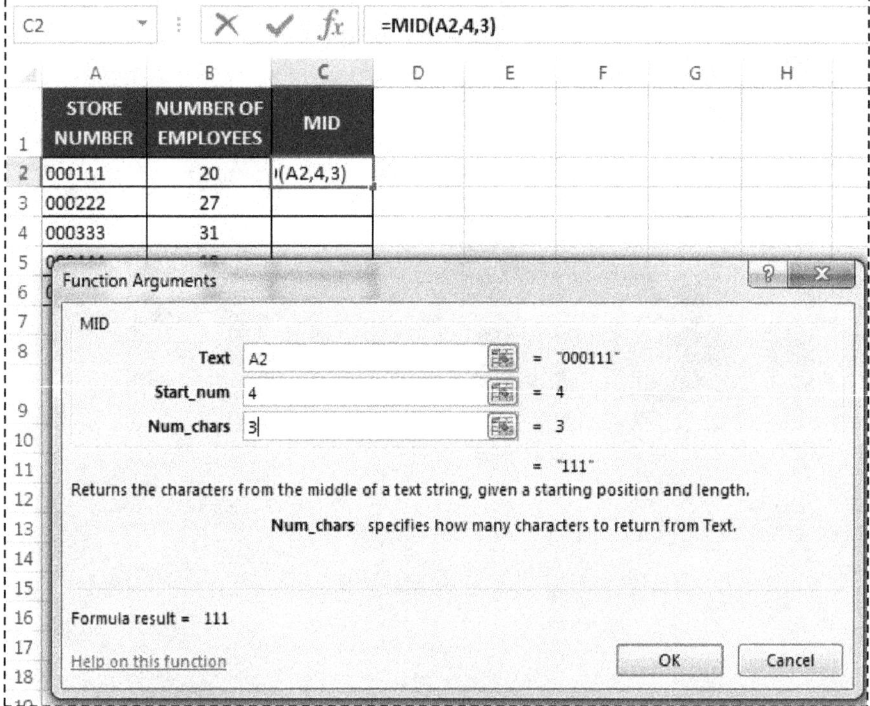

3. **Text** box click cell '**A2**' or enter **A2**
4. **Start_num** enter the number **4**, this is the position where the store number begins
5. **Num_chars** box enter the number **3**, this is the number of characters we want returned
6. Click the '**OK**' button

7. Copy the **MID** formula down cells '**C3**' thru '**C6**'

	A	B	C
1	STORE NUMBER	NUMBER OF EMPLOYEES	MID
2	000111	20	111
3	000222	27	222
4	000333	31	333
5	000444	18	444
6	000555	35	555

We now have a list of store numbers that do not contain the three leading zeros.

(PART 5) - CHAPTER 20

FORMULAS = IF & NESTED IF STATEMENTS

Formula:

- IF

Definition:

- **IF** formulas allow you test conditions and return one value *if true* and another *if false.*
- **NESTED IF** formulas allow you test conditions and return one value *if true* and another *if false*, if certain criteria is met.

Quick Example:

```
Formula Syntax:
IF(logical_test, value_if_true, [value_if_false])

logic_test required, value_if_true required,
value_if_false optional
```

Basic IF formula:

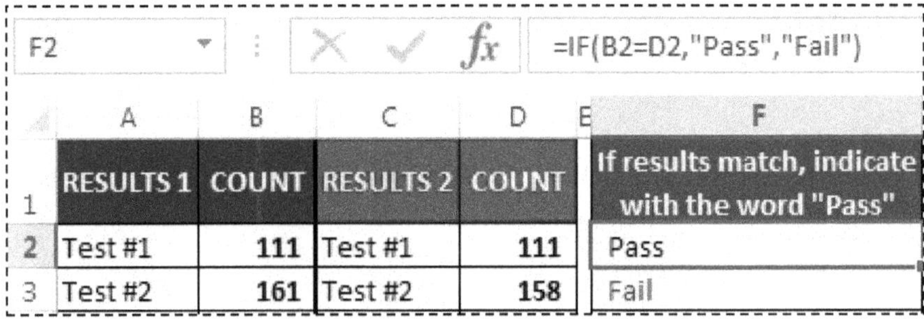

F2 =IF(B2=D2,"Pass","Fail")

	A	B	C	D	E	F
1	RESULTS 1	COUNT	RESULTS 2	COUNT		If results match, indicate with the word "Pass"
2	Test #1	111	Test #1	111		Pass
3	Test #2	161	Test #2	158		Fail

Nested IF formula:

F4 | fx | =IF(B4=D4,"Pass",IF(B4-D4>5,"BIG FAIL","Fail"))

	A	B	C	D	E	F
1	RESULTS 1	COUNT	RESULTS 2	COUNT		IF results match = **Pass** IF results DO NOT match = **Fail** IF results DO NOT match and the difference is greater than 5 = **BIG FAIL**
2	Test #1	111	Test #1	111		Pass
3	Test #2	161	Test #2	158		Fail
4	Test #3	183	Test #3	175		BIG FAIL
5	Test #4	243	Test #4	243		Pass
6	Test #5	263	Test #5	260		Fail

Scenario:

IF formulas are a very powerful tool for doing all types of analysis, let's walk through some examples:

1. You're a data analyst working on a project and need to compare test results
2. You've created a report and want a way to double check your formulas are calculating correctly
3. You need to evaluate if a sales person needs additional training based on their closing sales percentage

Detailed Example How To Use The Formula:

You're data analyst working on a project and need to compare test results.

1. If the results match between the two datasets, indicate with the word **'Pass'.**
2. If the results DO NOT match, show with the word **'Fail'.**

Sample Data:

	A	B	C	D	E	F
1	RESULTS 1	COUNT	RESULTS 2	COUNT		IF results match indicate with the word "Pass", otherwise label "Fail"
2	Test #1	111	Test #1	111		
3	Test #2	161	Test #2	158		
4	Test #3	183	Test #3	175		
5	Test #4	243	Test #4	243		
6	Test #5	263	Test #5	260		

1. Place your cursor in cell **'F2'**
2. From the toolbar select **Formulas : Insert Function**

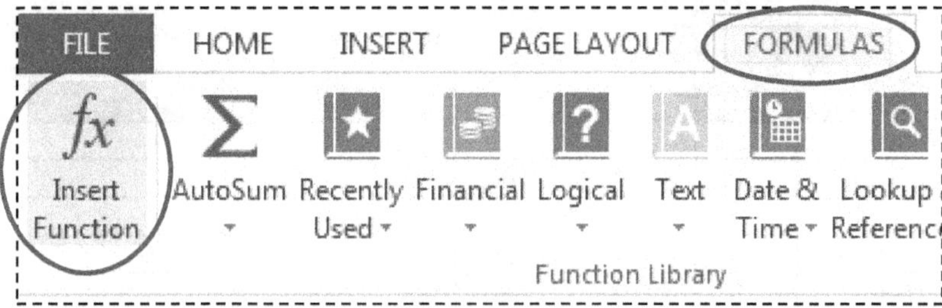

3. Type "**IF**" in the 'Search for a function:' dialogue box
4. Click the '**Go**' button

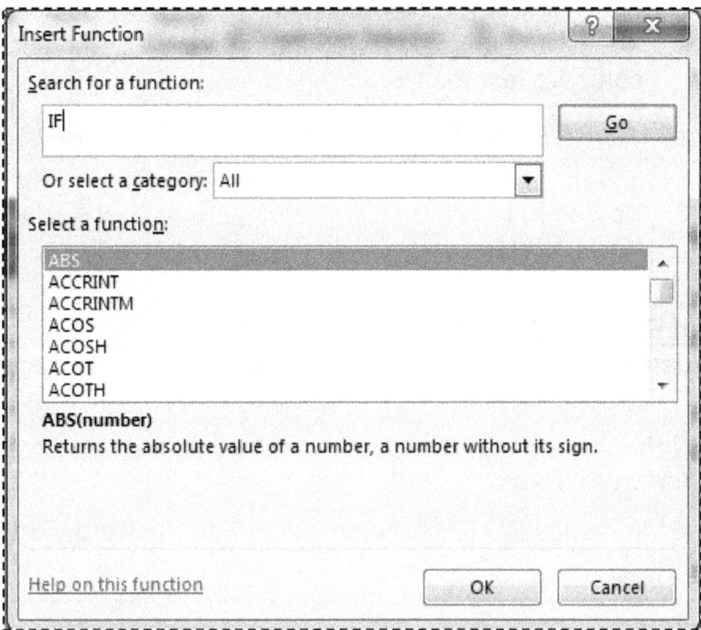

The following dialogue box should now appear:

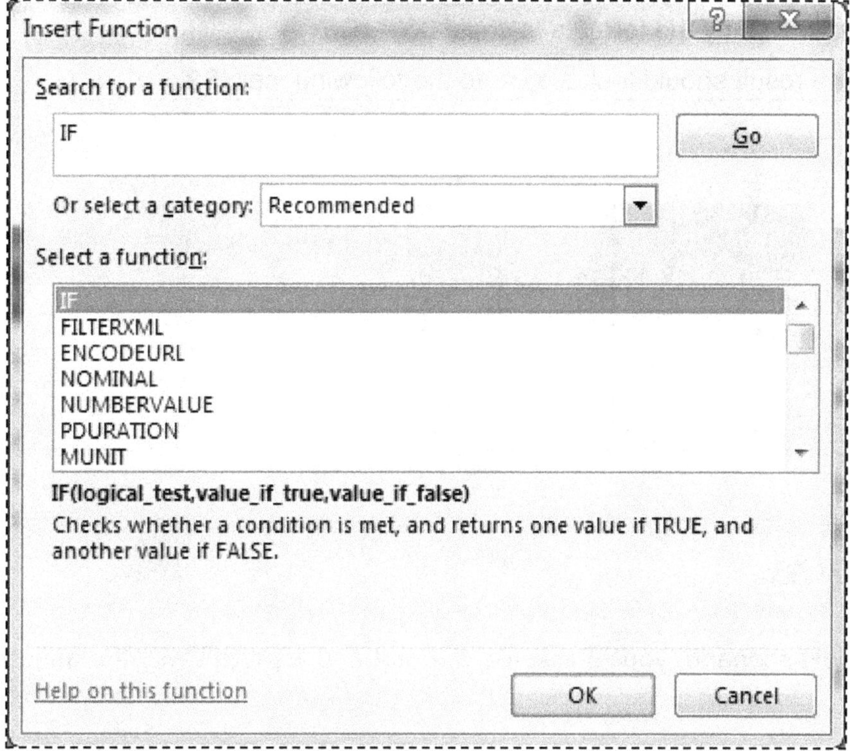

5. Click the '**OK**' button:
6. In the dialogue type the following:
    a. **Logical_test** = B2=D2
    b. **Value_if_true** = "Pass"
    c. **Value_if_false** = "Fail"

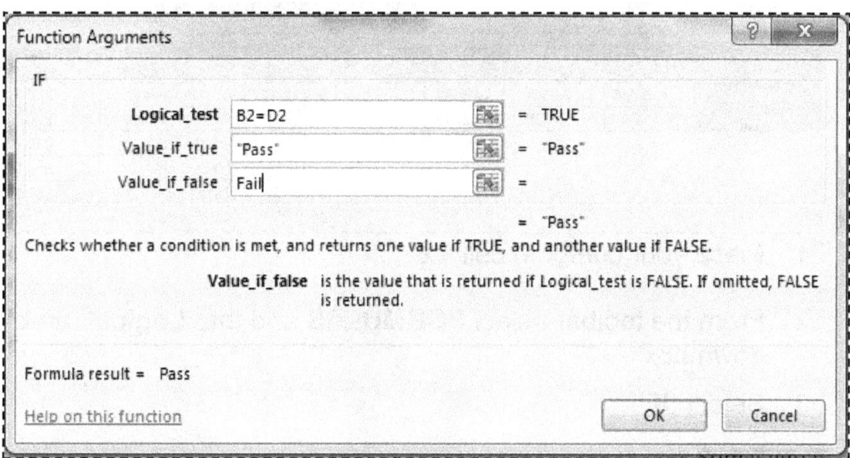

7. Click the '**OK**' button
8. Copy the formula to cells '**C3**' – '**C6**'

The result should look similar to the following, cell **'F2'**:

F2 =IF(B2=D2,"Pass","Fail")

	A	B	C	D	E	F
1	RESULTS 1	COUNT	RESULTS 2	COUNT		IF results match indicate with the word "Pass", otherwise label "Fail"
2	Test #1	111	Test #1	111		Pass
3	Test #2	161	Test #2	158		Fail
4	Test #3	183	Test #3	175		Fail
5	Test #4	243	Test #4	243		Pass
6	Test #5	263	Test #5	260		Fail

We've now compared two datasets and indicated if the results passed or failed.

Next scenario, you've created a report and want to verify the annual sales are correct.

We can accomplish this by summing the results of all the sales associates and comparing it to the total annual sales.

Sample data:

	F G	H	I	J	K	L	M	N	O
1	ANNUAL SALES								
2	CURRENT YR	Q1	Q2	Q3	Q4	ANNUAL		SALES PERSON	SALES
3	Actual Sales	$ 2,646	$ 23,586	$ 49,375	$ 107,505	$ 183,112		Graham, Peter	$22,708
4	Percent of Sales	1.4%	12.9%	27.0%	58.7%			Simpson, Helen	$20,258
5								Smith, Jack	$10,339
6								Steller, Alex	$50,925
7								Tanner, Joe	$15,276
8								Winchester, Billy	$63,606

1. Place your cursor in cell '**L6**'
2. From the toolbar select **FORMULAS** and the **'Logical'** drop-down box
3. Select **'IF'**

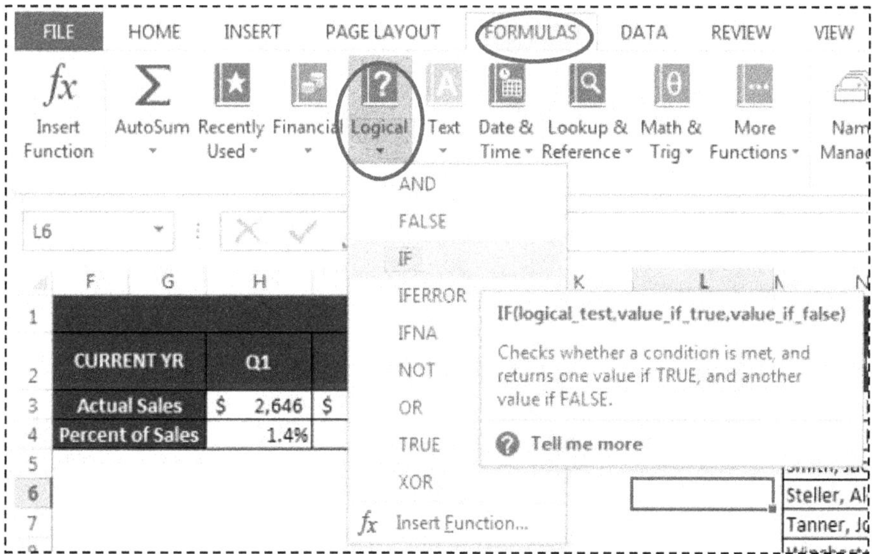

The following dialogue should now appear:

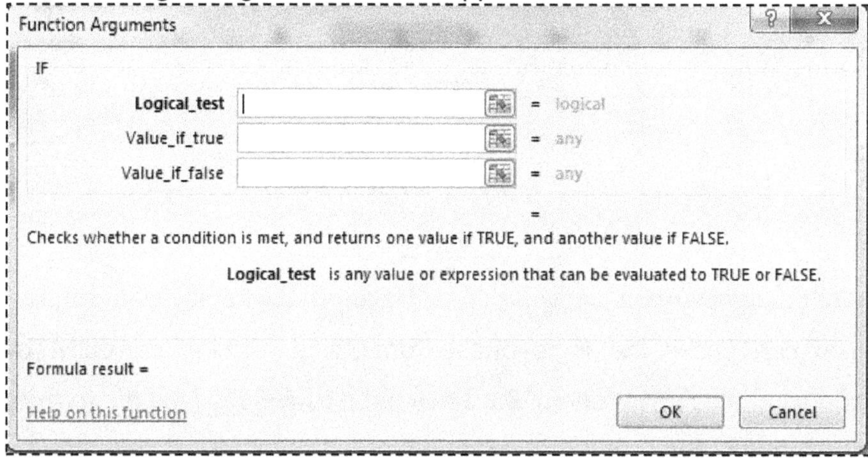

4. In the dialogue type the following:
    a. **Logical_test** = `SUM(O3:O8)=L3`
    b. **Value_if_true** = `Balance`
    c. **Value_if_false** = `Error in formula`

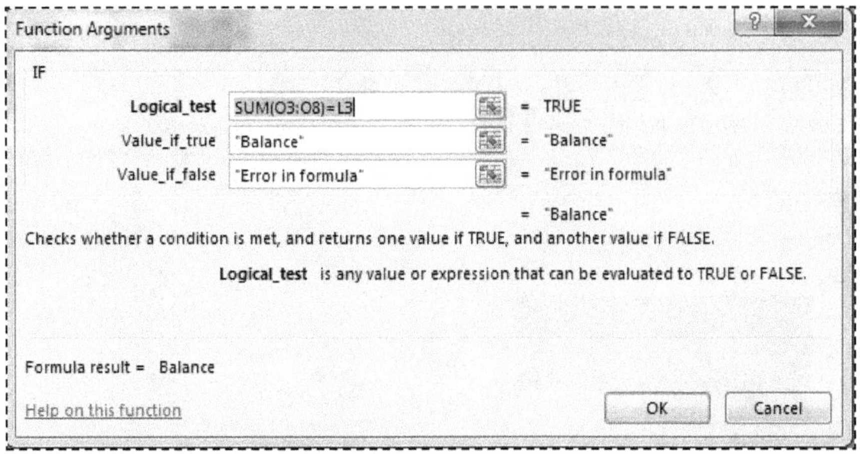

5. Click the '**OK**' button

	F	G	H	I	J	K	L	M	N	O
1	ANNUAL SALES									
2	CURRENT YR		Q1	Q2	Q3	Q4	ANNUAL		SALES PERSON	SALES
3	Actual Sales		$ 2,646	$ 23,586	$ 49,375	$ 107,505	$ 183,112		Graham, Peter	$22,708
4	Percent of Sales		1.4%	12.9%	27.0%	58.7%			Simpson, Helen	$20,258
5									Smith, Jack	$10,339
6							Balance		Steller, Alex	$50,925
7									Tanner, Joe	$15,276
8									Winchester, Billy	$63,606

```
=IF(SUM(O3:O8)=L3,"Balance","Error in formula")
```

Our results balance, we've verified the annual sales are correct.

You can check the logic of the formula is working correctly, by changing a value for one of the sales people. **NOTE:** *how the formula now states* ***"Error in formula"***.

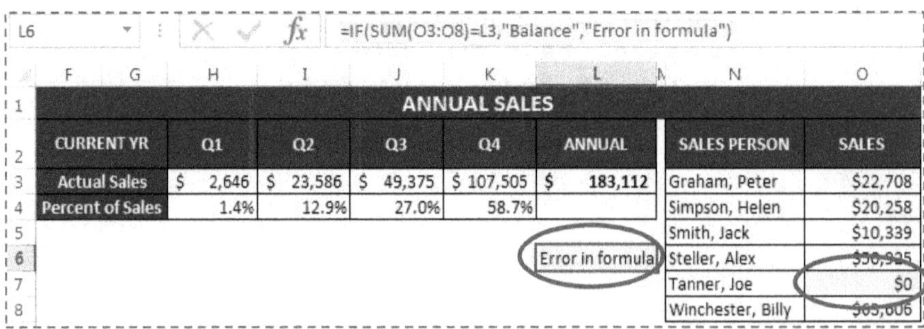

L6 =IF(SUM(O3:O8)=L3,"Balance","Error in formula")

	F	G	H	I	J	K	L	M	N	O
1	ANNUAL SALES									
2	CURRENT YR		Q1	Q2	Q3	Q4	ANNUAL		SALES PERSON	SALES
3	Actual Sales		$ 2,646	$ 23,586	$ 49,375	$ 107,505	$ 183,112		Graham, Peter	$22,708
4	Percent of Sales		1.4%	12.9%	27.0%	58.7%			Simpson, Helen	$20,258
5									Smith, Jack	$10,339
6							Error in formula		Steller, Alex	$50,925
7									Tanner, Joe	$0
8									Winchester, Billy	$63,606

In our last example, we will examine **Nested IF** statements to determine, if a sales person needs additional training based on their closing sales percentage.

Using the associate's sales closing percentage, we will determine, if they are an "Achiever" and could mentor others. If the sales person is "Meeting expectations," or is falling behind and "Needs Additional Training." The criteria for our evaluation is as follows, for sales closing percent:

- 85% or higher = **Achiever**
- 70 - 84% = **Meeting Expectations**
- 69% or less = **Needs Training**

Unfortunately, the capabilities of the formula wizard do not extend very well for Nested IF functions. Therefore, I will breakdown the formula to describe how it works, basically we'll be entering a series of ***If - Then statements***.

Sample data ***with results****:*

```
=IF(E3>=0.85,"Achiever",IF(E3>=0.7,"Meeting Expectations",IF(E3>=0.69,"Needs Training","Needs Training")))
```

D	E	F	G	H	I	J
SALES PERSON	% OF CLOSED SALES	85%< Achiever 70 - 84%> Meets Expectations 69%< Needs Additional Training				
Dower, John	60%	Needs Training				
Wilson, John	75%	Meeting Expectations				
Williams, Abbey	77%	Meeting Expectations				
Taylor, Sarah	70%	Meeting Expectations				
Graham, Peter	88%	Achiever				
Simpson, Helen	49%	Needs Training				
Smith, Jack	70%	Meeting Expectations				
Steller, Alex	85%	Achiever				
Tanner, Joe	80%	Meeting Expectations				
Winchester, Billy	66%	Needs Training				

A good way to start devising the formula is to write out your conditions using a format similar to the following:

❶ **IF** *column '**E**' value is equal to or greater than 85%* **THEN** *Achiever*

❷ **IF** *column '**E**' value is between 70-84%* **THEN** *Meeting Expectations*

❸ **IF** *column '**E**' value equal to or less than 69%* **THEN** *Needs Training*

❹ **OTHERWISE** (all other closing percentages) *Needs Training*

In Excel®, these conditions represent a series of logic tests, with each being separated by a comma. Please see the illustration below.

1. Begin with your ❶ first IF condition and enter into cell **'F3'** as:
   - `=IF(E3>=0.85,"Achiever",` (**<u>NOTE:</u>** the comma)

2. Next, we add the ❷ second condition as:
   - `IF(E3>=0.7,"Meeting Expectations",`

3. The ❸ third IF condition:
   - `IF(E3>=0.69,"Needs Training",`

4. Lastly, the otherwise condition ❹:
   - `"Needs Training"`

5. Close the formula with four closing parenthesis **))))** as there were four conditions

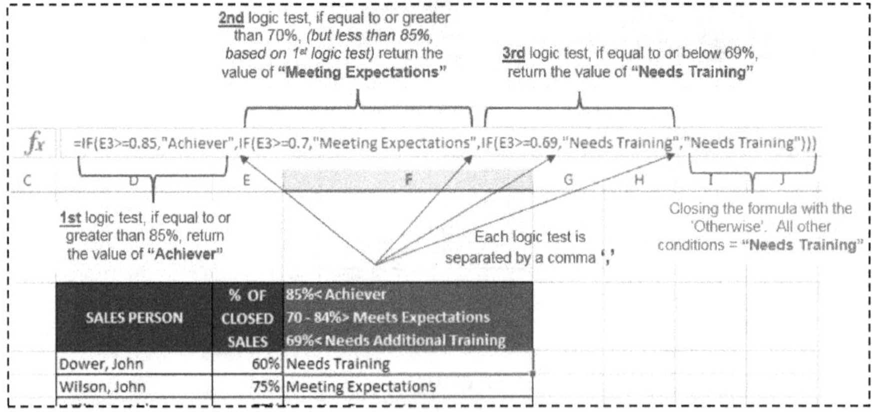

```
=IF(E4>=0.85,"Achiever",IF(E4>=0.7,"Meeting Expectations",
IF(E4>=0.69,"Needs Training","Needs Training")))
```

```
=IF(E3>=0.85,"Achiever",IF(E3>=0.7,"Meeting
Expectations",IF(E3>=0.69,"Needs Training","Needs
Training")))
```

It can be a little confusing how you enter the percent conditions. As the second and third conditions (if statements) are being influenced by the preceding if condition.

*For example, Excel® knows that **'E3>=0.7'** is really **'.70 - .84,'** because the preceding statement is **'E3>=0.85'.***

To finish the exercise, copy the formula down to cells **'F4'** thru **'F12'** and you will have determined if a sales person needs additional training based on their closing sales percentage.

```
=IF(E3>=0.85,"Achiever",IF(E3>=0.7,"Meeting Expectations",IF(E3>=0.69,"Needs Training","Needs Training")))
```

D	E	F	G	H	I	J
SALES PERSON	% OF CLOSED SALES	85%< Achiever 70 - 84%> Meets Expectations 69%< Needs Additional Training				
Dower, John	60%	Needs Training				
Wilson, John	75%	Meeting Expectations				
Williams, Abbey	77%	Meeting Expectations				
Taylor, Sarah	70%	Meeting Expectations				
Graham, Peter	88%	Achiever				
Simpson, Helen	49%	Needs Training				
Smith, Jack	70%	Meeting Expectations				
Steller, Alex	85%	Achiever				
Tanner, Joe	80%	Meeting Expectations				
Winchester, Billy	66%	Needs Training				

(PART 6) - CHAPTER 21
FORMULA = VLOOKUP

Formula:

- VLOOKUP

Definition:

- The VLOOKUP formula allows you to search for and return a value from another Excel® list to a new Excel® list based on a matching lookup value.

Quick Example:

```
Formula Syntax:
VLOOKUP (lookup_value, table_array, col_index_num,
[range_lookup])

All parameters are required, except for
[range_lookup]
```

	A	B	C	D
1	SALES PERSON ID	SALES	VLOOKUP FORMULA	RESULT
2	200	469	=VLOOKUP(A2,Sheet2!A2:B6,2,FALSE)	Graham, Peter

The VLOOKUP formula is made-up of *four* parts:

❶ lookup value:

This is the field you want to find (match) typically located on another tab or spreadsheet.

In the example below, **'A2'** is selected which has the Sales Person ID value of **'200'**. I will look to match this value on the tab labeled **'Sheet2'.** Sales Person Name is the value I want to look-up and be returned to the tab labeled **'Sheet1'**.

❷ table_array:

This is the spreadsheet (tab) and range of cells that are searched for the ❶ lookup_value. The field you want to match must be in the first column of the range of cells you specify in the ❷ table_array.

In the example below, I'm searching the tab labeled **'Sheet2'** with the cell range of **'A2:B6'**.

❸ col_index_num:

Is the column that contains the value you want returned.

In the example below, column **'2'** of the tab labeled **'Sheet2'** contains value of Sales Person Name that I want returned to the tab labeled **'Sheet1'**.

❹ range_lookup:

Is the optional value of **'TRUE'** or **'FALSE'**. The value of **'FALSE'** will return an *exact* match, while **'TRUE'** will return an *approximate* match. Most users enter **'FALSE'** for this parameter.

Below, I have entered **'FALSE'** for an exact match.

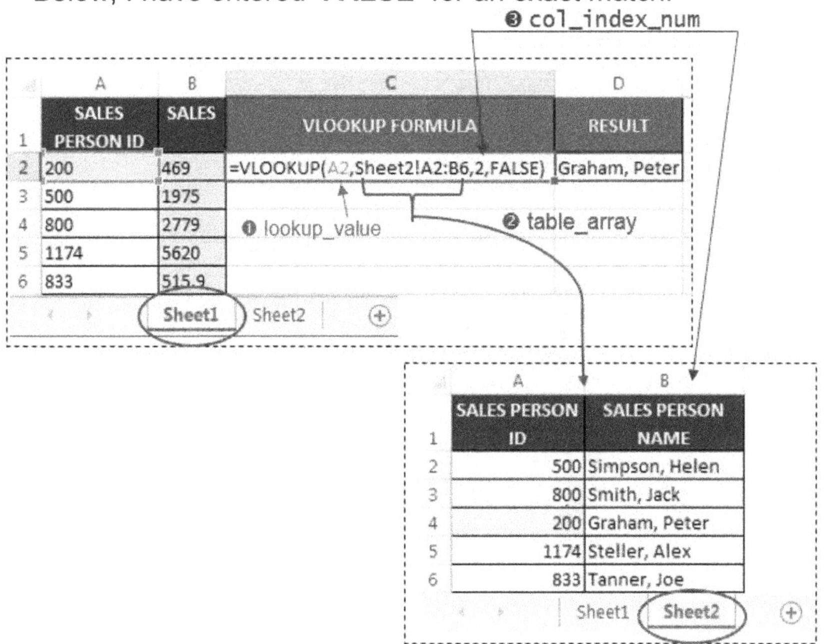

Scenario:

You've been asked to provide a list of the first quarter sales by month, for each sales person. You run a query from the sales database and generate an Excel® report. Unfortunately, the database only contains the sales person's ID, but not their name. You use a VLOOKUP formula to pull the Sales Person's Name from an existing Excel® spreadsheet to the new sales report.

Detailed Example How To Use The Formula:

*To download a free copy of the Excel® file used in this scenario please go to: http://bentonexcelbooks.my-free.website/sample-data-files select the file for **Chapter 21 (VLOOKUP)** in the **'The Microsoft Excel Step-By-Step Training Guide Book Bundle'** section*

Sample data (Sales Report with ID only):

	A	B	C	D
1	SALES PERSON ID	Jan	Feb	Mar
2	200	$ 869	$ 1,092	$ 1,550
3	500	$ 1,975	$ 2,274	$ 2,719
4	800	$ 2,779	$ 3,002	$ 3,460
5	833	$ 7,716	$ 8,015	$ 8,460
6	1174	$ 5,620	$ 5,843	$ 6,301

Sheet1 Sheet2

Sample data (Sales Person Name):

	A	B
1	SALES PERSON ID	SALES PERSON NAME
2	800	Smith, Jack
3	200	Graham, Peter
4	1174	Steller, Alex
5	500	Simpson, Helen
6	833	Tanner, Joe

Sheet1 Sheet2

1. On **'Sheet1'**, Insert a new column between columns **'A'** & **'B,'** label it "**SALES PERSON NAME**"
2. Next, apply the '**VLOOKUP**' formula for 'Sales Person Name' by clicking in cell '**B2**'

	A	B	C	D	E
1	SALES PERSON ID	SALES PERSON NAME	Jan	Feb	Mar
2	200		$ 869	$ 1,092	$ 1,550
3	500		$ 1,975	$ 2,274	$ 2,719
4	800		$ 2,779	$ 3,002	$ 3,460
5	833		$ 7,716	$ 8,015	$ 8,460
6	1174		$ 5,620	$ 5,843	$ 6,301

3. From the toolbar select **Formulas : Insert Function**

4. Type "**VLOOKUP**" in the **'Search for a function:'** dialogue box

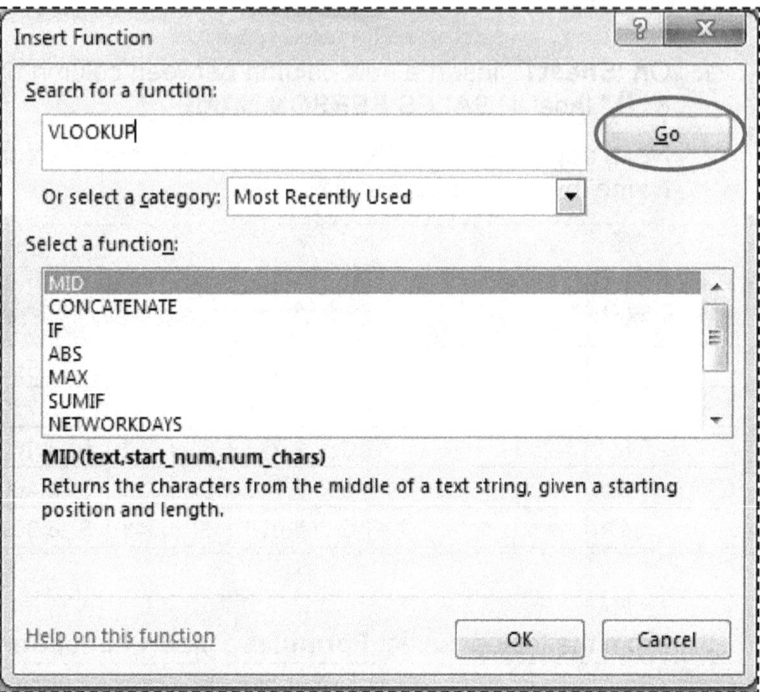

5. Click the '**Go**' button

The following dialogue box should now appear:

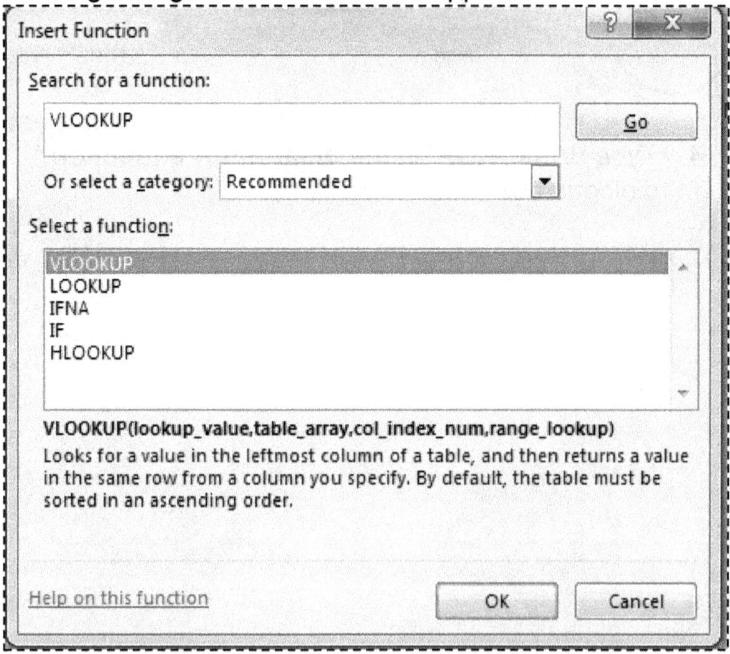

6. Click the '**OK**' button
7. Click cell '**A2**' or enter **A2** in the dialogue box for the **'Lookup_value'** *(the sales person ID is the field we'll lookup on **'Sheet2'**)*
8. For **'Table_array'**, click on the tab **'Sheet2'** and highlight cells **'A2:B6'** *(this is the range of cells we're searching)*
9. Enter the number **2** for '**Col_index_num'** *(this is the column with the sales person's name)*
10. For '**Range_lookup'** enter **FALSE**
11. Click the '**OK**' button

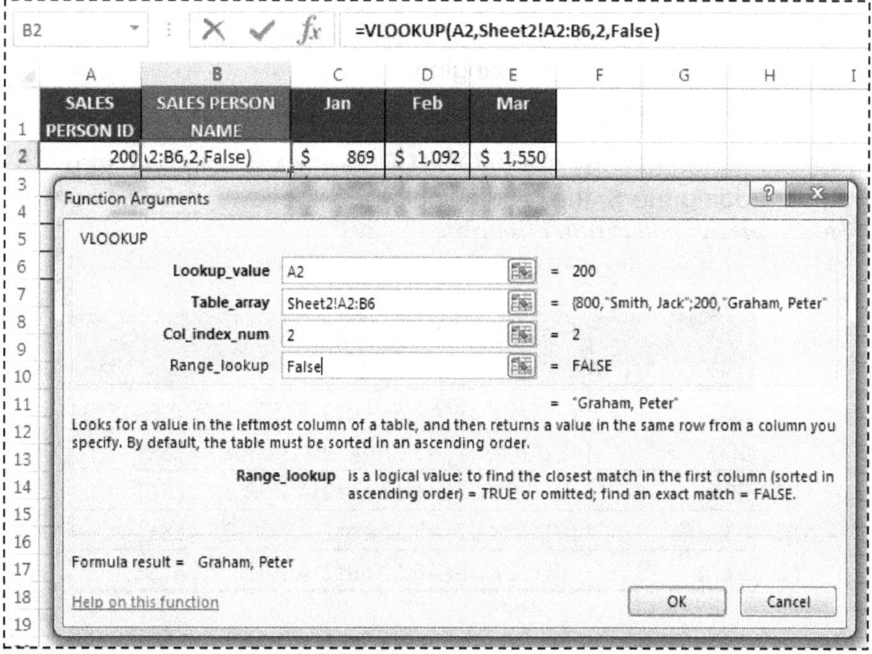

The following should be the result:

B2 =VLOOKUP(A2,Sheet2!A2:B6,2,FALSE)

	A	B	C	D	E	F
1	SALES PERSON ID	SALES PERSON NAME	Jan	Feb	Mar	
2	200	Graham, Peter	$ 869	$ 1,092	$ 1,550	
3	500		$ 1,975	$ 2,274	$ 2,719	
4	800		$ 2,779	$ 3,002	$ 3,460	
5	833		$ 7,716	$ 8,015	$ 8,460	
6	1174		$ 5,620	$ 5,843	$ 6,301	

12. We need to do one additional step before we can copy this formula down to cells '**B3**' thru '**B6.**' We must add the dollar symbol **$** to the **'Table_array'**. This will prevent our cell range from changing:

    =VLOOKUP(A2,Sheet2!**$A$2:$B$6**,2,FALSE)

If we attempted to copy the VLOOKUP formula to cells '**B3**' thru '**B6,**' without adding the **$**, the result would be as follows, ***NOTE:*** *how the **'Table_array'** cell range changes:*

	A	B
1	SALES PERSON ID	SALES PERSON NAME
2	200	=VLOOKUP(A2,Sheet2!$A$2:$B$6,2,FALSE)
3	500	=VLOOKUP(A3,Sheet2!A3:B7,2,FALSE)
4	800	=VLOOKUP(A4,Sheet2!A4:B8,2,FALSE)
5	833	=VLOOKUP(A5,Sheet2!A5:B9,2,FALSE)
6	1174	=VLOOKUP(A6,Sheet2!A6:B10,2,FALSE)

We would also receive an error in cells **'B4'** & **'B6'**

	A	B	C	D	E
1	SALES PERS	SALES PERSON NAME	Jan	Feb	Mar
2	200	Graham, Peter	$ 869	$ 1,092	$ 1,550
3	500	Simpson, Helen	$ 1,975	$ 2,274	$ 2,719
4	800	#N/A	$ 2,779	$ 3,002	$ 3,460
5	833	Tanner, Joe	$ 7,716	$ 8,015	$ 8,460
6	1174	#N/A	$ 5,620	$ 5,843	$ 6,301

13. After adding the **$** to the **'Table_array'**, copy the VLOOKUP formula to cells '**B3**' thru '**B6'**

We have successfully looked-up and added the Sales Person Name to the quarterly sales report. We can now provide a list of the first quarter sales by month, for each sales person.

	A	B	C	D	E
1	SALES PERS	SALES PERSON NAME	Jan	Feb	Mar
2	200	Graham, Peter	$ 869	$ 1,092	$ 1,550
3	500	Simpson, Helen	$ 1,975	$ 2,274	$ 2,719
4	800	Smith, Jack	$ 2,779	$ 3,002	$ 3,460
5	833	Tanner, Joe	$ 7,716	$ 8,015	$ 8,460
6	1174	Steller, Alex	$ 5,620	$ 5,843	$ 6,301

Alternatively, for the **'Table_array'** you may enter the columns **A:B** (`Sheet2!A:B`) instead of the range of cells (`Sheet2!$A$2:$B$6`), if the *entire column* contains the data you want returned, this would eliminate the need to complete **step 12**.

Let's walk through another example, this time using columns for the **'Table_array'** instead of the range of cells. In this example, I will also demonstrate another option to enter the VLOOKUP formula.

Scenario:

You've now been asked to include the **sales region** to the list of the first quarter sales by month, for each sales person.

Detailed Example How To Use The Formula:

*Sample data (Sales Report with ID & **Name**):*

	A	B	C	D	E
1	SALES PERS	SALES PERSON NAME	Jan	Feb	Mar
2	200	Graham, Peter	$ 869	$ 1,092	$ 1,550
3	500	Simpson, Helen	$ 1,975	$ 2,274	$ 2,719
4	800	Smith, Jack	$ 2,779	$ 3,002	$ 3,460
5	833	Tanner, Joe	$ 7,716	$ 8,015	$ 8,460
6	1174	Steller, Alex	$ 5,620	$ 5,843	$ 6,301

Sheet1 Sheet2

*Sample data (Sales Person Name & **Region**):*

	A	B	C
1	SALES PERSON ID	SALES PERSON NAME	REGION
2	800	Smith, Jack	East
3	200	Graham, Peter	West
4	1174	Steller, Alex	Central
5	500	Simpson, Helen	East
6	833	Tanner, Joe	West

Sheet1 Sheet2

1. On **'Sheet1'**, Insert a new column between columns **'B'** & **'C,'** label it "**REGION**"
2. Next, apply the '**VLOOKUP**' formula for 'REGION' by clicking in cell '**C2**'

	A	B	C	D	E	F
1	SALES PERS	SALES PERSON NAME	REGION	Jan	Feb	Mar
2	200	Graham, Peter		$ 869	$ 1,092	$ 1,550
3	500	Simpson, Helen		$ 1,975	$ 2,274	$ 2,719
4	800	Smith, Jack		$ 2,779	$ 3,002	$ 3,460
5	833	Tanner, Joe		$ 7,716	$ 8,015	$ 8,460
6	1174	Steller, Alex		$ 5,620	$ 5,843	$ 6,301

3. From the toolbar select **Formulas**
4. Click the drop-down box for **Lookup & Reference**
5. Select **VLOOKUP**

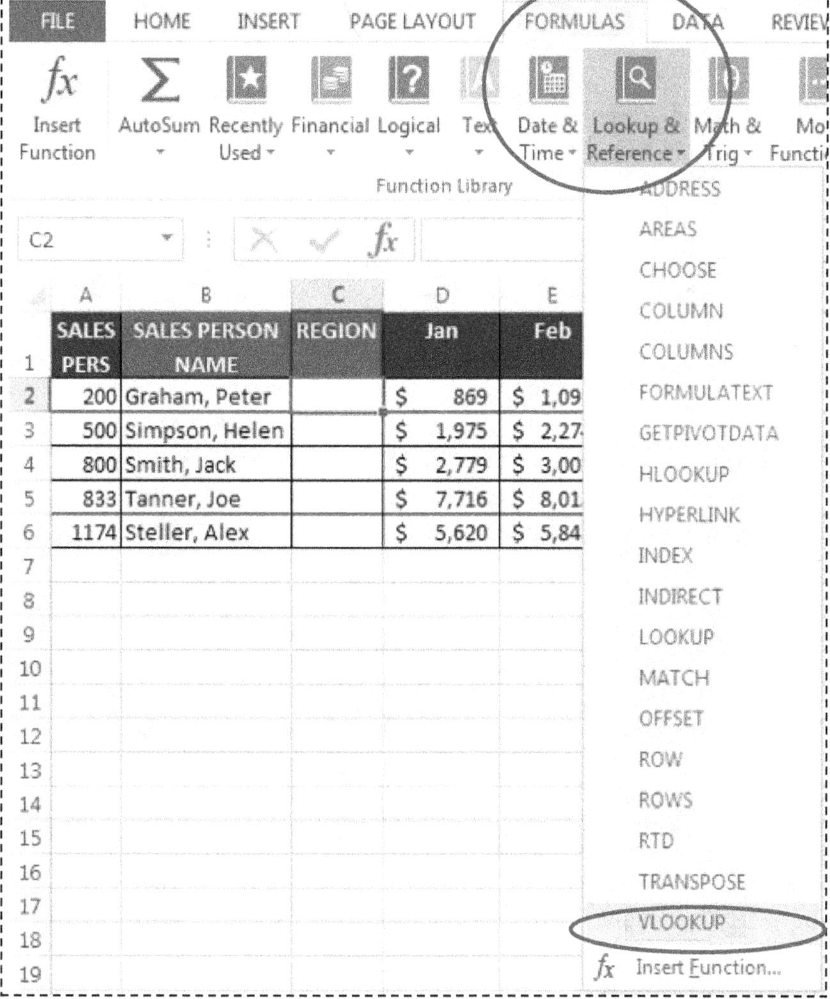

6. Click cell '**A2**' or enter **A2** in the dialogue box for the **'Lookup_value'** *(the sales person ID is the field we'll lookup on **'Sheet2'**)*
7. For **'Table_array'**, click on the tab **'Sheet2'** and highlight columns **'A:C'** *(this is the range of cells we're searching)*
8. Enter the number **3** for '**Col_index_num'** *(this is the column with the sales person's region)*
9. For '**Range_lookup'** enter **FALSE**
10. Click the '**OK**' button

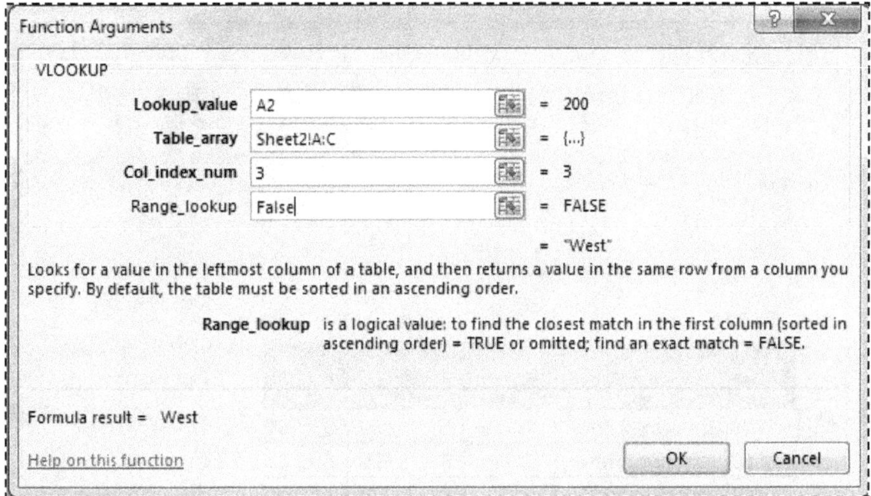

The following should be the result:

C2 =VLOOKUP(A2,Sheet2!A:C,3,FALSE)

	A	B	C	D	E	F	G
1	SALES PERS	SALES PERSON NAME	REGION	Jan	Feb	Mar	
2	200	Graham, Peter	West	$ 869	$ 1,092	$ 1,550	
3	500	Simpson, Helen		$ 1,975	$ 2,274	$ 2,719	
4	800	Smith, Jack		$ 2,779	$ 3,002	$ 3,460	
5	833	Tanner, Joe		$ 7,716	$ 8,015	$ 8,460	
6	1174	Steller, Alex		$ 5,620	$ 5,843	$ 6,301	

11. Copy this formula down to cells '**C3**' thru '**C6**'

The following should be the result:

	A	B	C	D	E	F
1	SALES PERS	SALES PERSON NAME	REGION	Jan	Feb	Mar
2	200	Graham, Peter	West	$ 869	$ 1,092	$ 1,550
3	500	Simpson, Helen	East	$ 1,975	$ 2,274	$ 2,719
4	800	Smith, Jack	East	$ 2,779	$ 3,002	$ 3,460
5	833	Tanner, Joe	West	$ 7,716	$ 8,015	$ 8,460
6	1174	Steller, Alex	Central	$ 5,620	$ 5,843	$ 6,301

We have successfully looked-up and added the Sales Person's **Region** to the quarterly sales report.

☑ **HELPFUL INFORMATION:**

When sending the results of a VLOOKUP to a customer or a co-worker, a common mistake beginners often make is including the VLOOKUP formula in the spreadsheet, rather than pasting the results as a value. This is a very easy thing to do, but depending on where the **Table_array** sheet or workbook is located can cause the following to happen.

1. Let's say in the example above, after adding the Sales Person Name & Region you deleted, '**Sheet2'**, because you no longer needed it.
    a. You saved the workbook without noticing the VLOOKUP formula is now broken.

   b. You emailed the spreadsheet results to the customer.

   c. When they open the spreadsheet, they likely would see an error in the results:

	A	B	C	D	E	F
1	SALES PERS	SALES PERSON NAME	REGION	Jan	Feb	Mar
2	200	#REF!	#REF!	$ 869	$ 1,092	$ 1,550
3	500	#REF!	#REF!	$ 1,975	$ 2,274	$ 2,719
4	800	#REF!	#REF!	$ 2,779	$ 3,002	$ 3,460
5	833	#REF!	#REF!	$ 7,716	$ 8,015	$ 8,460
6	1174	#REF!	#REF!	$ 5,620	$ 5,843	$ 6,301

2. Another common scenario, if the **Table_array** was located in a separate workbook.

   a. You saved the workbook without issue.

   b. You emailed the spreadsheet results to a co-worker.

   c. When they open the spreadsheet, they likely would see a **!SECURITY WARING** message about the file being linked to another workbook:

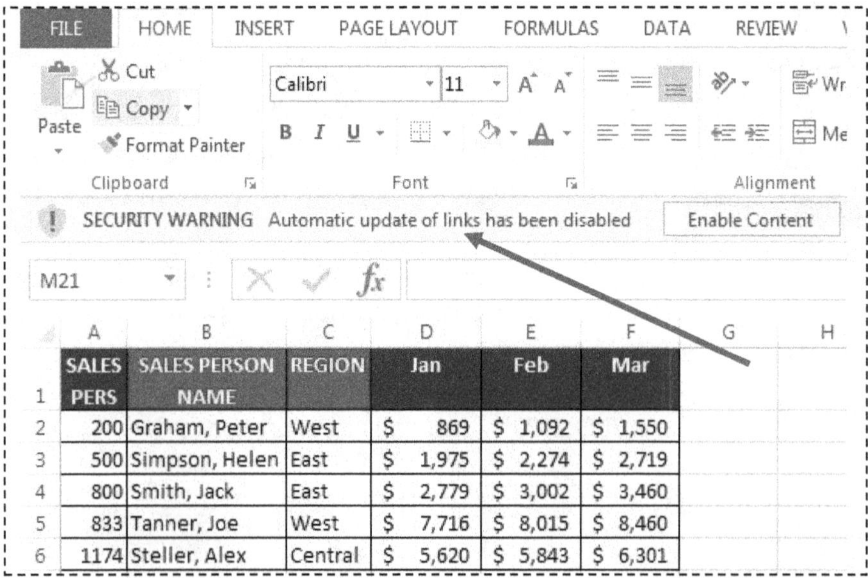

	A	B	C	D	E	F
1	SALES PERS	SALES PERSON NAME	REGION	Jan	Feb	Mar
2	200	Graham, Peter	West	$ 869	$ 1,092	$ 1,550
3	500	Simpson, Helen	East	$ 1,975	$ 2,274	$ 2,719
4	800	Smith, Jack	East	$ 2,779	$ 3,002	$ 3,460
5	833	Tanner, Joe	West	$ 7,716	$ 8,015	$ 8,460
6	1174	Steller, Alex	Central	$ 5,620	$ 5,843	$ 6,301

d. If they clicked the **'Enable Content'** button, they may receive the following message:

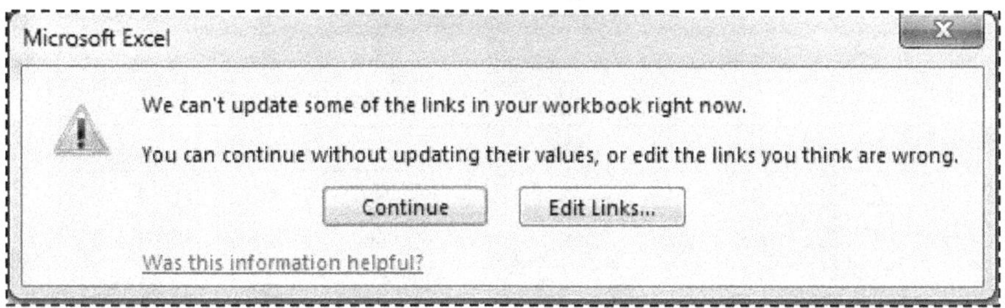

In either scenario, it could cause confusion, rework, or even lead the customer to have questions about you or the company / department you represent.

One of the easiest ways to address this issue is to **simply paste your VLOOKUP results as a value**. In the example above, we would:

1. Highlight cells '**B2**' thru **'C6'**
2. Click the '**Copy'** button or **CTL+C** from your keyboard
3. **Right click** and from the menu select **'Paste Special...'**
4. Select the **'Values'** radio button
5. Click the **'OK'** button

Please see screenshot below for an example:

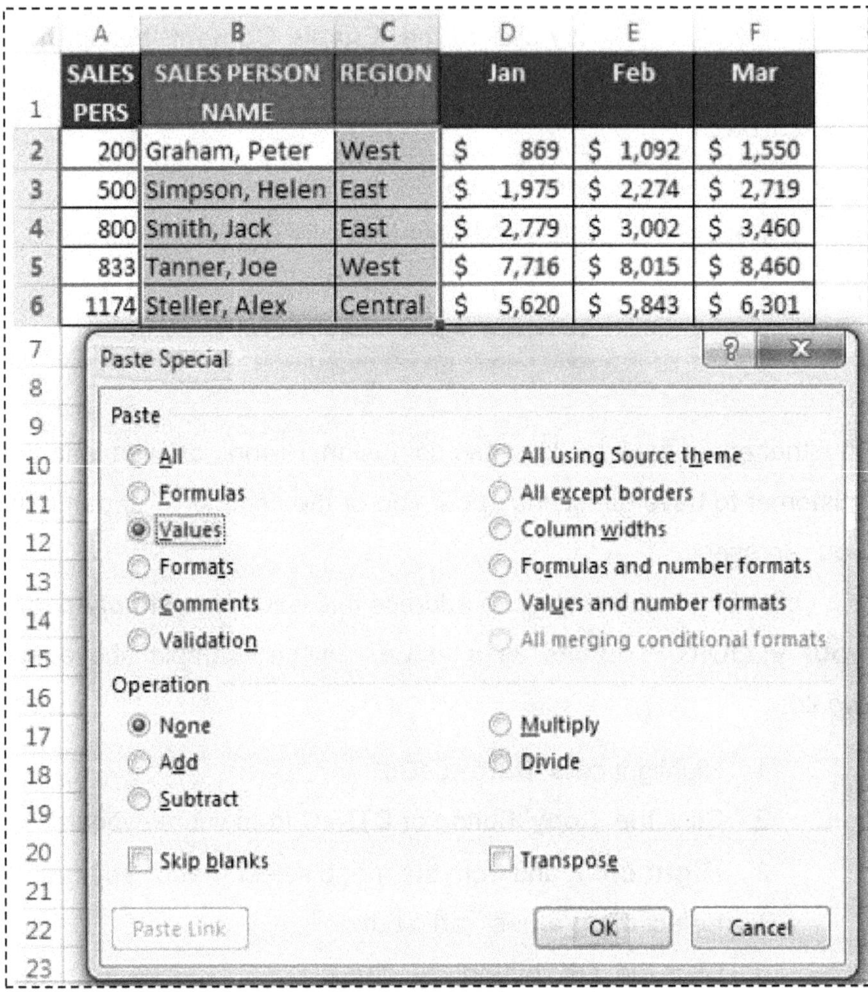

The VLOOKUP results are intact without any risk of error when you send them to a customer or a co-worker.

(PART 6) - CHAPTER 22

ENHANCED VLOOKUP FORMULAS

In this chapter we will extend the VLOOKUP functionality and examine some challenges that arise when using the VLOOKUP formula such as:

1. What to do when you attempt to lookup a value in the **table_array**, but none exists
2. What to do when you don't have a unique **lookup_value**
3. When the unique **lookup_value** is listed more than once in the **table_array**

This chapter also introduces a new formula, **IFERROR**.

Formula:

- IFERROR

Definition:

- IFERROR returns a value you specify if *(in our case the* VLOOKUP*)* formula evaluates an error such as: #N/A, #VALUE!, #REF!, #DIV/0!, #NUM!, #NAME?, or #NULL! Otherwise IFERROR will return the result of the *(*VLOOKUP*)* formula.

Quick Example:

```
Formula Syntax:
IFERROR(value, value_if_error)
All parameters are required
```

B4	=IFERROR(VLOOKUP(A4,Sheet2!A:C,2,FALSE),"Name Not Found")								
	A	B	C	D	E	F	G	H	I
1	SALES PERS	SALES PERSON NAME	REGION	Jan	Feb	Mar			
2	200	Graham, Peter	West	$ 869	$ 1,092	$ 1,550			
3	500	Simpson, Helen	East	$ 1,975	$ 2,274	$ 2,719			
4	800	Name Not Found	#N/A	$ 2,779	$ 3,002	$ 3,460			
5	833	Tanner, Joe	West	$ 7,716	$ 8,015	$ 8,460			
6	1174	Steller, Alex	Central	$ 5,620	$ 5,843	$ 6,301			

Scenario:

You've been asked to provide a list of the first quarter sales by month, for each sales person. However, *if* the Sales Person's name is not available, display the text **"Name Not Found".** You use a combination formula of IFERROR & VLOOKUP to develop this sales report.

Detailed Example How To Use The Formula:

To download a free copy of the Excel® file used in this scenario please go to: *http://bentonexcelbooks.my-free.website/sample-data-files select the file for* ***Chapter 22 (IFERROR)*** *in the* ***'The Microsoft Excel Step-By-Step Training Guide Book Bundle'*** *section*

Sample data (Sales Report with ID only):

	A	B	C	D	E
1	SALES PERS	SALES PERSON NAME	Jan	Feb	Mar
2	200		$ 869	$ 1,092	$ 1,550
3	500		$ 1,975	$ 2,274	$ 2,719
4	800		$ 2,779	$ 3,002	$ 3,460
5	833		$ 7,716	$ 8,015	$ 8,460
6	1174		$ 5,620	$ 5,843	$ 6,301

Sheet1 | Sheet2

Sample data (Sales Person Name):

	A	B	C
1	SALES PERSON ID	SALES PERSON NAME	REGION
2	200	Graham, Peter	West
3	1174	Steller, Alex	Central
4	500	Simpson, Helen	East
5	833	Tanner, Joe	West

Sheet1 | Sheet2

1. Select cell **'B2'** on **'Sheet1'**
2. Add the **VLOOKUP** formula:

   =VLOOKUP(A2,Sheet2!A:C,2,FALSE)

The following should be the result:

B2 | *fx* =VLOOKUP(A2,Sheet2!A:C,2,FALSE)

	A	B	C	D	E	F
1	SALES PERS	SALES PERSON NAME	Jan	Feb	Mar	
2	200	Graham, Peter	$ 869	$ 1,092	$ 1,550	
3	500		$ 1,975	$ 2,274	$ 2,719	
4	800		$ 2,779	$ 3,002	$ 3,460	
5	833		$ 7,716	$ 8,015	$ 8,460	
6	1174		$ 5,620	$ 5,843	$ 6,301	

3. Copy this formula down to cells '**B3**' thru '**B6**'

Note: the error **#N/A** in cell **'B4'**, this is because on the **table_array (Sheet2)** there is no Sales Person ID for ID# 800

	A	B	C	D	E
1	SALES PERSON ID	SALES PERSON NAME	Jan	Feb	Mar
2	200	Graham, Peter	$ 869	$ 1,092	$ 1,550
3	500	Simpson, Helen	$ 1,975	$ 2,274	$ 2,719
4	800	#N/A	$ 2,779	$ 3,002	$ 3,460
5	833	Tanner, Joe	$ 7,716	$ 8,015	$ 8,460
6	1174	Steller, Alex	$ 5,620	$ 5,843	$ 6,301

We were asked to provide a list of the first quarter sales by month, for each sales person. However, *if* the Sales Person's name is not available, display the text **"Name Not Found".** To address this requirement of *if the Sales Person's name is not found, display the text **"Name Not Found"*** we will add the function **IFERROR** to our **VLOOKUP** formula.

4. Select cell **'B2'** on **'Sheet1'**
5. Add the **IFERROR** formula to the existing **VLOOKUP** function:

```
=IFERROR(VLOOKUP(A2,Sheet2!A:C,2,FALSE),"Name Not Found")
```

The following should be the result:

B2 =IFERROR(VLOOKUP(A2,Sheet2!A:C,2,FALSE),"Name Not Found")

	A	B	C	D	E
1	SALES PERSON ID	SALES PERSON NAME	Jan	Feb	Mar
2	200	Graham, Peter	$ 869	$ 1,092	$ 1,550
3	500	Simpson, Helen	$ 1,975	$ 2,274	$ 2,719
4	800	#N/A	$ 2,779	$ 3,002	$ 3,460
5	833	Tanner, Joe	$ 7,716	$ 8,015	$ 8,460
6	1174	Steller, Alex	$ 5,620	$ 5,843	$ 6,301

6. Copy this formula down to cells '**B3**' thru '**B6**'

Note: the previous error of **#N/A** in cell **'B4'** is gone and now displays **"Name Not Found"**

	A	B	C	D	E
1	SALES PERSON ID	SALES PERSON NAME	Jan	Feb	Mar
2	200	Graham, Peter	$ 869	$ 1,092	$ 1,550
3	500	Simpson, Helen	$ 1,975	$ 2,274	$ 2,719
4	800	**Name Not Found**	$ 2,779	$ 3,002	$ 3,460
5	833	Tanner, Joe	$ 7,716	$ 8,015	$ 8,460
6	1174	Steller, Alex	$ 5,620	$ 5,843	$ 6,301

You've now created a list of the first quarter sales by month, for each sales person and when the Sales Person's name is not available, the text **"Name Not Found"** is displayed.

☑ HELPFUL INFORMATION:

The ***IF***ERROR formula was introduced in Microsoft® Excel® version 2007, prior to this, many of us would use ***IS*ERROR**. I include an example of **IS**ERROR in this book, because I still see many people use this formula in spreadsheets today. In the exercise above, someone may use the **IS**ERROR formula to accomplish the same thing as **IF**ERROR, below is an example of the how the formula would be written:

```
=IF(ISERROR(VLOOKUP(A2,Sheet2!A:C,2,FALSE)),"Name Not Found",(VLOOKUP(A2,Sheet2!A:C,2,FALSE)))
```

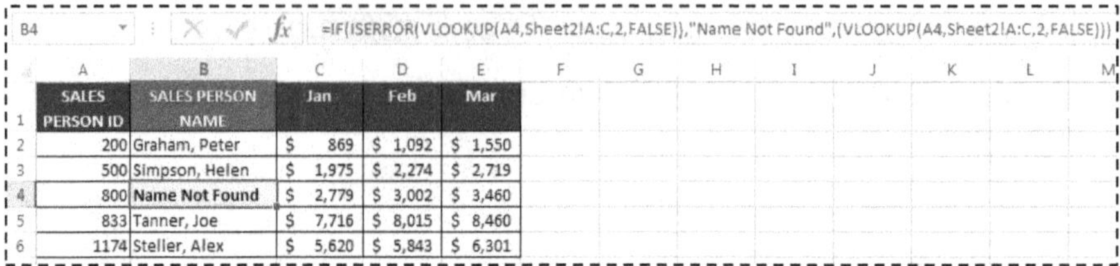
B4 =IF(ISERROR(VLOOKUP(A4,Sheet2!A:C,2,FALSE)),"Name Not Found",(VLOOKUP(A4,Sheet2!A:C,2,FALSE)))

SALES PERSON ID	SALES PERSON NAME	Jan	Feb	Mar
200	Graham, Peter	$ 869	$ 1,092	$ 1,550
500	Simpson, Helen	$ 1,975	$ 2,274	$ 2,719
800	**Name Not Found**	$ 2,779	$ 3,002	$ 3,460
833	Tanner, Joe	$ 7,716	$ 8,015	$ 8,460
1174	Steller, Alex	$ 5,620	$ 5,843	$ 6,301

As you can see **IF**ERROR greatly simplifies this type of functionality.

Another common issue that arises when using the VLOOKUP formula is occasionally you will *not* have a unique **lookup_value**. In all of the previous examples, we used a unique sale person ID number. **What would we do if all we had was a list of first and last names?** To tackle this question, we're going to use the **CONCATENATE** formula. Please see chapter 19, page 159 for more information on the **CONCATENATE** formula.

Scenario

You've been given a list of employees and their first quarter sales results and need to lookup what sales region each employee belongs too. You attempt to use the VLOOKUP formula, however upon further review of the two files, you see that the sales report contains only the sales person's first and last name, but not their sales person ID number. Therefore, you're not sure what the unique **lookup_value** should be. You're unable to lookup based on first or last name alone, because more than one employee has the either the same first or last name. You decide to use the CONCATENATE function to create a unique **lookup_value**.

Detailed Example How To Use The Formula:

Sample data (Sales Report with no Sales Person ID):

*To download a free copy of the Excel® file used in this scenario please go to: http://bentonexcelbooks.my-free.website/sample-data-files select the file for **Chapter 22 (Sales Report)** in the **'The Microsoft Excel Step-By-Step Training Guide Book Bundle'** section.*

	A	B	C	D	E
1	SALES PERSON FIRST	SALES PERSON LAST	Jan	Feb	Mar
2	Peter	Danner	$ 4,449	$ 7,048	$ 5,746
3	Maggie	Graham	$ 3,973	$ 6,251	$ 7,719
4	Peter	Graham	$ 1,975	$ 2,274	$ 2,719
5	Helen	Simpson	$ 7,716	$ 8,015	$ 8,460
6	Alex	Steller	$ 2,779	$ 3,002	$ 3,460
7	Joe	Tanner	$ 5,620	$ 5,843	$ 6,301
8	Elizabeth	Winchester	$ 869	$ 1,092	$ 1,550

Employee data:

*To download a free copy of the Excel® file used in this scenario please go to: http://bentonexcelbooks.my-free.website/sample-data-files select the file for **Chapter 23 (Employee Data)***

	A	B	C	D	E
1	SALES PERSON ID	SALES PERSON LAST	SALES PERSON FIRST	SALES REGION	MANAGER ID
2	100	Winchester	Elizabeth	West	50
3	200	Graham	Peter	West	50
4	300	Steller	Alex	Central	30
5	400	Simpson	Helen	East	40
6	500	Tanner	Joe	West	50
7	600	Graham	Maggie	Central	30
8	700	Danner	Peter	East	40

1. Insert a column on the sales report before '**SALES PERSON FIRST'**
2. Label the new **column 'A'** as 'VLOOKUP ID' *(this column is going to become our new **lookup_value**)*

The sales report should now look similar to the following:

	A	B	C	D	E	F
1	VLOOKUP ID	SALES PERSON FIRST	SALES PERSON LAST	Jan	Feb	Mar
2		Peter	Danner	$ 4,449	$ 7,048	$ 5,746
3		Maggie	Graham	$ 3,973	$ 6,251	$ 7,719
4		Peter	Graham	$ 1,975	$ 2,274	$ 2,719
5		Helen	Simpson	$ 7,716	$ 8,015	$ 8,460
6		Alex	Steller	$ 2,779	$ 3,002	$ 3,460
7		Joe	Tanner	$ 5,620	$ 5,843	$ 6,301
8		Elizabeth	Winchester	$ 869	$ 1,092	$ 1,550

3. In cell **'A2'** apply the following CONCATENATED formula:

```
=C2&" - "&B2
```

A2 | =C2&" - "&B2

	A	B	C	D	E	F
1	VLOOKUP ID	SALES PERSON FIRST	SALES PERSON LAST	Jan	Feb	Mar
2	Danner - Peter	Peter	Danner	$ 4,449	$ 7,048	$ 5,746
3		Maggie	Graham	$ 3,973	$ 6,251	$ 7,719
4		Peter	Graham	$ 1,975	$ 2,274	$ 2,719
5		Helen	Simpson	$ 7,716	$ 8,015	$ 8,460
6		Alex	Steller	$ 2,779	$ 3,002	$ 3,460
7		Joe	Tanner	$ 5,620	$ 5,843	$ 6,301
8		Elizabeth	Winchester	$ 869	$ 1,092	$ 1,550

4. Copy this formula to cells **'A3'** – **'A8'**
5. Insert a column between columns **'C'** & **'D'** label **'REGION'**

	A	B	C	D	E	F	G
1	VLOOKUP ID	SALES PERSON FIRST	SALES PERSON LAST	REGION	Jan	Feb	Mar
2	Danner - Peter	Peter	Danner		$ 4,449	$ 7,048	$ 5,746
3	Graham - Maggie	Maggie	Graham		$ 3,973	$ 6,251	$ 7,719
4	Graham - Peter	Peter	Graham		$ 1,975	$ 2,274	$ 2,719
5	Simpson - Helen	Helen	Simpson		$ 7,716	$ 8,015	$ 8,460
6	Steller - Alex	Alex	Steller		$ 2,779	$ 3,002	$ 3,460
7	Tanner - Joe	Joe	Tanner		$ 5,620	$ 5,843	$ 6,301
8	Winchester - Elizabetl	Elizabeth	Winchester		$ 869	$ 1,092	$ 1,550

6. Go to the employee data file, insert a column on the sales report before '**SALES PERSON ID'**
7. Label the new **column 'A1'** as 'VLOOKUP ID' *(this column is going to become our new **lookup_value**)*

The sales report should now look similar to the following:

	A	B	C	D	E	F
1	VLOOKUP ID	SALES PERSON ID	SALES PERSON LAST	SALES PERSON FIRST	SALES REGION	MANAGER ID
2		100	Winchester	Elizabeth	West	50
3		200	Graham	Peter	West	50
4		300	Steller	Alex	Central	30
5		400	Simpson	Helen	East	40
6		500	Tanner	Joe	West	50
7		600	Graham	Maggie	Central	30
8		700	Danner	Peter	East	40

8. In cell '**A2'** apply the following CONCATENATED formula:

```
=C2&" - "&D2
```

A2 | fx | =C2&" - "&D2

	A	B	C	D	E	F
1	VLOOKUP ID	SALES PERSON ID	SALES PERSON LAST	SALES PERSON FIRST	SALES REGION	MANAGER ID
2	Winchester - Elizabeth	100	Winchester	Elizabeth	West	50
3		200	Graham	Peter	West	50
4		300	Steller	Alex	Central	30
5		400	Simpson	Helen	East	40
6		500	Tanner	Joe	West	50
7		600	Graham	Maggie	Central	30
8		700	Danner	Peter	East	40

9. Copy this formula to cells **'A3' – 'A8'**
10. If you haven't already done so, please **SAVE** both files
11. Go back to the sales report, select cell '**D2'**, and apply the following VLOOKUP formula:

```
=VLOOKUP(A2,'[Employee Data.xlsx]Employee'!$A:$F,5,FALSE)
```

12. Copy this formula to cells '**D3**' – **'D8'**

D2 =VLOOKUP(A2,'[Employee Data.xlsx]Employee'!$A:$F,5,FALSE)

	A	B	C	D	E	F	G
1	VLOOKUP ID	SALES PERSON FIRST	SALES PERSON LAST	REGION	Jan	Feb	Mar
2	Danner - Peter	Peter	Danner	East	$ 4,449	$ 7,048	$ 5,746
3	Graham - Maggie	Maggie	Graham	Central	$ 3,973	$ 6,251	$ 7,719
4	Graham - Peter	Peter	Graham	West	$ 1,975	$ 2,274	$ 2,719
5	Simpson - Helen	Helen	Simpson	East	$ 7,716	$ 8,015	$ 8,460
6	Steller - Alex	Alex	Steller	Central	$ 2,779	$ 3,002	$ 3,460
7	Tanner - Joe	Joe	Tanner	West	$ 5,620	$ 5,843	$ 6,301
8	Winchester - Elizabetl	Elizabeth	Winchester	West	$ 869	$ 1,092	$ 1,550

13. Highlight cells **'D2'** – '**D8**', **COPY**, and **PASTE AS A VALUE** the **region** information
14. After you paste as a value, you may delete **column 'A'** on the sales report

	A	B	C	D	E	F
1	SALES PERSON FIRST	SALES PERSON LAST	REGION	Jan	Feb	Mar
2	Peter	Danner	East	$ 4,449	$ 7,048	$ 5,746
3	Maggie	Graham	Central	$ 3,973	$ 6,251	$ 7,719
4	Peter	Graham	West	$ 1,975	$ 2,274	$ 2,719
5	Helen	Simpson	East	$ 7,716	$ 8,015	$ 8,460
6	Alex	Steller	Central	$ 2,779	$ 3,002	$ 3,460
7	Joe	Tanner	West	$ 5,620	$ 5,843	$ 6,301
8	Elizabeth	Winchester	West	$ 869	$ 1,092	$ 1,550

You now have a list of employees, their first quarter sales results, and sales region.

☑ **HELPFUL INFORMATION:**

While the **CONCATENATE** function is helpful when you do not have a unique **lookup_value** for your VLOOKUP formula, there are **risks** with this option. In the example above, if our data sample was larger, there would a higher probability of more than one person having the same first and last name combination. However, sometimes this can't be avoided, the risks are outweighed by the value the VLOOKUP brings to task efficiency. The next section discusses the implications of what happens when you have same **lookup_value** listed more than once.

When the unique lookup_value is listed more than once on the table_array, the VLOOKUP will always return the value for *the first* unique lookup_value it finds in the table_array. Let's walk through an example.

Using similar sample data as the above for sales and employee, we'll again lookup the employee's sales region:

Sample data (Sales Report with two entries for the same *Sales Person ID)*:

SALES REPORT:

	A	B	C	D	E
1	SALES PERSON ID	SALES PERSON FIRST	SALES PERSON LAST	REGION	Jan
2	700	Peter	Danner		$ 4,449
3	600	Maggie	Graham		$ 3,973
4	200	Peter	Graham		$ 1,975
5	400	Helen	Simpson		$ 7,716
6	300	Alex	Steller		$ 2,779
7	500	Joe	Tanner		$ 5,620
8	100	Elizabeth	Winchester		$ 869
9	300	Butler	Catherine		$ 1,588

EMPLOYEE DATA:

	A	B	C	D	E
1	SALES PERSON ID	SALES PERSON LAST	SALES PERSON FIRST	SALES REGION	MANAGER ID
2	100	Winchester	Elizabeth	West	50
3	200	Graham	Peter	West	50
4	300	Steller	Alex	Central	30
5	400	Simpson	Helen	East	40
6	500	Tanner	Joe	West	50
7	600	Graham	Maggie	Central	30
8	700	Danner	Peter	East	40
9	300	Butler	Catherine	East	40

Hopefully, there are system controls in place to prevent a sales person ID from being added more than once. However, I've seen situations where this can happen, especially when migrating data from another system or importing employee information from an acquisition.

SALES REPORT:

D6 =VLOOKUP(A6,'[Employee Data.xlsx]Employee'!$A:$E,4,FALSE)

	A	B	C	D	E
1	SALES PERSON ID	SALES PERSON FIRST	SALES PERSON LAST	REGION	Jan
2	700	Peter	Danner	East	$ 4,449
3	600	Maggie	Graham	Central	$ 3,973
4	200	Peter	Graham	West	$ 1,975
5	400	Helen	Simpson	East	$ 7,716
6	300	Alex	Steller	Central	$ 2,779
7	500	Joe	Tanner	West	$ 5,620
8	100	Elizabeth	Winchester	West	$ 869
9	300	Butler	Catherine	Central	$ 1,588

As you can see from the screenshot above, the VLOOKUP will always return the value for the first unique **lookup_value** it finds in the **table_array**.

☑ **HELPFUL INFORMATION:**

To address this you could apply the **CONCATENATE** function to the sales person's ID, first, and last name, and make that the unique **lookup_value**. However, if you're in a position to do so, the best practice would be change the employee's sales person ID.

An easy way to identify duplicate values is use CONDITIONAL FORMATTING. For example, using the employee sample data:

1. Highlight **column 'A'**
2. From the toolbar select **HOME**: **Conditional Formatting**
3. From the drop-down box, select the **option 'Highlight Cells Rules'** then **'Duplicate Values...'**

EMPLOYEE DATA:

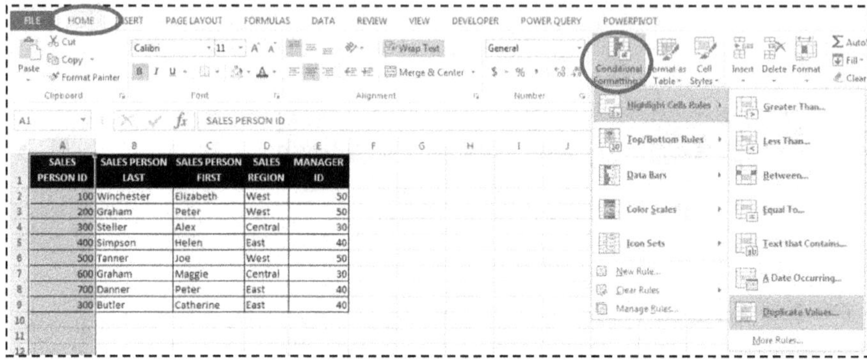

The following dialogue box should appear:

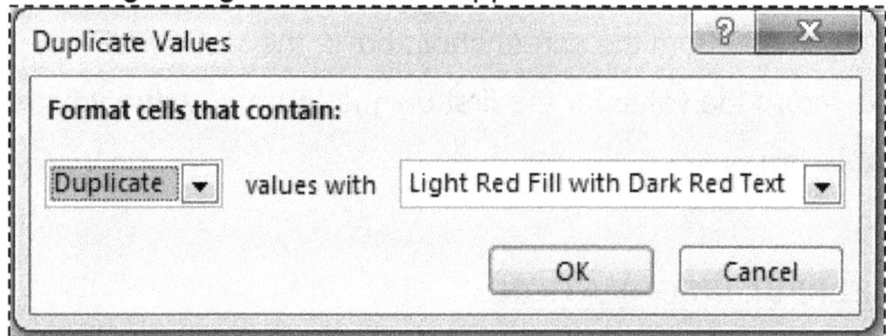

Click the '**OK'** button

The following rows should now be highlighted:

	A	B	C	D	E
1	SALES PERSON ID	SALES PERSON LAST	SALES PERSON FIRST	SALES REGION	MANAGER ID
2	100	Winchester	Elizabeth	West	50
3	200	Graham	Peter	West	50
4	300	Steller	Alex	Central	30
5	400	Simpson	Helen	East	40
6	500	Tanner	Joe	West	50
7	600	Graham	Maggie	Central	30
8	700	Danner	Peter	East	40
9	300	Butler	Catherine	East	40

To remove the Conditional Formatting:

3. From the toolbar select **HOME : Conditional Formatting:**

4. Select '**Clear Rules**' and either option:
   c. Clear Rules from Select Cells
   d. Clear Rules from Entire Sheet

Please see screenshot below for an example.

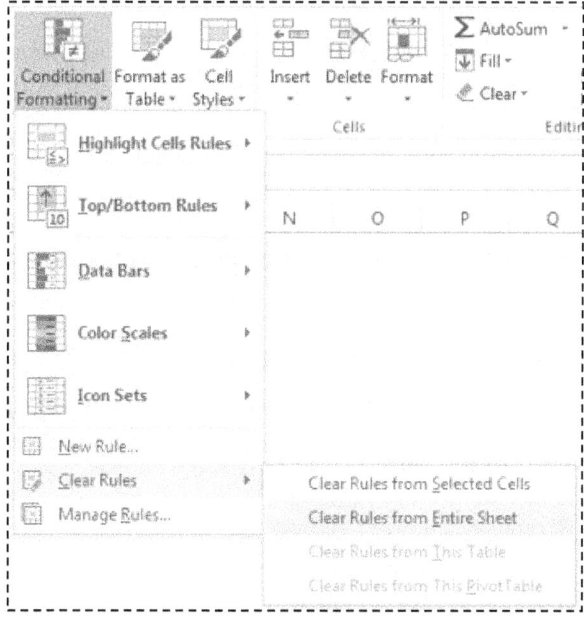

(PART 6) - CHAPTER 23

APPLYING THE VLOOKUP ACROSS MULTIPLE SHEETS OR WORKBOOKS

To apply the VLOOKUP formula across multiple workbooks or sheets, we will again use the **IFERROR** function, please see chapter 22, page 193 for the syntax.

Scenario:

A new sales management position has been created to oversee three sales regions. This new manager has been given a list of employee IDs, but does not know each employee's name and sales region. He has asked you to pull together all the employee data and create a consolidated report for him.

Detailed Example How To Use The Formula:

To download a free copy of the Excel® file used in this scenario please go to: *http://bentonexcelbooks.my-free.website/sample-data-files* *select the file for* ***Chapter 23 (Manager's Report)*** *in the* ***'The Microsoft Excel Step-By-Step Training Guide Book Bundle'*** *section.*

Sample data:
Workbook #1 (Manager's Report)
Manger's Report with Employee ID:

	A	B	C	D
1	EMPLOYEE ID	SALES PERSON LAST	SALES PERSON FIRST	SALES REGION
2	100			
3	200			
4	300			
5	301			
6	400			
7	500			
8	600			
9	700			
10	702			

Manager's Report

To download a free copy of the Excel® file used in this scenario please go to:
http://bentonexcelbooks.my-free.website/sample-data-files
*select the file for **Chapter 23 (Employee Data)** in the **'The Microsoft Excel Step-By-Step Training Guide Book Bundle'** section.*

Sample data:
Workbook #2 Employee Data
Employee data contained on 3 sheets (tabs):

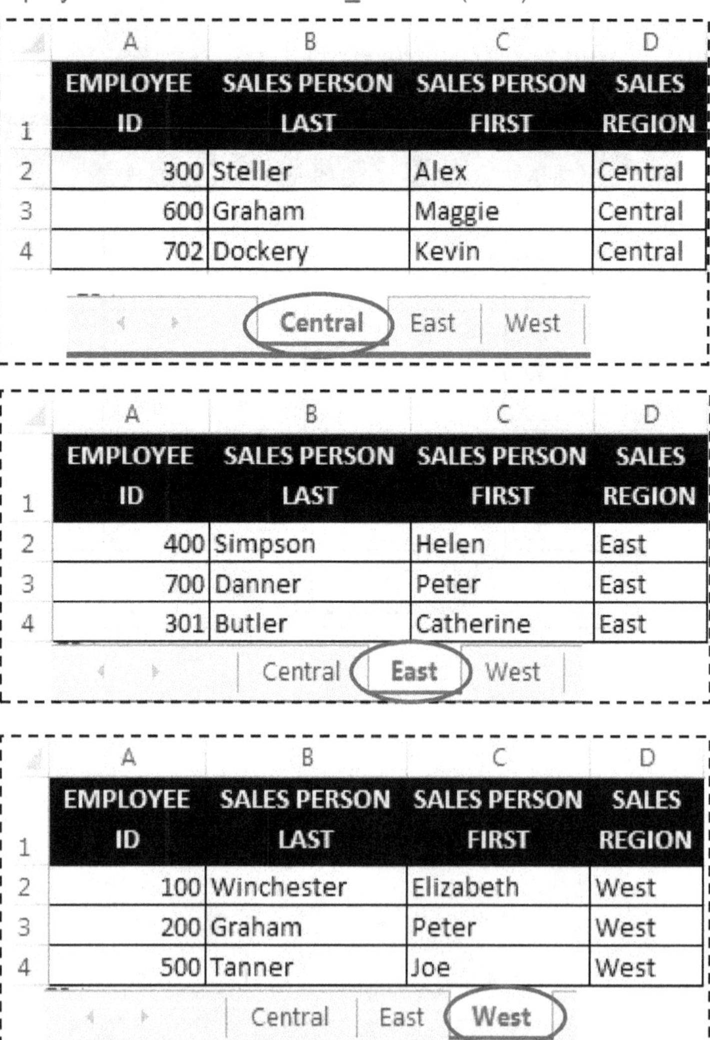

EMPLOYEE ID	SALES PERSON LAST	SALES PERSON FIRST	SALES REGION
300	Steller	Alex	Central
600	Graham	Maggie	Central
702	Dockery	Kevin	Central

EMPLOYEE ID	SALES PERSON LAST	SALES PERSON FIRST	SALES REGION
400	Simpson	Helen	East
700	Danner	Peter	East
301	Butler	Catherine	East

EMPLOYEE ID	SALES PERSON LAST	SALES PERSON FIRST	SALES REGION
100	Winchester	Elizabeth	West
200	Graham	Peter	West
500	Tanner	Joe	West

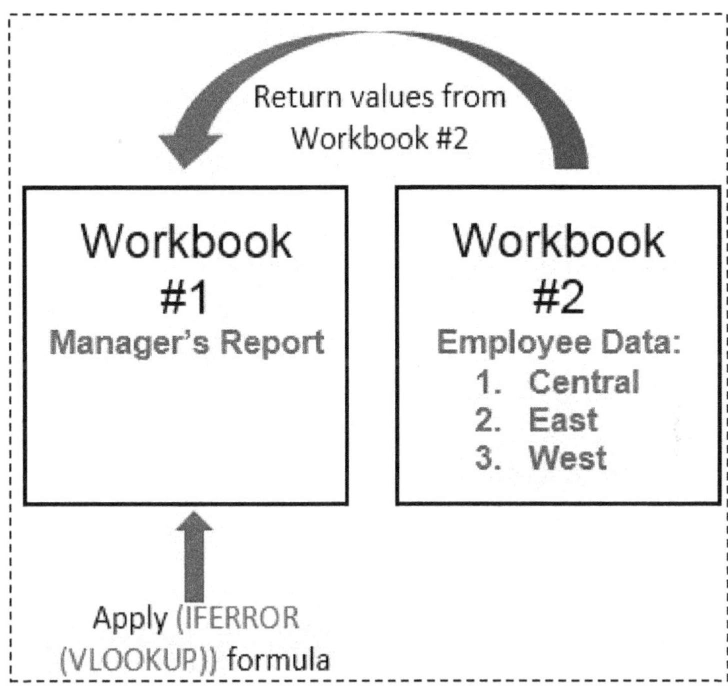

We're going to build a nested VLOOKUP formula, by the time we're done it is going be very long. However, by building step-by-step, we will minimize errors. Also, if we run into problems it will be easier to troubleshoot, because we know the previous parts we built are working.

1. Begin by going to workbook #1 (Manager's Report) and click cell 'B2'
2. Enter the following VLOOKUP formula:

```
=VLOOKUP(A2,'[Employee Data.xlsx]Central'!$A:$D,2,FALSE)
```

You'll receive the **#N/A** message, this is <u>OK</u> and to be expected. We'll address this as we go.

Workbook #1 (Manager's Report)

B2 =VLOOKUP(A2,'[Employee Data.xlsx]Central'!$A:$D,2,FALSE)

	A	B	C	D	E	F	G	H
1	EMPLOYEE ID	SALES PERSON LAST	SALES PERSON FIRST	SALES REGION				
2	100	#N/A						

3. Copy the above VLOOKUP formula down to cells **'B3'** – '**B10'**

Rows 4, 8, & 10 should now have values:

Workbook #1 (Manager's Report)

	A	B	C	D
1	EMPLOYEE ID	SALES PERSON LAST	SALES PERSON FIRST	SALES REGION
2	100	#N/A		
3	200	#N/A		
4	300	Steller		
5	301	#N/A		
6	400	#N/A		
7	500	#N/A		
8	600	Graham		
9	700	#N/A		
10	702	Dockery		

4. Next, we'll add the **IFERROR** function to the **VLOOKUP** formula, please go back to cell **'B2'** and enter the following:

```
=IFERROR(VLOOKUP(A2,'[Employee
Data.xlsx]Central'!$A:$D,2,FALSE),"Name Not Found")
```

5. Copy the updated IFERROR & VLOOKUP formula to cells **'B3' – 'B10'**

Workbook #1 (Manager's Report)

B2 =IFERROR(VLOOKUP(A2,'[Employee Data.xlsx]Central'!$A:$D,2,FALSE),"Name Not Found")

EMPLOYEE ID	SALES PERSON LAST	SALES PERSON FIRST	SALES REGION
100	Name Not Found		
200	Name Not Found		
300	Steller		
301	Name Not Found		
400	Name Not Found		
500	Name Not Found		
600	Graham		
700	Name Not Found		
702	Dockery		

Next, we'll extend the IFERROR and VLOOKUP formula, to search the *second tab* called 'East' on Workbook #2 (Employee Data).

6. Please go back to cell **'B2'** and enter the following:

```
=IFERROR(VLOOKUP(A2,'[Employee
Data.xlsx]Central'!$A:$D,2,FALSE),IFERROR(VLOOKUP(A2,'[Emp
loyee Data.xlsx]East'!$A:$D,2,FALSE),"Name Not Found"))
```

I know the above formula is difficult to read, I've attempted highlight the section that was added for the **'East'** tab on Workbook #2. Please also note, the additional parenthesis) at the end of the formula.

7. Copy the updated IFERROR & VLOOKUP formula to cells **'B3' – 'B10'**

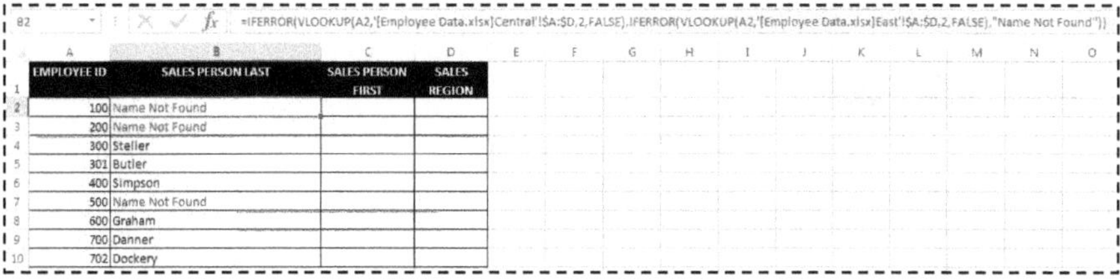
B2 =IFERROR(VLOOKUP(A2,'[Employee Data.xlsx]Central'!$A:$D,2,FALSE),IFERROR(VLOOKUP(A2,'[Employee Data.xlsx]East'!$A:$D,2,FALSE),"Name Not Found"))

EMPLOYEE ID	SALES PERSON LAST	SALES PERSON FIRST	SALES REGION
100	Name Not Found		
200	Name Not Found		
300	Steller		
301	Butler		
400	Simpson		
500	Name Not Found		
600	Graham		
700	Danner		
702	Dockery		

```
=IFERROR(VLOOKUP(A2,'[Employee Data.xlsx]Central'!$A:$D,2,FALSE),
IFERROR(VLOOKUP(A2,'[Employee Data.xlsx]East'!$A:$D,2,FALSE),"Name
Not Found"))
```

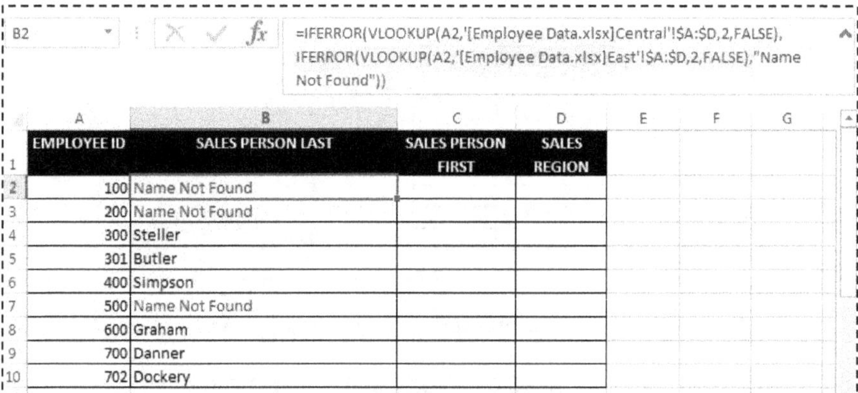

EMPLOYEE ID	SALES PERSON LAST	SALES PERSON FIRST	SALES REGION
100	Name Not Found		
200	Name Not Found		
300	Steller		
301	Butler		
400	Simpson		
500	Name Not Found		
600	Graham		
700	Danner		
702	Dockery		

Almost done, we'll now add the final IFERROR and VLOOKUP formula, to search the *third tab* called 'West' on Workbook #2 (Employee Data).

8. Please go back to cell **'B2'** and enter the following:

```
=IFERROR(VLOOKUP(A2,'[Employee
Data.xlsx]Central'!$A:$D,2,FALSE),IFERROR(VLOOKUP(A2,'[
Employee
Data.xlsx]East'!$A:$D,2,FALSE),IFERROR(VLOOKUP(A2,'[Emp
loyee Data.xlsx]West'!$A:$D,2,FALSE),"Name Not
Found")))
```

9. Copy the updated IFERROR & VLOOKUP formula to cells **'B3' – 'B10'**

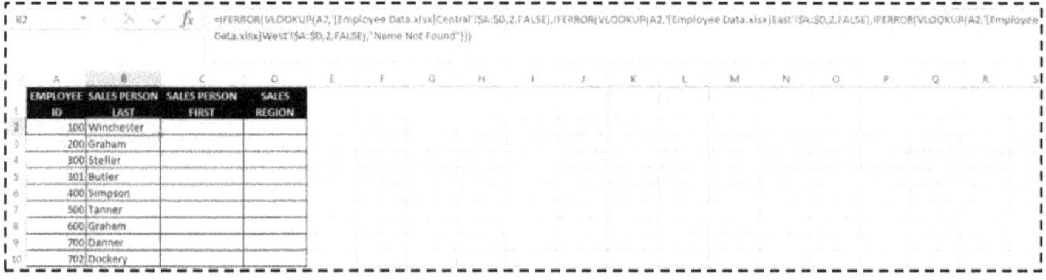

EMPLOYEE ID	SALES PERSON LAST	SALES PERSON FIRST	SALES REGION
100	Winchester		
200	Graham		
300	Steller		
301	Butler		
400	Simpson		
500	Tanner		
600	Graham		
700	Danner		
702	Dockery		

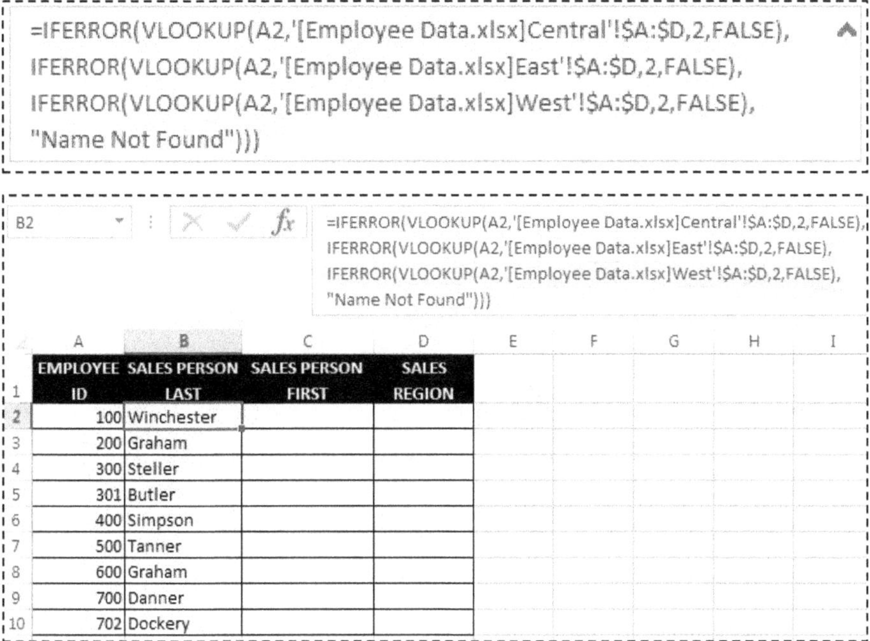

```
=IFERROR(VLOOKUP(A2,'[Employee Data.xlsx]Central'!$A:$D,2,FALSE),
IFERROR(VLOOKUP(A2,'[Employee Data.xlsx]East'!$A:$D,2,FALSE),
IFERROR(VLOOKUP(A2,'[Employee Data.xlsx]West'!$A:$D,2,FALSE),
"Name Not Found")))
```

EMPLOYEE ID	SALES PERSON LAST	SALES PERSON FIRST	SALES REGION
100	Winchester		
200	Graham		
300	Steller		
301	Butler		
400	Simpson		
500	Tanner		
600	Graham		
700	Danner		
702	Dockery		

Great job! If you had trouble, don't worry, this was a complex nested IF VLOOKUP formula. You'll get better with practice. It often still takes me a couple of tries to get the formula correct and I have had years of experience. It is very easy to miss a comma or parenthesis with these advanced functions. Your skill level will improve with repetition.

To complete the scenario, we're going to copy the formula to the **'SALES PERSON FIRST'** & **'REGION'** columns on workbook #1 (Manager's Report).

10. Before we begin copying the IFERROR & VLOOKUP formula, we need to add the **dollar $** symbol to the **lookup_value**. Please see below for an example.

11. On workbook #1 (Manager's Report) click cell **'B2'**

12. For each VLOOKUP, before the lookup_value, add the **$**:

```
=IFERROR(VLOOKUP($A2,'[Employee Data.xlsx]Central'!$A:$D,2,FALSE),IFERROR(VLOOKUP($A2,'[Employee Data.xlsx]East'!$A:$D,2,FALSE),IFERROR(VLOOKUP($A2,'[Employee Data.xlsx]West'!$A:$D,2,FALSE),"Name Not Found")))
```

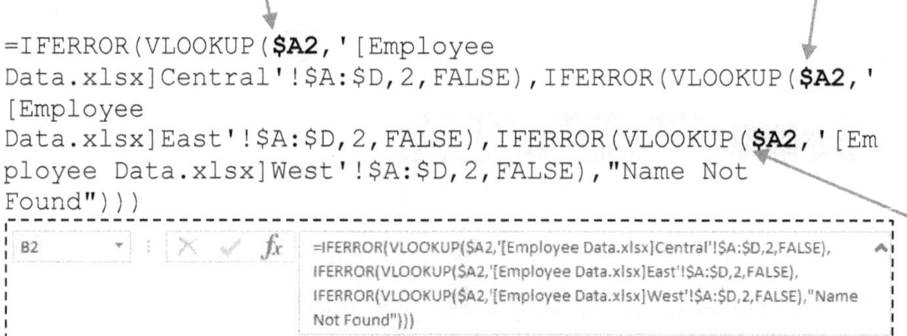

13. Copy the updated IFERROR & VLOOKUP formula to cell **'C2'**

14. In cell **'C2'** change the **col_index_num** for all VLOOKUP formulas to **3**

```
=IFERROR(VLOOKUP($A2,'[Employee Data.xlsx]Central'!$A:$D,3,FALSE),IFERROR(VLOOKUP($A2,'[Employee Data.xlsx]East'!$A:$D,3,FALSE),IFERROR(VLOOKUP($A2,'[Employee Data.xlsx]West'!$A:$D,3,FALSE), "Name Not Found")))
```

```
=IFERROR(VLOOKUP($A2,'[Employee Data.xlsx]Central'!$A:$D,3,FALSE),
IFERROR(VLOOKUP($A2,'[Employee Data.xlsx]East'!$A:$D,3,FALSE),
IFERROR(VLOOKUP($A2,'[Employee Data.xlsx]West'!$A:$D,3,FALSE),"Name
Not Found")))
```

C2 | =IFERROR(VLOOKUP($A2,'[Employee Data.xlsx]Central'!$A:$D,3,FALSE),IFERROR(VLOOKUP($A2,'[Employee Data.xlsx]East'!$A:$D,3,FALSE),IFERROR(VLOOKUP($A2,'[Employee Data.xlsx]West'!$A:$D,3,FALSE),"Name Not Found")))

	A	B	C	D	E	F	G	H	I
1	EMPLOYEE ID	SALES PERSON LAST	SALES PERSON FIRST	SALES REGION					
2	100	Winchester	Elizabeth						
3	200	Graham							
4	300	Steller							
5	301	Butler							
6	400	Simpson							
7	500	Tanner							
8	600	Graham							
9	700	Danner							
10	702	Dockery							

15. Copy the updated IFERROR & VLOOKUP formula to cells **'C3' – 'D10'**, please note to copy the formula to **column 'D10'**

It is OK, that **column 'D'** is displaying the same values as **column 'C'**, we'll fix this in the next steps.

	A	B	C	D
1	EMPLOYEE ID	SALES PERSON LAST	SALES PERSON FIRST	SALES REGION
2	100	Winchester	Elizabeth	Elizabeth
3	200	Graham	Peter	Peter
4	300	Steller	Alex	Alex
5	301	Butler	Catherine	Catherine
6	400	Simpson	Helen	Helen
7	500	Tanner	Joe	Joe
8	600	Graham	Maggie	Maggie
9	700	Danner	Peter	Peter
10	702	Dockery	Kevin	Kevin

16. Select cell **'D2'**
17. Change the **col_index_num** for all VLOOKUP formulas to **4**
18. Copy the updated IFERROR & VLOOKUP formula in cell **'D2'** to cells **'D3'** – **'D10'**

```
=IFERROR(VLOOKUP($A2,'[Employee
Data.xlsx]Central'!$A:$D,4,FALSE),IFERROR(VLOOKUP($A2,'
[Employee
Data.xlsx]East'!$A:$D,4,FALSE),IFERROR(VLOOKUP($A2,'[Em
ployee Data.xlsx]West'!$A:$D,4,FALSE),"Name Not
Found")))
```

```
=IFERROR(VLOOKUP($A2,'[Employee Data.xlsx]Central'!$A:$D,4,FALSE),
IFERROR(VLOOKUP($A2,'[Employee Data.xlsx]East'!$A:$D,4,FALSE),
IFERROR(VLOOKUP($A2,'[Employee Data.xlsx]West'!$A:$D,4,FALSE),"Name
Not Found")))
```

D2 | fx | =IFERROR(VLOOKUP($A2,'[Employee Data.xlsx]Central'!$A:$D,4,FALSE), IFERROR(VLOOKUP($A2,'[Employee Data.xlsx]East'!$A:$D,4,FALSE), IFERROR(VLOOKUP($A2,'[Employee Data.xlsx]West'!$A:$D,4,FALSE),"Name Not Found")))

	A	B	C	D	E	F	G	H	I
1	EMPLOYEE ID	SALES PERSON LAST	SALES PERSON FIRST	SALES REGION					
2	100	Winchester	Elizabeth	West					
3	200	Graham	Peter	West					
4	300	Steller	Alex	Central					
5	301	Butler	Catherine	East					
6	400	Simpson	Helen	East					
7	500	Tanner	Joe	West					
8	600	Graham	Maggie	Central					
9	700	Danner	Peter	East					
10	702	Dockery	Kevin	Central					

The final report should look similar to the following:

	A	B	C	D
1	EMPLOYEE ID	SALES PERSON LAST	SALES PERSON FIRST	SALES REGION
2	100	Winchester	Elizabeth	West
3	200	Graham	Peter	West
4	300	Steller	Alex	Central
5	301	Butler	Catherine	East
6	400	Simpson	Helen	East
7	500	Tanner	Joe	West
8	600	Graham	Maggie	Central
9	700	Danner	Peter	East
10	702	Dockery	Kevin	Central

Congratulations! You've successfully applied a VLOOKUP formula across multiple tabs and workbooks.

You've completed the scenario, the new manager has been given a consolidated report that lists the ID, name, and sales region for all of his employees.

(PART 6) - CHAPTER 24

VLOOKUP TROUBLESHOOTING

While the VLOOKUP and associated formulas are very useful and quite powerful, it can be challenging and sometimes frustrating to learn them. Why a VLOOKUP is not returning the correct value can puzzle even the most experienced users. This chapter addresses some of the most common VLOOKUP errors and how to resolve them. The areas reviewed are:

1. Why I am receiving the **#N/A error message**?
2. My **lookup_value** is the same as the match value in the **table_array**, why is my VLOOKUP formula not returning a value?
3. Why am I getting the **#REF error message**?
4. My VLOOKUP formula was working, but now I'm getting the wrong values, why?

ERROR / ISSUE: Why I am receiving the **#N/A error message**?

There are a number of reasons why you'll get the **#N/A error message,** but the most likely cause, especially for beginners is:

- The field you want to match, the **lookup_value**, IS NOT the FIRST COLUMN in the range of cells you specify in the **table_array**.

Let's take a closer look, in the example below, the VLOOKUP formula is fine, but since we're matching on the 'SALES PERSON ID', this column needs to be FIRST in the table_array.

SHEET 1:

A2 | =VLOOKUP(B2,Sheet2!A:C,2,FALSE)

	A	B	C	D	E	F
1	SALES PERSON NAME	SALES PERSON ID	Jan	Feb	Mar	
2	#N/A	200	$ 869	$ 1,092	$ 1,550	

SHEET 2 (table_array):

	A	B	C
1	SALES PERSON NAME	SALES PERSON ID	REGION
2	Graham, Peter	200	West
3	Steller, Alex	1174	Central
4	Simpson, Helen	500	East
5	Tanner, Joe	833	West

Solution: Make the 'SALES PERSON ID', the first column in the table_array.

SHEET 2 (table_array):

	A	B	C
1	SALES PERSON ID	SALES PERSON NAME	REGION
2	200	Graham, Peter	West
3	1174	Steller, Alex	Central
4	500	Simpson, Helen	East
5	833	Tanner, Joe	West

SHEET 1:

A2 =VLOOKUP(B2,Sheet2!A:C,2,FALSE)

	A	B	C	D	E	F
1	SALES PERSON NAME	SALES PERSON ID	Jan	Feb	Mar	
2	Graham, Peter	200	$ 869	$ 1,092	$ 1,550	

ERROR / ISSUE: Why I am getting the **#N/A error message**? My **lookup_value** IS the FIRST COLUMN in the range of cells specified in the table_array. What else could be wrong?

The next two examples can be a little more tricky to understand as they involve formatting issues, such as *extra spaces* and/or mis-matched *case* of the lookup_value.

Let's first review the issue of extra spaces in the lookup_value or table_array. When I first started using VLOOKUP formulas, I was having trouble getting one to work. I literally spent hours trying to figure out why it wasn't working. After banging my head against my desk, I realized there were extra spaces in my lookup_value. Most of the time you can't see extra spaces, especially if they are after the lookup_value, but these invisible nuisances will cause your VLOOKUP to fail. Below is an example:

- Can you see the **extra spaces** in the below screenshot?

SHEET 1:

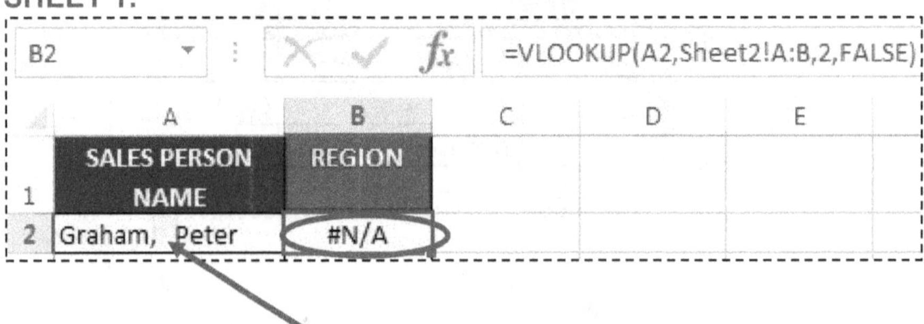

B2 =VLOOKUP(A2,Sheet2!A:B,2,FALSE)

	A	B	C	D	E
1	SALES PERSON NAME	REGION			
2	Graham, Peter	#N/A			

Solution: First identify where the extra spaces are and then remove them.

To identify the where the extra spaces are, I use the **LEN** formula. The **LEN** formula *counts the number characters* in a cell. In the below example we can see that:

- In **sheet 1** for the lookup_value, the LEN formula is indicating more characters compared to what is contained in the table_array. The names:
  - Graham, Peter should only be 13 characters
  - Simpson, Helen should only be 14 characters

Although I can't easily see these extra spaces (characters), they exist and are causing my VLOOKUP to fail.

SHEET 1:

	A	B	C
1	SALES PERSON NAME	REGION	LEN
2	Graham, Peter	#N/A	15
3	Simpson, Helen	#N/A	16

SHEET 2 (table_array):

	A	B	C
1	SALES PERSON NAME	REGION	LEN
2	Graham, Peter	West	13
3	Simpson, Helen	East	14

Now that I know where the problem is, I will remove these extra spaces by using the **TRIM** formula. The **TRIM** formula *removes all extraneous spaces* from a cell, except for single spaces between words.

SHEET 1:

D2 | fx =TRIM(A2)

	A	B	C	D
1	SALES PERSON NAME	REGION	LEN	TRIM
2	Graham, Peter	#N/A	15	Graham, Peter
3	Simpson, Helen	#N/A	16	Simpson, Helen

Next, I will **paste as a value** the results of the TRIM formula into **column 'A'** and this will fix the VLOOKUP error.

SHEET 1:

	A	B	C
1	SALES PERSON NAME	REGION	LEN
2	Graham, Peter	West	13
3	Simpson, Helen	East	14

ERROR / ISSUE: Why else would I be getting the **#N/A error message**?

A similar formatting issue that will cause a VLOOKUP to fail is related to mis-matched *case* of the lookup_value.

Below is an example:

- The last name of GRAHAM, Peter is all **uppercase**
- The entire name of simpson, helen is **lowercase**

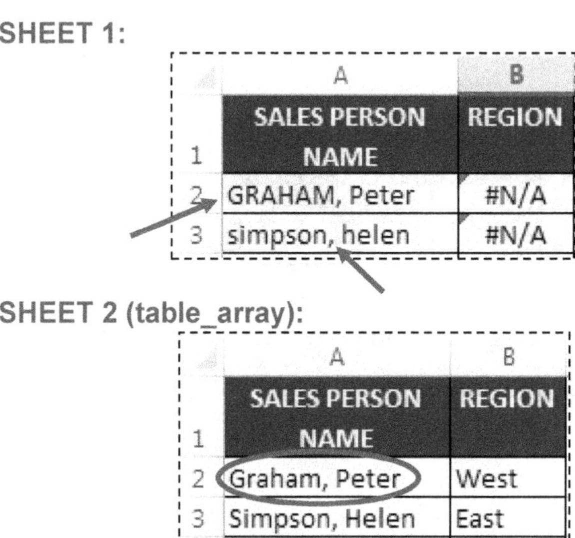

SHEET 1:

	A	B
1	SALES PERSON NAME	REGION
2	GRAHAM, Peter	#N/A
3	simpson, helen	#N/A

SHEET 2 (table_array):

	A	B
1	SALES PERSON NAME	REGION
2	Graham, Peter	West
3	Simpson, Helen	East

Solution: Use a text function to make the case formatting consistent with the table_array.

In the below example, I will use the formula **PROPER** to change the lookup_value. You may also use formulas **UPPER** or **LOWER** if you choose:

SHEET 1:

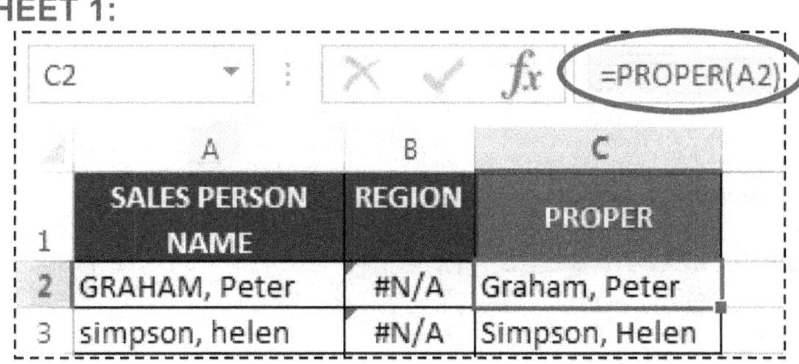

C2 =PROPER(A2)

	A	B	C
1	SALES PERSON NAME	REGION	PROPER
2	GRAHAM, Peter	#N/A	Graham, Peter
3	simpson, helen	#N/A	Simpson, Helen

Next, I will **paste as a value** the results of the **PROPER** formula into **column 'A'** and this will fix the VLOOKUP error.

SHEET 1:

B2 =VLOOKUP(A2,Sheet2!A:B,2,FALSE)

	A	B	C	D	E
1	SALES PERSON NAME	REGION	PROPER		
2	Graham, Peter	West	Graham, Peter		
3	Simpson, Helen	East	Simpson, Helen		

ERROR / ISSUE: Why am I getting the **#REF** error message?

Like the #N/A error message, there are a number of reasons why you'll get the **#REF error message,** but one of the more common causes is:

- The **table_array** range of cells is incorrect.

In the example below, the VLOOKUP in sheet 1 is referencing ***2 columns*** in the table_array. The **#REF error** is because the **col_index_num** is referencing *column 3*, but that column is NOT included in the table_array.

Please see below screenshots:

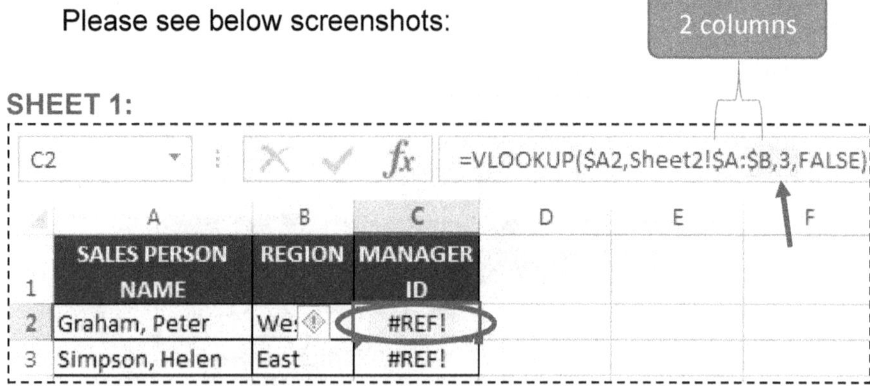

	A	B	C	D	E	F
1	SALES PERSON NAME	REGION	MANAGER ID			
2	Graham, Peter	We:	#REF!			
3	Simpson, Helen	East	#REF!			

SHEET 2 (table_array):

	A	B	C
1	Number of Columns:		
2	1	2	3
3	SALES PERSON NAME	REGION	MANAGER ID
4	Graham, Peter	West	50
5	Simpson, Helen	East	40

Solution: Change the table_array to include the correct number of columns.

SHEET 1:

C2 =VLOOKUP($A2,Sheet2!$A:$C,3,FALSE)

	A	B	C	D	E	F
1	SALES PERSON NAME	REGION	MANAGER ID			
2	Graham, Peter	West	50			
3	Simpson, Helen	East	40			

ERROR / ISSUE: My VLOOKUP formula was working, but now I'm getting the wrong values, why?

Again, there can be a number of reasons why a VLOOKUP will suddenly stop working, but one of the more common causes is:

- Someone has inadvertently added or deleted columns in the **table_array** range of cells.

In the example below, REGION *was* being populated correctly. Let's say, you reviewed this report on a Friday, but then on the following Monday, when you opened the same report, the results were different. Why?

SHEET 1 (correct on Friday):

	A	B	C
1	SALES PERSON NAME	REGION	MANAGER ID
2	Graham, Peter	West	50
3	Simpson, Helen	East	40

SHEET 1 (incorrect on Monday):

	A	B	C
1	SALES PERSON NAME	REGION	MANAGER ID
2	Graham, Peter	100	West
3	Simpson, Helen	200	East

After reviewing the table_array, you discover someone has added **two new columns**; 'SALES PERSON ID' and 'HOME OFFICE LOCATION'.

SHEET 2 (table_array)

	A	B	C	D	E
1	SALES PERSON NAME	SALES PERSON ID	HOME OFFICE LOCATION	REGION	MANAGER ID
2	Graham, Peter	100	Seattle	West	50
3	Simpson, Helen	200	London	East	40

Solution: Adjust your VLOOKUP formula to account for the newly inserted columns. Please see example below:

SHEET 1

B2 | =VLOOKUP($A2,Sheet2!$A:$E,4,FALSE)

	A	B	C	D	E	F
1	SALES PERSON NAME	REGION	MANAGER ID			
2	Graham, Peter	West	50			
3	Simpson, Helen	East	40			

CHAPTER 25

EXCEL® SHORTCUTS & TIPS

The following lists some of the most common Microsoft® Excel® shortcuts:

DESCRIPTION	COMMANDS
FORMATTING	
CTRL+B	Applies or removes **bold** formatting
CTRL+I	Applies or removes *italic* formatting
CTRL+U	Applies or removes underlining formatting
FUNCTION	
CTRL+A	Selects (highlights) the entire worksheet
CTRL+C	Copies the contents of selected (highlighted) cells
CTRL+X	Cuts the selected cells
CTRL+V	Pastes the contents of selected (highlighted) cells, including cell formatting
CTRL+F	Displays the Find and Replace dialog box, with the **Find** tab selected
CTRL+H	Displays the Find and Replace dialog box, with the **Replace** tab selected
CTRL+K	Displays the Insert Hyperlink dialog box for new hyperlinks or the Edit Hyperlink dialog box for selected existing hyperlinks
CTRL+N	Creates a new blank workbook
CTRL+O	Displays the dialog box to open a file
CTRL+S	Saves the active file with its current file name, location, and file format
CTRL+P	Displays the Print dialog box
CTRL+Z	The undo function will reverse the last command or to delete the last entry you typed
ESC	Cancels an entry in the active cell or 'Formula Bar'

NAVIGATION	
CTRL+PageUp	Switches between worksheet tabs, from **left-to-right**
CTRL+PageDown	Switches between worksheet tabs, from **right-to-left**
CTRL+↓	Goes to the last row with content for the active column
CTRL+↑	Goes to the first row with content for the active column
CTRL+→	Goes to the last column with content for the active row
CTRL+Home	Goes to cell A1 of the active worksheet
Shift + F3	Opens the Excel formula window
EDITING	
F7	Runs Spellcheck
Shift + F7	Opens the thesaurus dialogue box

☑ Helpful Tip:

Below are two ways to change a currency symbol. In the following examples, I will demonstrate the **British Pound £** and **Euro €**:

1. Select the cells you would like to change the currency, in this example, cells '**B2**' – '**B6**' are highlighted:

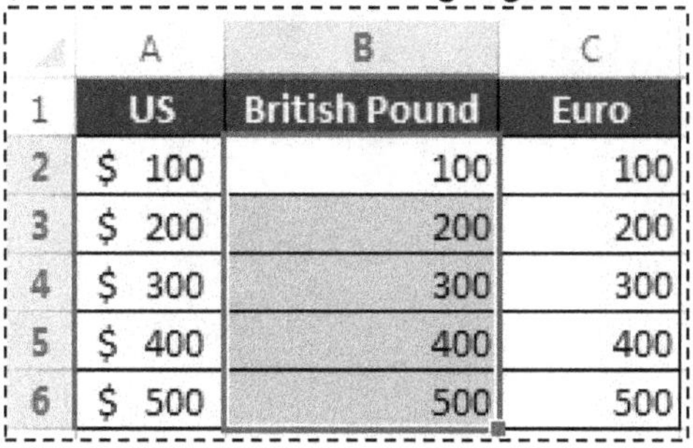

	A	B	C
1	US	British Pound	Euro
2	$ 100	100	100
3	$ 200	200	200
4	$ 300	300	300
5	$ 400	400	400
6	$ 500	500	500

2. From the **'HOME'** toolbar click the drop-down box for **$**
3. Select one of the currency's listed, in this example, **'£ English (United Kingdom)'** was selected

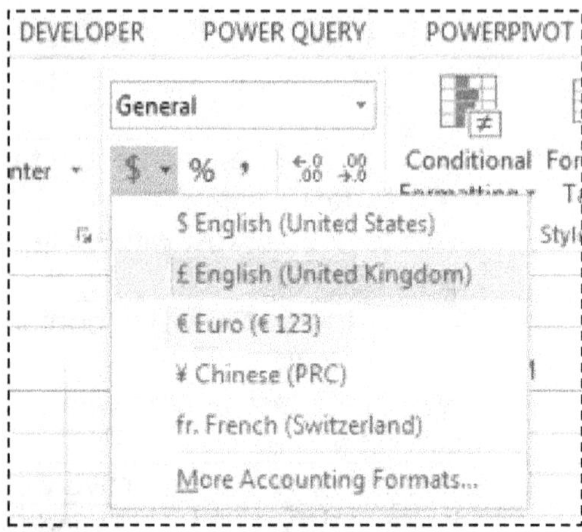

Alternatively, if your desired currency is not listed in the **'HOME'** toolbar **$** drop-down box, you can:

1. Select the cells you would like to change the currency
2. Right click and select **'Format Cells…'**:

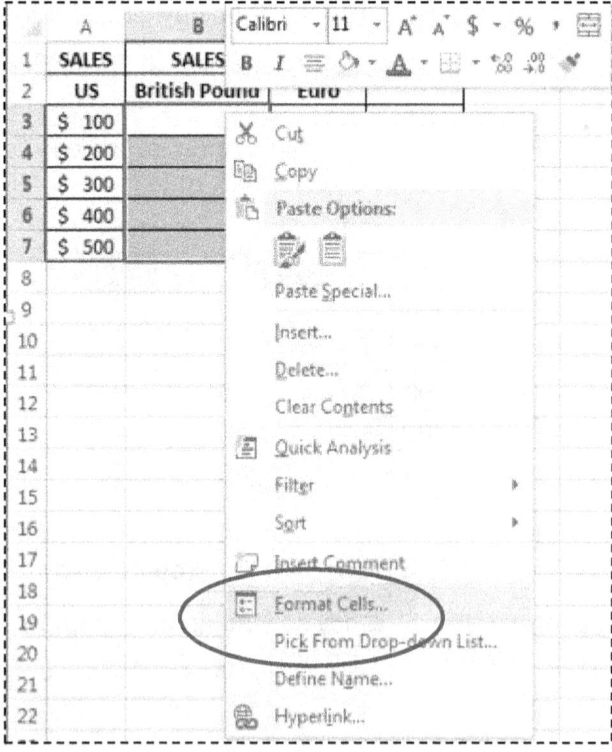

3. Select the tab **'Number'**
4. **'Category:' 'Currency'**
5. In the **'Symbol'** drop-down box select your desired currency, in this example, ***'£ Engilsh (United Kingom)'*** was selected:

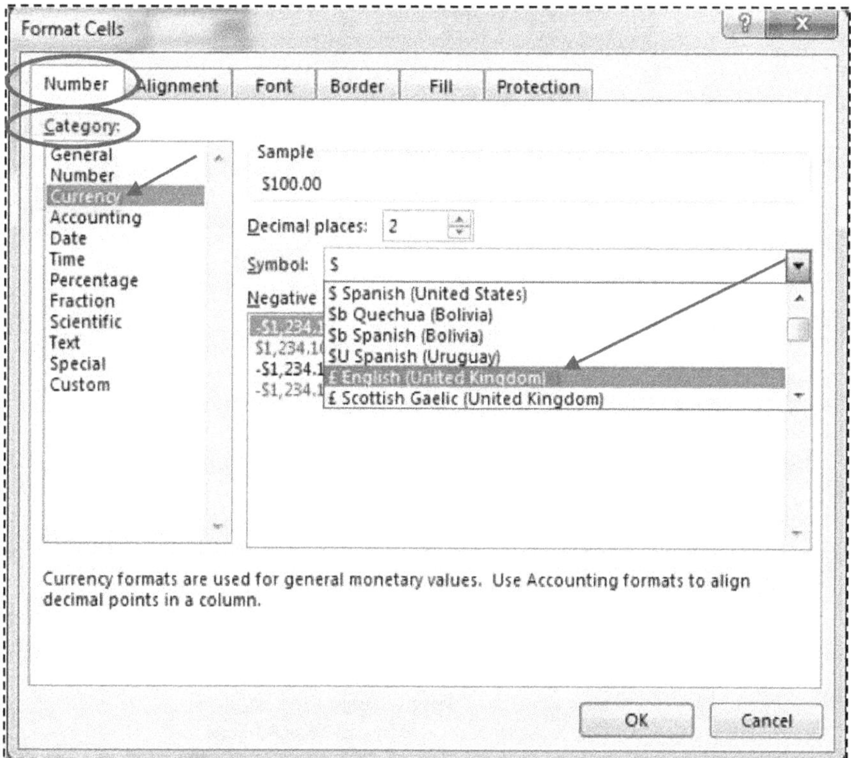

6. Click the **'OK'** button
7. Repeat the preferred method above, this time for the '**Euro €'** currency

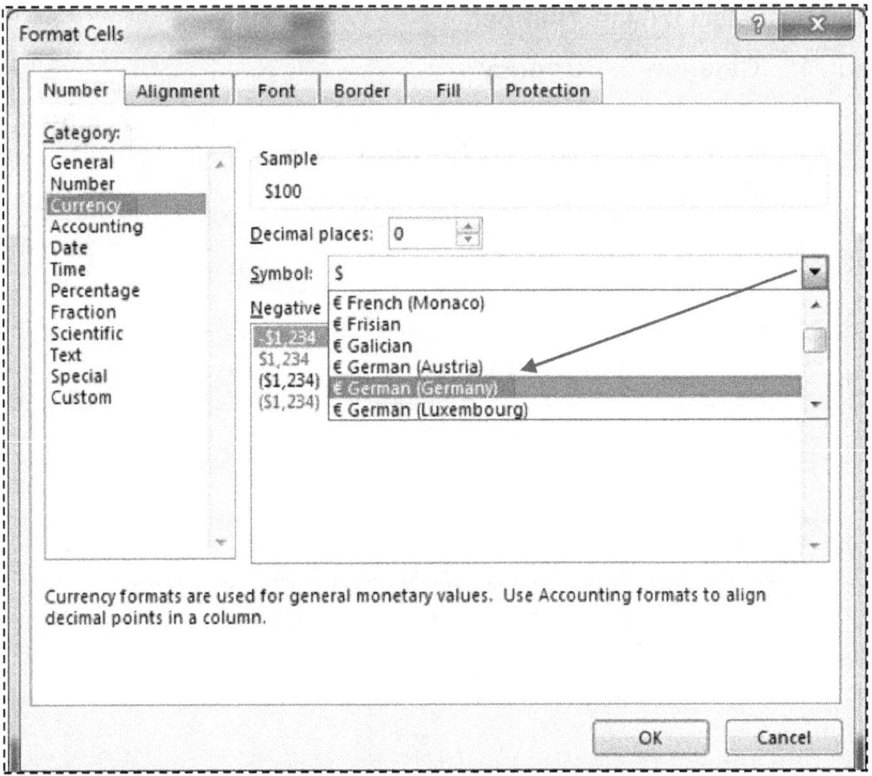

We now have currency displayed in the **British Pound £** and **Euro €**:

	A	B	C
1	US	British Pound	Euro
2	$ 100	£100	100 €
3	$ 200	£200	200 €
4	$ 300	£300	300 €
5	$ 400	£400	400 €
6	$ 500	£500	500 €

A Message From The Author

Thank you for purchasing and reading this book! Your feedback is valued and appreciated! Please take a few minutes and leave a review.

www.ingramcontent.com/pod-product-compliance
Lightning Source LLC
Chambersburg PA
CBHW071419050326
40689CB00010B/1904

9781518628757